YALE LAW LIBRARY SERIES IN LEGAL HISTORY AND REFERENCE

T0334867

PAUL W. KAHN

Origins of Order

Project and System in the

American Legal Imagination

NEW HAVEN AND LONDON

Yale UNIVERSITY PRESS

Published with support from the Lillian Goldman Law Library, Yale Law School, and with assistance from the Mary Cady Tew Memorial Fund.

Yale University Press books may be purchased in quantity for educational, business, or promotional use. For information, please e-mail sales.press@yale.edu (U.S. office) or sales@yaleup.co.uk (U.K. office).

Set in Janson type by Westchester Publishing Services.

Library of Congress Control Number: 2019935199
ISBN 978-0-300-24341-3 (hardcover : alk. paper)
ISBN 978-0-300-26148-6 (paperback)

A catalogue record for this book is available from the British Library.

10 9 8 7 6 5 4 3 2 1

For the sum of modern intellectual history constitutes the antagonism between the mechanical and the organic, art and nature, the will to form and the givenness of forms, between labor and rest.

—Hans Blumenberg, "Imitation of Nature:
Toward a Prehistory of the Idea of the Creative Being,"
trans. Anna Wertz, 12 *Qui Parle* 17, 23 (2000)

CONTENTS

PREFACE: PROJECT, SYSTEM, AND THE LEGAL IMAGINATION

The term "law" has always had to do double duty. On the one hand, laws are made through a political process. On the other hand, laws are discovered as a system already operating in the world. The legislative output of Congress is the first sort of law; the laws of thermodynamics are the second. When we focus on the social, however, the line becomes blurred. The social order is the site of our legislative projects, yet the very point of social science is to discover systemic laws operating within the community independently of anyone's project of law creation.[1] My ambition in this book, in simplest terms, is to explore this ambiguity in law as it shows itself in American political and legal thought over the long nineteenth century, the period from the American founding to the Lochner Court of the early twentieth century. Over the course of that century, there is a general shift from thinking of law—particularly constitutional law—as the product of a project to thinking of law as an immanent system.

I do not pursue a traditional history of constitutional law. My interest is rather to use the formations of law to explore the modern social imaginary. That there is a connection between modernity and a certain attitude toward law has long been evident in political theory and political practice. Modern political theory begins with the idea of a social contract: an idealized image of a constitution. Modern political practice begins from the idea that a state should have a constitution that both creates power and controls it for the sake of citizen rights. Both the theory and the practice of politics put law at the foundation of their enterprises. Of course, the actual relationship of law to political practice is complex and shifting. My inquiry is not into the history of that relationship itself, but rather into how it has been imagined. How we think about law tells us a great deal about what it means to be modern. Thinking about law has itself been the generative source of much of what we mean by modernity.

Modernity is not just a historical period, it is a way or ways of thinking about self and society. Modern thinking is characterized by an endless questioning of the self, both what it is and what it should be. Today, the question of what it should be becomes a question of how it came to be. Our paradigmatic forms of self-explanation are backward-looking; we have become writers of histories. Not just political history and biography, but histories of every discipline, of every art form, and of every social practice. This endless writing and rewriting of history is both an exercise in self-discovery and a continual reimagining of modernity as a break with the past. I follow that pattern of inquiry. I propose to investigate the shifts within the legal imaginary as it developed over the nineteenth century. I hope to use the legal inquiry as a metonym for exploring tensions—perhaps irresolvable—within the larger social imagination of modernity.

To be modern is to be endlessly trying to answer this question of the origin of modernity. Origin, however, has at least two meanings: historical and conceptual. Investigations of the past can attempt to identify either the causes of or the reasons for the way we construct political narratives—including accounts of law. In this work, my primary concern is conceptual. I use history to identify conceptual possibilities. I argue that in imagining the legal order, we are, in Wittgenstein's phrase, held "captive" by pictures.[2] In the case of law, it is actually two pictures: project and system.

Modernity's concern with its own origin is part of a larger effort to take responsibility for self and community. There is a fear that without a proper understanding of history, we will be governed by "accident and force."[3] Self-creation is thought to be inseparable from self-knowledge. Accordingly, modernity is an attitude toward self-construction that looks to the past in order simultaneously to free and to realize the self. The modern self occupies its future by treating its past as a resource.

The modern self aspires, accordingly, to self-creation: each of us would make a *project* of our own life. Revolution in practice and social contract in theory are both political responses to this need for autonomy. Alongside this aspiration for project, however, we find a skeptical response that de-links progress from project. On this view, political, social, and even psychological order are not the consequence of a deliberate intervention; their complexities are beyond the capacities of any human intention to create. Order is more like a language, which has *systemic* order, but is not the product of a project. It develops on its own; it develops through us, but not by us. This tension between self-creation and immanent order appears at multiple sites, one of which is the contest over the meaning and nature of law.[4]

Law has a special regard for the past, but again that regard can be seen as either liberating or constraining. Courts purport to decide present cases on the basis of past acts of law creation and pronouncement. The very point of a constitution is to create a structure that endures. To endure is to be continually reapplied. Knowledge that the law will be applied is what makes the project of constitutional creation possible.[5] Yet, were law to be strictly bound to the past, it would become our prison, rather than an expression of our capacity for self-government.[6] The most serious problems of legal interpretation as well as of legal theory arise just here: to live as a part of a system of order that precedes us and that we have obligations to support, while also living in the law as a practice of freedom. Can law be our project if it is also a system that claims us? Contemporary constitutional law has been struggling with this problem at least since Alexander Bickel gave it the name "the counter-majoritarian difficulty."[7] The problem, however, has much deeper roots, for it puts into issue the relationship of revolution—the free project of the people—to constitution—the system of law.

This problem takes different forms of expression at different times. Today, we worry about the countermajoritarian difficulty, while at the end of the nineteenth century scholars worried about the majoritarian difficulty: a fear of reckless action by popular majorities.[8] The general problem echoes the great medieval, theological debate over the place of reason and will in God's nature. Is God to be understood as the perfection of reason or as the possessor of an absolutely free will? If God's will is not bound by reason's laws, how can he be both wise and good? If he is bound, how is he free? Is God's creation a project to be understood by reference to the particular intent of God's will? Or is creation a system that realizes the order of reason itself? Are the laws of nature to be explained as God's project or reason's system?

In this book, I examine this tension between project and system in nineteenth-century thought about legal order. One view of the relationship of knowledge to practice is expressed in the idea of a constitution as the product of a popular will informed by political science. Political projects call upon political theory as a normative inquiry into what politics should be. I will call this way of imagining law that of the "project." A popular political project is a choice of the people to construct a legal order, informed by an idea or a theory. Opposed to the idea of law as a political project is an idea of law as a social system. To study the social is to inquire into an immanent order that arises spontaneously from within society. This immanent order lies behind the multitude of discrete acts and events that occupy our attention in daily life. Social science reveals an order of law that is the result of no one's intention. Modern social science will invent a new vocabulary to describe and a new method to discover that which the ordinary actor does not see or plan, yet which is immanent in the behavior of a population.[9]

Here, then, is a deep puzzle of modernity, for we are simultaneously committed to the ideas of project and of system, to forms of self-knowledge that enable and disable political action. To understand a project, we have to deploy the conceptual tools of narrative. We must know what actors intend and for what reasons they have made their choices. To understand a system, we have to deploy the tools of structural analysis. We have to treat populations, not individuals, which means that we must distinguish anecdotal accounts from immanent order. These are not just different tools, but different world views respecting what it means to live under law.

Modern public law begins with the idea of revolution, which is the imagined moment of taking responsibility for the project that is our collective political life. For this reason, revolution is always on the agenda of modern political communities. We need little reminder of this today, after decolonization, the color Revolutions, and the Arab Spring. Even when there is no practical possibility of revolution, the question remains: should we throw off our past and begin anew? The absence of revolution must itself be seen as a choice.

Modern revolution is always linked to a constitutional project. The constitution represents the political decision to invest in one possible future. Choosing one possibility, the decision excludes others.[10] A constitution combines moral and political theory, on the one hand, with an assertion of self-government, on the other; it combines reason and will. The former is universal; the latter, particular. Between the political universal and the particular constitution, there must be an act of will by the community.[11] A constitution is not just a legal order of rights—for example, human rights—imposed upon a political community. Rather, modern constitutional creation claims legitimacy as the authentic act of the people. It is their project. Because this project begins from theory, the study of law becomes a part of the project.

While modernity is the age in which the possibility of revolution appears as an issue of political morality, it is simultaneously an age of social science. The idea of the social as system suggests that we do not ordinarily know what we are doing or even who we are. Our ordinary beliefs do not amount to knowledge claims. They are only impressions, like that of the sun rising. On this view, rather than agents controlling our lives through projects, we are parts of a system revealed only by the methods of the social scientist. What used to be termed "fate" has become the object of scientific investigation of the laws of the social. This can leave us with a sense that we are no more in control of our lives than was Oedipus. Of course, the laws of a social system are not like the laws of thermodynamics. They are subject to pathologies that block their "natural" operation. For this reason, the study of law as system is put to use in practices of repair. While on the project view, the social is subordinate to politics, on the system view, the political is subordinate to the social.

This tension of project and system tended to take a theological form in the seventeenth and early eighteenth centuries. In the twentieth century, it tended to take a psychological form in the clash between ideas of personal authenticity and of social role. In the nineteenth century, the site of this tension was often in arguments over the nature of law. By looking at the development of American legal thought in the nineteenth century, I want to explore the reach of these master narratives of project and system. Neither can wholly displace the other; each generates distinct problems, even as each offers solutions to problems created by the other. Indeed, we would be wrong to think of the tension between them as a problem to be resolved. The fecundity of our commitment to self-government arises out of the diverse accounts we deploy to explain ourselves. This is no less true today than it was in the nineteenth century.

My inquiry proceeds in three parts. Part I sets out the terms of the analysis. I explore the conceptual shape of each of the paradigmatic forms: project and system. I elaborate their meanings by looking first at the theological uses of these forms of the imagination—uses that long preceded their deployment in accounts of law—and then at a series of paradigmatic texts, beginning with Thomas More's *Utopia* and ending with Alexis de Tocqueville's *Democracy in America*. I emphasize that project and system begin not as sophisticated theoretical accounts but as basic elements of the imagination that we deploy in our ordinary affairs. We all have projects—individual and group, large and small. We all also make use of an elementary idea of a natural system in order to understand an organism. A living being has an immanent order that it maintains as long as it is alive. It is not a mere aggregate, yet it is no one's project. The organism grows into itself as if it had an idea of where it was going. That is the idea of immanence and spontaneity characteristic of a system. Its extension to the society in the form of the social sciences was one of the prominent features of the nineteenth century.

Having set forth the basic shape of project and system as forms of the imagination, I proceed in Parts II and III to put these conceptual models to work. Part II explores the project character of the

American legal imaginary in the first half of the nineteenth century. The era begins with the grand project of constitutional construction and ends with the Civil War. Part III looks at the emergence and significance of the systemic imagination in the second half of the nineteenth century. This is an era marked by the theorizing of an "unwritten" constitution. Such a constitution is no one's project. It arises spontaneously and is immanent in the social. I end with a conclusion that speaks to the continuing significance of the distinction of project and system within contemporary debates in law and politics.

ACKNOWLEDGMENTS

I have been thinking about projects and systems ever since I wrote my first book, *Legitimacy and History: Self-Government in American Constitutional Theory.* Only in the last few years, however, did I come to see how central this distinction was to my own thought and to the broader project of law and social theory. That realization was linked to my focus on the function of narrative in the social imaginary. Increasingly, I asked: what kind of story do we tell when we explain law and politics? In fact, we tell stories of project and stories of system. This book emerged when I took up the problem of explaining why that is the case. Conversations with Robert Post, Owen Fiss, Tony Kronman, Daniel Markovits, and David Grewal greatly helped me to clarify my ideas. I had particular help with the manuscript from my colleagues Bruce Ackerman and Sam Moyn. I owe a great deal to friends and colleagues outside of Yale as well, including Kiel Brenan-Marquez, Ryan Mitchell, Benjamin Berger, Olivier Beaud, Miguel Maduro, Amnon Lev, and Daniel Bonilla. Over the past few years, I have taken advantage of any number of speaking invitations to talk about these ideas and put them to use on different problems. Particularly helpful were opportunities afforded me at Cornell Law School, the Michel-Villey Institute for Legal Culture and Philosophy of Law at Paris 2 Panthéon Assas University, Osgood Hall in Toronto, the Law Faculty of the University of Lisbon, and at the European University Institute in Florence. I would also like to thank Patrick McCormick, Dylan Kolhoff, Wajdi Mallat, and Michael Masciandaro. Finally, I remain grateful for the contribution of Barbara Mianzo, without whose help it would be difficult for me to get anything done in a timely manner.

INTRODUCTION: ON METHOD, OR WHAT PHILOSOPHY HAS TO OFFER

In the *Phaedrus*, Socrates is asked by his companion whether he is sympathetic to contemporary efforts to explain the gods and their acts as only figurative representations of natural forces—for example, the wind and rain. Socrates responds that pursuing such explanations would be an endless task. Accordingly, he sticks to a simpler and more accessible object of inquiry: himself.[1] In modern terms, he suggests that it is easier to understand a free act than a caused event. Given the success of modern science, this sounds counterintuitive. Yet, it takes only a moment to realize that no scientific explanation is ever complete because it can never reach the origin of a causal sequence. Everything is quite literally linked to everything else from the perspective of causal inquiry. Science is, therefore, never done; no account can be certain that further inquiry will not reveal other causes.

Socrates' answer suggests not just that an inquiry into nature would be endless—something that we have turned into a virtue of the scientific method—but that it would be without point. If the myth of Boreas and the young girl is nothing but a figurative representation of the natural force of the wind, what difference could it make to any of us? There is no moral to be drawn from a gust of wind. A myth, however, is not just a poor representation of a set of physical causes; it is an account that calls for a deliberate response. It tells a story and represents a way of living—for good and for bad.

Socrates' rejection of the naturalist account of myth tells us that there is nothing "natural" about the scientific imagination. Nature as the object of our knowledge has a history, just as forms of art and religious belief have histories.[2] Of course, unlike Socrates, we cannot be dismissive of the claims of science, for philosophy's claim to the high ground of an education worth having is deeply contested today. The traditional inquiries of philosophy seem increasingly out of place for the same reasons that undermined theology. First, a loss of faith that there is an object to which the representations of the discipline attach.[3] Theology becomes literature once faith disappears. Second, the rise of awareness of cultural and religious diversity. Theology becomes cultural studies when we cannot separate beliefs from believers. Today, we cannot suppress the knowledge that our religious tradition is just one of many, in which case the only thing special about it may be that it is our own.

Philosophy confronts these same two challenges. The philosophical tradition of inquiry fails to produce texts that meet the test for reliable knowledge claims. Are philosophical texts only literature to be studied alongside fiction? If philosophical texts are not science, is their effort to make universal claims about the self and the good anything other than a practice of cultural hegemony? Does Western philosophy stand in the same relationship to other traditions of reflection as Western religion stands to non-Western religions? Is philosophy too destined for the cultural studies department?

Philosophy has, for the most part, given up the aspiration to describe the essential nature of man or to identify universal values. Modern philosophy yields the space for such universal claims to new, specialized disciplines such as cognitive science, linguistics, game theory, and evolutionary biology. Philosophy in the Socratic tradition instead takes us as we are, asking about *our* beliefs and practices. Philosophy is a practice of interpreting those beliefs and practices.

Philosophy takes us as we are, but not in the sense that it is satisfied with whatever we report. We may not understand ourselves very well; often we don't understand others. Interpreting ourselves, however, we have no choice but to examine the reasons we offer to each other in order to explain and to persuade. The reasons we offer in such accounts have their own histories, which link the individual to the community and the community to the individual. We occupy a symbolic order—actually, multiple symbolic orders—that inform us before we utter a first sentence or make a first decision. We look out upon the world from a particular position; we are never not looking and we are always somewhere.[4] Philosophy, as I pursue it, begins here: the object of its inquiries is the social imaginary as we find it at work in our ordinary life of cultural reproduction.[5]

We operate within a sort of horizon constituted by the forms of the understanding as they are put to work by the imagination.[6] These forms, while necessary for us, do not represent an abstract necessity. My parents are contingent from an abstract perspective, but to me they are absolutely necessary. The same is true of my language, my nation, my family, my professional role, and my expectations for myself and my polity. Together, all of these elements constitute my world. Philosophy helps us to see the contingent character of that world. Seeing that contingency may allow us to value it differently, but not because we have reached some neutral ground from which to make judgments. There is no such ground.

Because we stand simultaneously as subjects within history and as interpreters of that history, we experience the double pull of necessity and contingency. Philosophy inquires into this contingent necessity as the "historical *a priori*": the categories of the imagination that give shape to our experience as meaningful to us.[7] Philosophy's task, as I pursue it, is to study the genealogy and conceptual architecture of the categories of the historical *a priori* that constitutes the social imaginary of modernity.[8] Project and system are two such categories.

These are not new categories in themselves. As I explain in Chapter 1, they are as old as the West. They are, however, put to new uses as political order separates itself from traditional religious order. Modern politics begins with the idea of revolution. That idea depends on the possibility of imagining politics as a secular, democratic project. The people can remake their political order based on an idea—a theory—of their rights and of the institutions that will realize their interests while respecting those rights. We have endless arguments about the theory, but we share the picture of a political project. It is the background condition of our theories, practices, and arguments.

A social imaginary is not a theory; it does not have the logical consistency of a theory. It is informed by narratives, examples, and practices, as much as by theory. It is the set of resources to which we ordinarily have recourse in explaining ourselves and persuading others. Among those resources is an idea of system that begins to be applied to social phenomena—society—in the seventeenth century. By the end of the nineteenth century, system is a part of the basic picture against which ideas of social order are developed. We are, after all, in the age of Darwin, Social Darwinists, Alexander von Humboldt, capitalism, and Marx.

Project and system views of law are in deep tension, as I will show, but this is not a tension that needs to be resolved at an abstract level. We live with multiple ways of imagining law and explaining ourselves. These different pictures contend at the retail level. They are put to use in efforts to explain and persuade. Consider, for example, a criminal trial in which the prosecutor argues that the defendant freely chose to pursue an illegal project, while the defense argues that the fault is in the system of education or housing or family within which the defendant grew up. We need both perspectives not just to understand the particular, but to imagine the broad character of social order, including law.

Over the course of the nineteenth century, there is a movement from project to system as the dominant way of imagining law, among American lawyers, judges, politicians, and scholars. The question of what causes shifts in the categories of the social imaginary is not one for philosophy.[9] To seek a cause is to deploy a category borrowed from the natural sciences. Scientists seek to account for change by identifying factors—causes—that are necessary conditions precedent to the events. For philosophy to follow that line of thought is to think that history is working itself out in a single direction, as if it could not be other than it is and has been. The teleological character of this approach is a remnant of a distinctly premodern conception of creation under the direction of God.

Philosophy can observe difference, but it cannot offer proof. When we say, for example, that the Reformation led to a change in attitudes toward science, we are not identifying a cause in a scientific sense. We are observing a difference and offering an interpretation that tries to make sense of an indefinite array of events, practices, beliefs, and individual innovations, no one of which we can say was necessary. We cannot say what would have been the case in the absence of any particular fact; we cannot isolate one factor and test its relevance. An interpretation, accordingly, does not identify causes; it offers reasons that can be more or less persuasive. What persuades may change over time. An interpretation, then, is as much about us as it is about its object of inquiry.

Just as philosophy does not offer causes, it does not adjudicate between project and system. One view is not right in itself, or more right than the other. At issue are ways of imagining law, not the truth of the law as an object independent of our imagining. Law simply is an interpretive practice. It is whatever we imagine it to be just to the degree that we can persuade others to see as we do. In the pages that follow, I do my best to articulate each of the imaginings of law that I address. I try to reconstruct the legal world as it is seen by the participants. I take no sides in their debates, for most of the time the participants did not see themselves as debating. They simply imagined the world as best they could as possibilities appeared in the context of particular concerns and controversies. We have no choice but to do the same.

Philosophy's contribution, then, is not to counter the accounts of causation that are offered by social scientists and historians, but to interpret the products of the social imaginary in order to expose the character and operation of the historical *a priori*. There is no special site for examination of the social imaginary, for it is equally present in the micro- and the macrocosm.[10] We can examine a text or a genre; we can look to an event or an era, a person or a group. The categories of the imagination are constantly replicated in our experience, and experience has no natural limits.

Nevertheless, law is a particularly fruitful place of inquiry, not only because of its importance to modern life, but because it produces readily available texts—texts that include both the laws themselves and reflections upon the law. Law in the modern era always develops within a theory of law. This is one of the ways in which law differs from custom. More broadly, law locates itself with respect to a theory of politics that grounds the legitimacy of law. Modern law includes this critical activity of arguing about what the law is and what it should be.[11] Arguing, we make use of the imaginative resources at hand.

Representations of law are everywhere. The philosophical task is to interrogate these representations in order to discover what they can tell us about how we imagine ourselves and our communities. When we take up that task, we are drawn in two directions at once: project and system.

PART 1

Project and System Before the Constitution

Biographies sometimes speak of miraculous years of creativity, after which things are never the same. Einstein had such a year in 1905. Miraculous years also happen in the history of thought and action: 1776 was such a year. Americans know it as the year of their national founding. In the history of social theory, 1776 is no less important for an entirely different reason. That was the year that Adam Smith published *The Wealth of Nations*, from which we date the beginning of modern economics.

Revolution and economics stand to each other as project to system. The relationship between these two ideas is a problem for law and politics, but more generally it is a problem of modernity. In the United States, over the course of the nineteenth century, attitudes toward law—particularly constitutional law—moved from a predominance of the idea of project to a predominance of system. Before the Civil War, law was seen within the lens of the project: the written Constitution was a project. After the War, law was seen through the lens of system: the true or real Constitution was unwritten and coincided in large part with the common law. A project of law begins in an intentional act; it is an effort to realize an idea or set of ideas. No one ever took as their project the creation of the system of the common law. Rather, judges decided individual cases, in the same way that individuals engage in particular economic transactions. Principles of order in a system are immanent and spontaneous; they arise independently of the motivating interests of those whose actions bring the system into being.[1]

7

The best-known shift in nineteenth-century thought was from thinking of the natural order as the result of God's project to thinking of it as a Darwinian system. Prior to the shift, if nature worked "according to a plan," if it manifested a lawfulness, that could only be the result of a deliberate project that shaped unintelligible matter according to an idea of order.[2] After the shift, order did not depend upon an idea that preceded its coming into being. The scientist's role was not to pursue natural theology but to investigate the immanent order of nature. That order no longer revealed the mind of God expressed in and through his project of creation. Darwin explained the possibility of complex systemic order without intention.

Darwinian ideas of evolution were hardly the first or the only ideas of system appearing in the nineteenth century. Indeed, Darwin was not even the first to develop an idea of evolution.[3] That century witnessed the dramatic growth of the social sciences, all of which share the goal of locating the immanent systems operating in human affairs. The social scientist studies principles of order as they emerge from the totality of individual beliefs and actions. The object of study is no longer the individual but society, which exhibits a unity and an organization distinct from the mere aggregation of individuals and individual actions.

These laws of the social do not precede their realization; they are no one's thoughts or intentions. Indeed, they may be wholly unknown to the persons whose activities they describe. They are constitutive of a new object of observation—society—of which the individual actor is only a part.[4] He or she is a part not by virtue of a deliberate choice or a plan in the form, for example, of a social contract. Rather, finding oneself to be part of the social whole is now constitutive of identity. Individual identity is thought of less as a matter of standing alone before God's final judgment to account for the project of one's life and more as a matter of standing with a community that has developed through history and will continue to develop after we are gone. Individuals will have to develop an ability to think of themselves in both ways: as capable of projects and as members of a society. Each perspective will generate a different account of citizen identity and a different account of law. Each will bring different ideas of legal interpretation and different ideas of citizen responsibilities.

Society is more than the aggregation of individual persons insofar as it demonstrates a new level of organization as a system. If there were no system to be discovered, if human events and behavior followed no laws when viewed collectively, what exactly would be the object of social science? There is no science of the particular; there is only a narrative of the single event. The unlimited reach of the modern social science approach rests on our unlimited capacity to take a systemic perspective on ourselves.

That our own lives—which strike us first of all and most of the time as constituted by decisions and acts in pursuit of our own interests—are constitutive parts of an intelligible system of social order is a startling idea. It is as startling as trying to reconcile our sense that we are free to decide upon our actions with our knowledge that every event is determined by a cause. In both cases, we are forced to consider the possibility that reality is not what appears in our ordinary experience. We are forced to take ourselves as one object of thought alongside other persons and events. We give up the first-person point of view on our projects and treat our own behavior as events requiring an explanation in an entirely different, third-person frame of reference. In the social sciences today, that explanation is likely to take a statistical form. We must see ourselves as elements of a population that displays an immanent order.[5]

Viewed from the perspective of natural science, human behavior is to be explained by reference to physical causes. The natural science of man is a form of materialism: we explain a movement, an action, or a thought by placing it within a sequence of material changes. We look, for example, to neural chemistry. Viewed from a social science perspective, our actions are explained when they are set within ordered patterns of events. New methods of study arise to support these new social disciplines. We learn about bell curves and regression analyses. Thus, the eighteenth and nineteenth centuries witnessed the development of statistics as a language of the social sciences.[6] The laws of the social take the form of laws of probability.

The social scientist's imagination of system, however, can no more displace our experience of project than the natural scientist's imagination of causation can displace our experience of freedom. This competition in the imagination is not just a matter of ordinary intuition against theory; it is implicated as well in matters of policy and social design. Despite the analyses of the social scientists, there is no area of human concern that we cannot think open—for good or bad—to re-formation through the deliberate adoption of a project. Polity, society, and even the self are never settled, but always open to projects of reform. Those projects gain stability when they take the form of law. To be incapable of imagining a project with respect to a certain domain of experience is to imagine an absence of freedom. There, we are bound by a different sort of law: one impervious to our projects.

As long as the tension between project and system has existed, there have been efforts to overcome it through synthesis. One modern form of this response has been to argue that inquiry into system provides the knowledge that allows for the better construction of projects. We do not have to choose between project and system; we never abandon our freedom to system. Rather, we freely adopt projects based on our awareness of social and natural systems. Projects adopted in ignorance of these systems are not likely to succeed. This response collapses system into project: systemic knowledge is put to use in projects. The opposite response collapses project into system. Here, projects are the mechanism by which a system realizes itself. On the former view, project needs system; on the latter, system needs projects. We might think of these efforts at synthesis as two forms of cooptation: project and system each try to coopt the other into a single worldview.[7]

The ambition for synthesis of project and system has taken both forms in American law. It is almost a commonplace to think of the original project of American constitutionalism as that of creating a machine that would "go of itself."[8] The project, in other words, was to create a system. For this, there is an obvious theological precedent: God's project of creation was thought by many in the early modern period to have been the bringing forth of a system—nature—the continuing order of which does not rely on successive interventions by a divine actor. The project of creation was, on this view, a one-time event; after that, the natural system sustains itself. This was not just a way of reconciling the new sciences with a theological commitment. It also expressed the continuing difficulty of imagining the possibility that order could arise independently of intention. Order expresses an idea; ideas require a subject with the capacity for thought. That nature was a system constituted proof of the existence of a God whose project was creation.

Kant gave philosophical expression to this idea of system as the end of a constitutional project. He thought a well-designed government could work even with a race of devils.[9] It would be a system that tended toward its own ends, with the qualities of repair and reproduction. No doubt some of the American framers also thought a well-designed constitution would have these organic qualities. Yet, for the most part, the analogy of constitutional construction that they deployed was to a machine—for example, a watch—not to an organism.[10] The watch's perfection is always measured by an idea outside of itself: when it breaks, it needs repair by someone with an idea of its end and its nature. A machine has no power of repair and reproduction.[11] It remains the product of a project; it is not a natural system.[12]

Efforts at synthesis moving in the opposite direction emerge by the middle of the nineteenth century. Now, projects of legal construction are only sites for the working out of the immanent logic—the laws—of a constitutional system that will appear wherever the Anglo-Saxon race is free to govern itself. The analogue of the political system is no longer the machine but the organism. An organism is not the product of an original project. It is born from another organism; it is not made.[13] Without need of an intentional act—an original project—the origins of law, like the origins of life, are lost. More precisely, they are lost because they no longer matter in the account, for systemic order is spontaneous.

The project-system tension is not resolved, then, but replicated in the contrasting analogies of political order to machine and to organism. Ultimately, a constitutionalism of project labors in the shadow of revolution—one machine can substitute for another—while a constitutionalism of system distrusts revolution because it will disrupt a natural, organic development.[14] Projects can be created anew; systems limit legitimate interventions to repair of pathology—even a social organism can get sick.[15] We will see that this contrast of project and system appears in a particular trope in nineteenth-century legal theory: the contrast of a written constitution and an unwritten constitution. Writing, the American founders created a machine; unwritten, the Anglo-American common-law constitution was an organic growth.

Ideas of project and system were hardly new in 1776. Having a project is a commonplace of ordinary experience. To formulate a plan in order to make something—alone or with others—is to pursue a project. The paradigmatic project in classical thought was the work of the craftsman—the exercise of a techné. If I build a house, I must direct my actions by reference to an idea of the house that I want to build. That idea will be informed by my general idea of the ends that a house serves, which can range from functional to aesthetic. There can be a theory of the house independent of any particular project. Architects might study that theory in the same way that the Founders studied political theory.

A project is always an effort to realize an idea that precedes it. A project that loses track of its idea becomes aimless or arbitrary action. A political project is no different in its structure; the idea precedes its construction in and through law and institutions. Any particular idea for a political project depends upon more general ideas regarding the ends of politics. These ideas can be considered prior to or apart from their realization in projects. For that reason, we find modern political theory develops in tandem with the modern political project of constitutional construction.

The ideas that inform a project can be further specified in terms of an end and a plan—in Aristotelian terms, the final and formal causes. Animals certainly act toward an end, but only people have plans. A project is not just a goal-directed activity. It is a special sort of directed activity: one in which the idea of the goal informs a plan apart from and prior to the actions intended to realize that end. We can describe an animal as hunting, but it has no theory of hunting by which it shapes a plan. It does not adopt a project; it acts toward an end.

A political project can be a one-time event—a founding, for example—or it can be open-ended. The project continues as long as we imagine practice to be informed and measured by the same plan. The plan grounds a double means-end rationality; first, in the relationship of plan to goal—the issue of design—and second, in the actual carrying out of the plan as a means of reaching a goal—the issue of effectiveness. Design rationality means that we can examine, criticize, and reform the plan by measuring it against its end. We might compare the relative merits of a number of different plans aiming at the same end. Effectiveness rationality means that we can judge the project's success as it is carried out. A plan that works well in theory may fail to be effective in fact. In that case, we may turn to what seems a second-best design that works better under the actual circumstances. Design and effectiveness rationality may not always point in the same direction.

The means-end rationality of a project works at different levels of generality. I can have long-term projects that are realized through many short-term projects. A student may say that his goal is to get a degree or perhaps to get a job for which the degree qualifies him. To realize that goal he adopts a plan that will include multiple subprojects with more limited ends. At any moment, his particular end may be no more than succeeding in a specific class, but that end functions as a means within the larger project; it has a place in the plan.

I cannot know what the student is doing without speaking to him and asking for an account. Absent access to the intentions of actors, we have no way of deploying the language of project—ends and plans—to describe what it is they have done or are doing. Because the ideas that inform a project are not observable, project discourse requires an intersubjective relationship. A project is a way of imagining and narrating a course of action by free agents, including ourselves. We refer to projects when asked to give an account of what we are doing. Our explanation offers narratives of projects that are grounded in reasons for our acting one way rather than another. If we do turn to the language of observable behavior to describe others, we are either confronting a pathology ("he did not know what he was doing" or "he was ill") or admitting our ignorance of the meaning of the action.

Taking up a project, I decide for an idea. That decision can always be abandoned, changed, or renewed. I might become convinced that the ideas upon which the project is based are not correct. Ideas are always subject to theoretical contestation. I may become convinced, for example, that a political project was based on an incorrect idea of justice. Or, I may decide the plan is not an effective way to realize that idea. In either case, flawed design or flawed effectiveness, I will have to amend or abandon the project. There is no virtue in sticking to a project regardless of these judgments about design and effectiveness.

Thus, offering a narrative of project, I think of myself as a free agent. A project always has about it a sense of a proposal, for even in the middle of a project one can change one's mind. Of course, calculations may change as costs are sunk, but the possibilities of reimagining the project are endless. Moreover, because projects intersect, we might find that our plans conflict. In that case, we will have to try to understand our priorities among projects.

Since a project is always directed by an idea and an idea only has an intentional quality when it is actually adopted by someone, we can always ask, Whose project is it? Projects don't exist absent commitments to the ideas that define those projects.[1] A project that belongs to no one remains only a possibility, unless and until someone makes it his or her own. This is what it means to say that a project is only possible for a free actor. Acting freely, I make the project my own.[2]

When we have no access to the person or persons to whom we ascribe a project—for example, they are long dead—our descriptions of their projects might be radically different from their own. We might say that the archaeological record shows that a particular community had the construction of a building as its project, but we don't know whether the project was the building of a temple or a dwelling.[3] We imagine them following a blueprint, but that may have been only one element of a plan that rested on religious, political, or familial ideas. Their theory of the house may have been radically different from our own. Not knowing why they acted as they did, we project onto them our own understanding of what it would mean to us to build such a structure. Doing so, we no doubt misrepresent them.[4]

The normative discourse surrounding a project will move within a pattern of ends, plans, and ownership. We might, for example, have disagreements over whether the end informing the project of lawmaking should be justice or security. We may further disagree about the nature of justice (justice as equality of outcomes or of opportunities?) or the meaning of security (security from what?). If we agree on an end, we might have disagreements over the plan. We might share a similar concept of justice, but still disagree on how to make this idea real in our social arrangements. We can disagree on plans—as in constitutional design—and on effectiveness—as in agency capture or political polarization. Finally, we might criticize the lawmaking project as not our own, arguing that it has not been the product of a democratic process. I might understand a law passed by the legislature as, for example, the successful project of lobbyists who gained control of the elected representatives.[5] I think of that law as something done to me by the government, rather than as something that we, the citizens, have done together.

Apart from this internal, normative order, a project can fail wholly or partially for any number of reasons that are external to it. A political project can be defeated by enemies or overcome by unforeseen events over which we have no control. Good ideas don't guarantee successful projects—not even when I appropriate the ideas as my own. Success depends as much on contingent matters of history as it does on getting one's theory right.

In classical thought, the idea of the project—techné—as a form of explanation was well established. Project was not, however, the antithesis of system. Rather, the relevant contrast was between a project and an activity done for its own sake. A project always has a goal outside of itself; it has, therefore, a beginning, a middle, and an end—a progress that marks the movement from idea to embodied form. The ethos of the techné is, accordingly, bound to time and to the risks of time. To pursue a project is always to expose the self to the risk that things might not go well, despite one's best efforts. This is no less true today. Classically, to be free of that risk was to achieve a kind of autonomy.[6] That was possible only by pursuing activities for their own sake. When plan was not separate from goal, action could be complete in itself and time no longer a threat.

Today, we might speak of "existing in the moment" to capture this idea of escaping from the endless possibility of project failure. One form of such an activity is contemplation, but there are many others. The distinction is not so much in what we are doing as in the reasons for our actions and the value we realize in pursuing the activity. A political practice, for example, might find its value in the activity of collective deliberation and public striving.[7] The same could be true of a sport. I might pursue an athletic practice for the joy it gives me quite independently of winning or losing a particular game. We can have the same sort of experience in the fine arts: a musical performance has a beginning, middle, and end, but it might be done for its own sake and appreciated as an activity. Of a project, we are satisfied when we accomplish our end. Of an activity, we might feel some disappointment when we reach the end.

The turn to system in the nineteenth century was not, however, a response to the time-bound character of goal-directed projects. The nineteenth century is not classical Greece. System is a form of explanation; it is not in itself an ethos or a way of living. The appeal to system was not an effort to escape the perils of time; rather, it was a different way to understand the nature of order. Action and project compete as first-person points of view. Both speak to intentions. System is a third-person point of view. This shift in perspective is not without political and legal consequences. It appeals, for example, to a different kind of expertise and thus a different sort of expert. The systemic account of politics affects our understanding of ourselves as citizens. Even more deeply, it affects our understanding of law: its origin, nature, and end.

The idea of system has an internal normative structure that is quite distinct from that of a project. We intuit this when we speak, for example, of equilibria, disturbances, or externalities. If a project is a striving to achieve an idea external to the acts constitutive of the project, then a system is a striving to maintain an immanent principle of order. Because system exists independently of intention, "striving" here has to be understood metaphorically. The nature of a system is to maintain itself.[8] We know this phenomenon most immediately as life.

To take up a project is to bring an idea into the world. The law of a system is not taken up, but discovered. To give a systemic account is to describe a reciprocal relationship—a lawful regularity—between parts and whole. That relationship informs the system even before its full realization in time and space—the oak tree already informs the acorn. In a project, the whole exists only as idea until the project is accomplished; in a system, the whole operates as a principle of order at every moment. A project proceeds toward a goal "bit by bit"; a system grows by becoming what it already is. It does so without the mediation of deliberate action by a subject. To have law without project is to imagine ideas without intention, or, in Kant's strange phrase about the beautiful, "purposefulness without a purpose. . . ."[9] These immanent principles of order are the laws that are the objects of scientific research. They are prior to the phenomena even though they have no existence prior to the events they inform.

We are most immediately familiar with systemic forms of explanation with respect to organisms. The organism has an immanent principle of order that determines the nature of its parts—organs—from the moment of conception. An organism is not an aggregation of parts that come into being independently of each other, put together according to a plan. Rather, an organism is a system of reciprocal relationships between parts and whole. The parts do not precede the whole, which means that their coming into being is a law-governed process. An organism reproduces itself according to its kind, again without the intervention of an actor whose project the organism is. We use these same forms of systemic explanation when we move from individual organisms to ecosystems, all the elements of which exist in relationship to each other and together constitute a whole that cannot be grasped as an aggregate. Just as projects can become elements within the plan of ever-larger projects, systems occupy ever-larger systems. A constitution is a system constituted by parts that are themselves systems—for example, the judiciary or executive branches.[10]

Although the idea of system is not new, its application to the social is a distinctively modern idea.[11] Individual persons seem, first of all and most of the time, to be pursuing projects at various levels of generality. They have ends in view and explain their behavior by setting forth their plans and choices. That these same phenomena can be explained as elements of a system following laws that are immanent, rather than chosen, is a startling idea. It requires a reorientation of the perspective from which we imagine ourselves and a reconstruction of the nature of an explanation.

When we appeal to system to explain the social, we take up a third-person point of view. We stand in relationship to ourselves as if we were merely another phenomenon to be explained by identifying the immanent principles of order of the populations of which we are a part. At least since Job, Westerners have struggled with the issue of the appropriate perspective to take on our own actions. What we see is not necessarily what God sees. This problem of "what does God see?" became for moderns the problem of science: what is the law behind the appearances?[12] In both cases, the epistemic claim is linked to a claim about the real. God and the scientist see differently from us because they see the truth. They see what is.[13]

To imagine a system, then, is to imagine order outside of the terms of a project. For this reason, we ask of a system not what its goal is, but what its laws are. We ask about functions, not choices. Thinking of the social as a system requires us to ask whether persons too perform functions that are not choices. The ambiguity of the term "function" captures the nature of a system. We say that an activity or process has a function in relation to something else, describing a relationship among parts to the whole. Thus, an organ has a function in relationship to the whole of an organism. We also say a function describes a lawful regularity, as when we say that x is a function of y. The functional character of systemic order means that it can be purposive without being anyone's purpose.

Understanding the social through the conceptual frame of system—law without project—opened a space for the most dramatic intellectual move of the nineteenth century: the theory of biological evolution. The felt necessity of a link of intelligible order to intentional act—order as the result of project—had sustained belief in creation. The world had to be God's project because absent a creator, there was no way that an idea could inform a whole prior to its coming into being. This was the basic idea behind the proof of God's existence from design: the order found in the world could only be the product of an idea, and an idea required a subject whose idea it was. But if the social could have a systemic order absent a project, then why not the natural order as well? And, of course, Darwinian theory is shot through with the language of markets: competition, comparative advantage, satisfaction of needs, and striving for success. Perhaps ironically, the social made possible our modern idea of nature.

The parts of a system are not trying to achieve ideas external to the system. Rather, their function is their contribution to the continuing realization of the system itself. This is true even if those parts are our own actions and the system is the social order.[14] The ethos of a system is not to accomplish an end, but to maintain itself. That does not mean there can be no change in a system short of exogenous shock; it does mean that the change must be explained in terms of the laws internal to the system—for example, growth. Change that is lawful is itself an expression of stability. The social is precisely ordered change. This is why the social as system opened up a model for biology as a system of evolution, while Newton's system of physical laws did not.

Systems, like projects, can be disturbed. When a project is disturbed, it needs repair or amendment through external intervention. The order of the project comes from without, which means that any correction requires a new appeal to an external source of order. When a watch breaks, we take it to the watchmaker for repair; when a law fails to accomplish its end, we return to the legislature for enactment of an amendment. A system, however, maintains itself against disturbance. It has a power of self-correction, self-amendment, or simply healing. An injured organism can heal itself; a disturbed economy will return to equilibrium; so too will a disrupted environment. To imagine the social within the pattern of system is to imagine patterns of self-correction or movement back to stability in response to disturbance.

Systems, like projects, can be analyzed at multiple levels. Disturbance at one level might be an expression of order at a higher level.[15] I might go bankrupt, but my failing personal finances might simultaneously be an expression of a well-functioning economic system. Of course, no system has limitless power; some disturbances are too great and the system fails.[16] Organisms die, environments collapse, economies fail, nations are defeated.

Just as we do not ask what a system is trying to achieve, we do not ask whose it is. It refers only to itself, not to anything outside of itself. Accordingly, to imagine a system is to imagine a bounded domain; a system has borders that distinguish an inside from an outside. The borders of a system reach as far as the relationships among its parts extend.

Disruption of a system can be a cross-border phenomenon: the entry of something new. If the system can absorb the new by incorporating it into its internal order, then the boundaries of the system may be effectively redrawn. What had been outside becomes a part of the systemic order of the whole.[17] Think, for example, of immigration. We might imagine immigrants—particularly undocumented—to disturb the internal order of the community. Our response, however, might be to reimagine the borders of the relevant system. We might move from thinking of the territorial state as the boundaries of the system to thinking of regions and their population flows as the system.

Project and system compete as ways of imagining the world and our place in it. We might think of project as practical and system as theoretical, but that does not do justice to the reach of these ideas. We can see the world as full of projects or as constituted by systems. For premoderns, the world itself was God's project. Today, we are more likely to view the natural order as system. Inevitably, however, we appeal to both system and project. In explaining ourselves and our social practices, project and system do not so much refer to different domains as to different forms of explanation. We are thoroughly familiar with the vocabularies of both forms of explanation.

Consider, for example, the human organism. We can understand the body as a system, the well-being of which is our experience of health. The expert in the systemic knowledge of the body is the biologist; the expert in its repair is the doctor. But there is nothing about the body itself that gives a privileged position to the doctor and the biological knowledge upon which she relies. One might make of the body a project, pushing it toward extremes of endurance or aesthetic expression. I might become a religious ascetic, treating the body in a most unhealthy manner from the perspective of the physician and her knowledge. If I am a prisoner on a hunger strike, I have turned the body into the site of a political project, in which case the doctor's view that I am harming myself now appears as a category mistake. The body, in short, is not one thing or another. It is a site of imaginative contestation between different attitudes, activities, and forms of explanation.

Whatever we might think of the ontological status of natural systems—a problem beyond the reach of this book—social systems occupy a position like that of our attitude toward the body. There is no single truth to discover; there are only different forms of explanation. For example, a language is a symbolic system: words gain their meaning only in their relationships to other words, which together constitute the whole of the language. Part and whole come into being at the same moment. We don't have individual words before we have a language. We cannot ask what a word "should mean," only what it does mean. We pursue that inquiry by noting how the word can be used to construct some propositions in contrast to others. The system has immanent principles of order: laws of grammar. They were no one's intentions. To identify these rules is to investigate the systemic character of the language: the relationship of the parts to each other, which together constitute a whole. Yet, the systemic character of language won't tell us what to say in any particular set of circumstances. It will not even tell us what language to use.

If we study language from the perspective of its use, we are taking up the perspective of project.[18] Some projects—for example, those of poets—take language itself as a project, just as the ascetic takes the body as a project. If we had no projects to make use of a language, it would simply disappear. Indeed, languages are dying at a rapid rate. Not because they have lost their systemic quality, but because they are no longer part of anyone's project. This fact can lead to a radical form of intervention in which preservation of the language actually becomes a project. At that point, we are operating not simply with a language, but for the sake of a language. The truth of language no more lies in system than in project.

The "facts" of our lives are not something separate from the way in which we imagine ourselves when we give an account. When we move from accounts of the domain of nature to those of the social, system and project become tools of persuasion. The manner in which we give an account of ourselves is never an innocent act. There is no right choice, but only a contestation over even the most basic elements of modern life, from the body to the law. Law, like language, has a systemic nature. But also like language, if law is no longer a field of projects—including the project of law itself—it will simply disappear.

Project and System in the Mind of God

The Judeo-Christian story of creation offers an archetypal account of a project. God's project differs from human projects in the dimension of power, not in its structure. The creation project has the same intentional quality as ordinary projects. The idea must precede the act. Of course, God has the power to realize his ideas without effort. Nevertheless, the project is to give material reality to an idea—a plan—that belongs to a subject capable of deliberation and intention. Realization is a process that takes time (even if not much), and it is one in which evaluation of effectiveness ("How did the project go?") is the final step of that process ("It was good."). God apparently is no more certain of how his project will turn out than the rest of us. Indeed, omnipotent as he may be, the project is not entirely a success.

A project, even the first project, must shape a material under the direction of an idea. The original project in this religious tradition differs from all others in that God must first create the material upon which the rest of the project will then be carried out. Thus, the opening words of Genesis are "In the beginning, God created the heaven and the earth." This is heaven and earth as material not yet informed by an idea. Without shape, they cannot be imagined; they are pure potential. This is the beginning that allows the project to go forward; the precondition of all projects.

Of this heaven and earth, the text states, "And the earth was without form, and void; and darkness was upon the face of the deep." Until the project of creation begins, there is nothing positive to be said of earth and sea: darkness and void speak only of absence. A world is that about which we can speak. We can speak intelligibly only of that which expresses some form; that is, an intelligible world is one that embodies an idea or ideas. In the Bible, ideas enter the world as the project of some subject. That first subject is God. Creation is his idea before it is our world.

After the somewhat awkward beginning of creating matter without form, the Genesis account describes a step-by-step effort to realize a project. God's project, despite his power, has the same tentativeness that every project has: there is always risk. Thus, from the very first step of rendering form—light—there is a juxtaposition of omnipotence and judgment. Creation by an omnipotent actor requires nothing more than the speaking of a proposition: "God said, Let there be light." But God seems not altogether certain that this is the direction the project should take. Accordingly, each step of creation is followed by a pause in order to evaluate: "And God saw the light, that it *was* good." It is as if he were a craftsman examining the quality of his work at the end of each day.[19] Having an omnipotent power to carry out a project does not eliminate the need to evaluate the outcome of the project. Between the idea and its execution is an act of will, and every act of will is subject to a normative evaluation. Indeed, the moment of evaluation implicit in the structure of the project carries with it the possibility that this may not have been God's first effort at creation. Is it possible that he judged his prior attempts to have turned out badly? Prior to Noah, did not God nearly come to that judgment with respect to his current project?

Does the evaluation of each day's creative effort suggest that he was open to changing his mind as he saw the results of his work? That this is a serious question becomes clear when the project comes to include man. God's original idea for a man does not quite work out: Adam is lonely. God solves that problem—with Eve—only to confront another problem in the independent judgment of the couple that he created. Once subjects with free wills are created, God is indeed forced to improvise—to change the plan—as he responds to what it is that they do. The project of world creation takes on a new character when it includes the problem of dealing with a free agent. As every parent knows, there is only so much "making" that can be done with one's children. They may be our project, but they are not *only* our project.

Theologically, the Genesis account leads us to ask why it took God six days to carry out this project. Why did an omnipotent God not make all of creation at once? Did he not have in mind the entirety of the plan when he started? The Genesis account has a temporal structure because projects have a temporal structure. That does not explain the number of days, but it does account for duration.

The creation myth is organized around the idea of a project. As such, it minimizes that element of creation that does not quite fit within the model of a project: "In the beginning." That beginning occurs before the creation of time. It has no measure because it represents no idea: it was "without form." The project is the bringing of an idea, which has no time or place, into material and temporal form. Only when an idea has been actualized can we speak of time and place. That transition not only begins time, but takes time. A transition that took no time would not be a project. We know what such nonproject myths of origin look like. Plato's myth in the *Phaedrus*, for example, speaks of the Ideas existing outside of the heavens and informing all that happens. The governing concept of that myth is not project, but memory: a metaphor for the soul's reaching back to the transcendental condition of becoming, which is the timeless Ideas. For Plato, we are in time, but the Ideas are not. For Genesis, God is in time right alongside us. That the Old Testament God occupies time—he is in history—is what makes miracles imaginable.

The Old Testament idea of God, then, is that of a subject with a project. That project extends to the entirety of the world—there is only one God. The project of creation begins with the natural world and ends with man. Man knows himself in the first instance as created, that is, as a subject whose being is defined by his relationship to God's project. The ethos of the project—of maker and made, of authority and dependence—informs the entirety of the Old Testament. That ethos includes God's responsibility toward his creation, as well as his power of judgment over that which he created. It also includes man's responsibility toward the source of his own creation.[20] Understanding oneself as created, even if created as a free subject, provides the ethical context for decision. Free will requires right choice, which is the choice responsive to the fact that our existence is a part of God's project. The fact of dependence grounds norms of obedience and respect. It also grounds the fear of God's justice were a subject to act against the order of God's project.

We see the ethos of project acted out as God deals with the most troublesome part of his creation: man. Disobedience in the Garden is fundamentally an effort to breach the line between creator—one who has a project—and created—the product of a project. Man's sin is to forget his place and to try to be like God. The tree from which he is commanded not to eat is the tree of knowledge of good and evil. Eating of the tree is represented as an effort to know what God knows. A knowledge of good and evil is a necessary condition of having any projects, for one only seeks to realize that which one believes to be good. God exiles man before he can also eat of the tree of life, becoming immortal and thus even more godlike.[21] Having become capable of his own projects by virtue of his sin, man's projects will take place on the hard ground outside of Eden. Unlike in the myth of the *Phaedrus*, man's projects are not a memory of Eden; rather, they remind us of the fall and of the difficult labor that is man's lot. Man is doomed to have projects that he cannot achieve, for what he wants most but cannot have is immortality. Every mortal project is an effort to bring order to the chaos of becoming; every project succumbs eventually to the disorder of time.

A free subject knowing good and evil can form projects of his own. Indeed, exile from the Garden requires projects in the form of taking care of the self, including raising a family. This immediately raises the question of how those projects intersect with God's project. It takes only the second generation to answer this question. Cain, who tills the soil, murders his brother Abel, who raises sheep, when God seems to favor Abel's sacrifice over that of Cain. Killing Abel, Cain takes away something that belongs only to God—human life, which was the endpoint of God's project. Because Cain knows the good, he should know better.

The failure of the original project was brought about by man's free will, to which God responded with punishment. A project among free subjects, however, cannot be unidirectional. It must take the form of a free exchange, that is, of something like a contract. A contract expresses the mutuality of a project or projects. God's relationship to Israel, after the covenant, includes this reciprocal element. Man must make himself a part of God's project, but God promises something in return: Israel will survive and become a great nation. The God of the Old Testament must learn how to deal with a free subject, just as man must learn how to deal with God.[22]

The reciprocity of projects among free subjects gives us a way of understanding Abraham's sacrifice, as well as Moses's covenant. Abraham is tested in his faith, but he acts with confidence in the reciprocal nature of the commitment to the project. God demands Abraham's only legitimate son, Isaac, but God has promised to make Abraham father of a great nation. The demand is paradoxical, but there has been no promise that God's acts will appear reasonable. Already God made it possible for Sarah to produce a son in her old age. That too was paradoxical. Abraham's faith, then, is the alignment of his will with God's project without any claim to know God's reasons.

For this same reason, when Moses receives the law on Mount Sinai, it must be read in its entirety to the assembled community before they can agree to it. The point here is not to evaluate God's formulation of the law against their own conceptions of the good. This is not a negotiation; there is no exchange of ideas about what the law should be or how best to realize their different ends. The content of the law is entirely God's project. He writes the law without consultation with Moses. Nevertheless, this is the reciprocity required among free agents, even when one stands in a hierarchical relationship to the other. A free agent knowingly contracts, even when he is in no position to reject the offer.[23] The structure of law in the Garden was simply that of command ("You must not eat."), but that failed. After Moses, if God's project is to succeed among free subjects, then God must respect the agency even of those whose very existence is owed to him.[24]

The normative claim here is not difficult to understand: it is the same as that found in the relationship between a parent and a grown child. To have a child may be part of the parents' project to create an enduring family, but for that project to succeed the child must come to adopt it as his own. He will only do that if parents and child enter into a reciprocal relationship of respect: a covenant. The child must make the project of the parents his own, but he cannot be coerced into that position. Projects intersect with free agency in what is formally a contract.[25] This hardly means that the contracting parties are in an equal position to bargain for their separate interests. The child may feel a moral obligation to enter the contract; he may feel he lacks the power to resist. Nor does it mean that each party has an independent project that is to form the basis of a negotiated compromise between their conflicting interests. These are secular ideas of contract modeled on market transactions involving objects or acts, the value of which is a matter of the subjective interest or taste of each of the parties. That entire model comes later. In the beginning, contract was covenant.

A covenant freely accepted is consistent with the idea that man "should" accept the covenant because he not only has projects, but is a part of God's project. He owes his life to the Creator, and one acknowledges that gift by entering the Covenant. The child does not choose which family to join. He has a special obligation to his own family—that which created him. Still, he must choose to be a part of that project into which he was born precisely because he is a subject with a free will. He *can* choose otherwise, even if it is the wrong choice. As I have written elsewhere, "Evil makes us human."[26]

The ethical problem of the project arises at this intersection with agency. The problem of the Jews is to understand themselves as simultaneously free and bound by God's project. To claim an autonomy independent of God would be to sin; but to fail to exercise agency would also be to sin. The answer is to freely bind oneself. This was Cain's failure and Noah's success. But for Noah, God was prepared to judge his project to be a failure, for men are evil despite their knowledge of the good. Just as an artist might destroy an unsuccessful work, God brings a flood to destroy his project. He destroys everything and everyone, except Noah and the occupants of the ark. The project must begin again with a new covenant.

A different variation on this problem of the ethos of project is introduced in the Book of Samuel, when the Israelites ask the prophet Samuel to select for them a king so they can defend themselves like other nations. Samuel advises against this and is angered by the rejection of his advice. God tells Samuel that the community is not rejecting Samuel as much as God, who has been their king. God too is angered by the demand, for it suggests that Israel will be the Jews' own project. Yet, despite his threats, God does not abandon the Israelites. Neither, for that matter do the Jews abandon God or his laws; the covenant remains. So, too, do the priests. The free act of commitment to God's project is performed in the daily prayer rituals as well as in the yearly cycle of rituals. Samuel, however, narrates the emergence of an autonomous zone of political projects.[27] That project and God's project are distinct, but occupy the same space; their relationship will present a problem from that point forward. As a relationship among free agents, neither project can be wholly subordinated to the other.[28]

All of these ideas of project and its ethos, of creator and an intergenerational commitment of the created, of hierarchy and agency, will appear in a secularized form in the constitutional project of the late eighteenth and nineteenth centuries. We are still living with this way of imagining our politics. That, however, is not all that we are living with, for system now competes with project.

Before the eighteenth century, it was difficult for those in the Judeo-Christian tradition to think of natural order as anything other than the consequence of an intentional act on the part of God.[29] A whole could precede its parts only as a representation to a subject. There was no other way to imagine the presence of an absence—the whole that was not yet there. Thus, the explosion of scientific insight into the lawfully ordered character of nature initially appeared not as a challenge to faith, but as proof of God's existence. If the universe exhibited an order in which every part stood in a lawfully ordered relationship with respect to every other part, one could only account for that by appealing to the idea of an omnipotent designer. If order went all the way down—as well as all the way up—then God was at work everywhere.

The alternative to this view of God's work was not a self-sustaining, immanent order, as if order came from nowhere and no one, but an idea of a potentially arbitrary God, who must also be an intervening God. A universe without lawful order everywhere would require constant external intervention simply to hold everything in its place. From Leibniz forward, however, philosophy is preoccupied with the idea that God's creative act was to create a *system* in which all of the parts interact with each other according to laws: an order in which the parts sustain the whole and the whole sustains the parts. That whole was both a metaphysical and a normative concept; it linked nature and morality. God's creation had to be good, even if it did not immediately appear that way to man. This was the principle behind Leibniz's *Theodicy*, which claimed that this is "the best of all possible worlds." That which appears bad to us—for example, an earthquake or a war—has its reasons, which would be visible from a systemic perspective.[30]

System linked natural and moral orders in a way that pushed out of view ideas of an interventionist God responding to man's deeds. We do not face divine power as Job did: the inexplicable acts of an intervening God. God's power is no longer independent of his creation. As far as we are concerned, that power is exhausted in creation. Nature was created as a single system of which we too are a part. The ethos of project demanded compliance with law—the covenant; that of system imagines that we need only realize our nature.[31] When Alexander Pope writes "whatever is, is right," he is not admonishing compliance with the covenant but rather the individual's pursuit of his own nature.[32]

There is in this theological idea of creation as system a remnant of the classical idea that reason is the principle of being, the sole force of order in the world. Plato illustrated the point with the divided line of the *Republic*: the task of philosophy is to move up from the images of Ideas to the pure Ideas. The material of the world contributes nothing to its intelligibility. Rather, it obscures our understanding and marks our lesser condition. Plato understood system as the unity of reason, the good, and the beautiful: whatever is—that is, truly is—must have all three qualities. In Judeo-Christian thought, unity is provided by the mind of God. Reason is not free of intention. The unity of the creator grounds the systemic reason of the created.

For Plato, the hierarchy of being grounds a hierarchy of morality. There is a necessary relationship between metaphysics and morality because the idea of the good is the ultimate point of knowing and being. The creator god of the Judeo-Christian tradition, however, is accountable not just for the reason of the universe, but for its material character as well. The distinction, so important to classical thought, of form from matter disappears when God creates *ex ni-hilo*.[33] God's creation is not a lesser form of something else. Thus, our experience is not a lesser version of that which we were meant to be—something that we recall from before our births. There cannot be the same Platonic impulse to disregard this world, once it is understood as entirely a product of God's will. The problematic character of this world is now located in its relationship to that other eternal world that is also part of God's creation. It is deficient measured against what is to come, not against a memory of what truly is.

Because the world's order expresses God's intention, that system must be good. Man's role is not to transcend this world by following reason, but to play his part in its order. Indeed, from the systemic perspective, the world expands to include the space and time beyond our earthly existence. Our nature is to be as a part of *that* system. Man is no longer seen primarily through Adam's sin against God's project. On the systemic view, God not only created nature, he created *our* nature. To have a nature and to be a part of nature are now seen as intimately connected. Our nature is to seek our own happiness. Because we are a part of nature, that act of self-regard must also express the perfection of the system.

Alexander Pope is representative of this worldview. No idea is more central to Pope's *Essay on Man*, published in 1734, than that of system.[34] In the very first stanza, Pope uses this idea to question the limited reach of man's reason:

> He, who through vast immensity can pierce,
> See worlds on worlds compose one universe,
> Observe how system into system runs,
> What other planets circle other suns,
> What varied being peoples every star,
> May tell why Heaven has made us as we are.
> But of this frame, the bearings, and the ties,
> The strong connections, nice dependencies,
> Gradations just, has thy pervading soul
> Looked through? or can a part contain the whole?

Here, we see the new sciences offered as support for a creative God, who works through what Pope later calls "general laws." Man cannot have a comprehensive view of the whole, because he is only a part. To believe that one perceives the entire order or that the universe exists for man is merely presumptuous. Such anthropocentric ideas are the object of Pope's repeated derision. System, for Pope, operates as both a metaphysical and a moral idea. He writes:

> Better for us, perhaps, it might appear,
> Were there all harmony, all virtue here;
> That never air or ocean felt the wind;
> That never passion discomposed the mind.
> But all subsists by elemental strife;
> And passions are the elements of life.
> The general order, since the whole began,
> Is kept in nature, and is kept in man.

Pope expresses the idea that nature refers to both an external and an internal order. Nature continually spans both metaphysics and morals; it is both fact and norm. Man's nature, then, contains the same double forces as nature. The two principles that govern man are reason and self-love. The former is a principle of limits; the latter is one of endless, diverse motions.

> Two principles in human nature reign;
> Self-love to urge, and reason, to restrain;
> Nor this a good, nor that a bad we call,
> Each works its end, to move or govern all
> And to their proper operation still,
> Ascribe all good; to their improper, ill.
> Self-love, the spring of motion, acts the soul;
> Reason's comparing balance rules the whole.

Pope pursues the ethos of system in representing the diversity of human natures, each of which pursues its own self-love, but all contributing to an order that emerges not as the end of their individual actions, but yet through their actions. There is no single hierarchy of goods; no single best way of life. Reason must work upon the plurality of forms of self-love:

> Yes, Nature's road must ever be preferred;
> Reason is here no guide, but still a guard:
> 'Tis hers to rectify, not overthrow,
> And treat this passion more as friend than foe:
> A mightier power the strong direction sends,
> And several men impels to several ends:
> Like varying winds, by other passions tossed,
> This drives them constant to a certain coast.
> Let power or knowledge, gold or glory, please,
> Or (oft more strong than all) the love of ease;
> Through life 'tis followed, even at life's expense;
> The merchant's toil, the sage's indolence,
> The monk's humility, the hero's pride,
> All, all alike, find reason on their side.

Pope's idea of system allows him to understand self-love as the source of energy in a larger order. The pursuit of individual interests will lead to social order because the whole is a well-ordered system. Thus, he writes, "The state of nature was the reign of God: / Self-love and social at her birth began." And a little later: "Thus God and Nature linked the general frame, / And bade self-love and social be the same." Reason leads self-love to realize its own good in a way that creates and sustains the system of the social. When Pope writes "Reason is here no guide," he is rejecting the model of project. In a system, the role of reason is to correct pathology or, as Pope writes "to rectify, not overthrow."

Project and system will compete as leading paradigms of modern thought; they will compete specifically in the American political imaginary. This nation begins with the Old Testament faith of the Puritans informed by the paradigm of project. Not surprisingly, they begin their errand to the wilderness by re-imagining a covenant: The Mayflower Compact. America is a project from that point forward. America, however, is simultaneously an expression of the Enlightenment and of the new sciences of nature and the social. Those sciences draw on the idea of system, not in distinction from faith but as an expression of a modern faith.

Secularization: Project and System

While the appearance in 1776 of distinctly modern ideas of project and system is only a coincidence, it is hardly surprising. Both developments—that politics can be a revolutionary project and that society is a system—are products of the secularization that characterized the Enlightenment. Secularization in the history of ideas refers to the reframing of concepts that had been put to theological purposes such that they now do their work within entirely human dimensions. Examples include sovereignty, sacrifice, and covenant.[35] Each of these terms had been embedded in a universe of meaning anchored by belief in God. Secularized, each has a place in a social imaginary that maintains the nation-state as a human order, independent of support from an intervening god. We may be a "nation under God," but we sacrifice for the state not for God. We are literally "under" God in the sense that he makes no appearance within our political practices. Some political rhetoric may still invoke God, but the modern state, unlike the Church, does not claim to represent or embody divine presence. The modern state represents us, We the People. Its laws have a political origin and a secular justification.

As politics and science turned away from God as an element of practice and explanation, long-deployed imaginative forms were reconceived. Where earlier, man and political order had been God's project, they were now secular projects. Hobbes's great work, *Leviathan*, captures this transformation in the locus of sovereign power: not God, but the citizens themselves create the sovereign through a mutual and reciprocal project of contracting in which they act only upon themselves. Politics—creating the Leviathan—is man's project alone. So much so that religious faith and practice become a part of that project, rather than the other way around.[36] Similarly, where previously the idea of a system "behind" appearances had been used to accomplish the task of theodicy, now system remains as an immanent order without need of a founding God. What had been theodicy becomes an economy in which, as Mandeville put it, "private vices [produce] public benefits."[37]

Systemic order stands, at first, in need of the directing hand of an omnipotent God: "the invisible hand."[38] Over the course of the nineteenth century, that need dissipates, becoming nothing more than a rhetorical invocation of God's providence. The role of the social will be to step into the place of the ontologically real system of the seventeenth and eighteenth century. That system had been grounded in God's reality. By the time of Durkheim at the end of the nineteenth century, the social is our God.[39]

Revolution and social science represent practical and theoretical dimensions of secularization. We no longer pursue a politics directed by revelation; we no longer study nature to fathom the mind of God. God's remaining role is projected to the margins—cosmological origins and ends, on the one hand, and private faith, on the other. These are the margins of time—the unfathomable duration of the universe— and of space—the nonpublic space of the private household. There is no expectation of miraculous, divine intervention in the life of the individual or the political community. There is no study of revelation that will help us to understand nature; no study of biblical texts to learn of a divinely sanctioned legal order. In parallel fashion, the methods of scientific study are extended to the individual and the community.[40] They have been naturalized. The modern conception of the social is a product of that naturalization.

In myth, God's creative powers are superhuman, but his reasons are of the same type that operate in the ordinary life-world. God loves, gets angry, forgives. Perhaps he even gets bored, which may have been why he created anything at all. He is all too human. Secularization entails the disappearance of this entire form of explanation. Nature is now seen as a system operating under laws that organize without intention. The alternative to God's creative power is not the chaos of unorganized matter; it is the lawful regularity of natural systems. A natural order that operates according to law has no need of God. Indeed, it excludes the possibility of a cognizable appearance of God. A God at the margins can be, and was, marginalized, for he can play no role in our explanations of nature or society.

The social sciences appear when this same transition from ordinary reasons of the life-world to systemic explanation occurs with respect to human behavior. To imagine natural phenomena as falling into systems of order is one thing; to imagine that human behavior falls into systems independent of our intentions is quite another. People do things for all sorts of reasons that they tell themselves and share with others. When we investigate the social, however, those reasons drop out as the terms of explanation. Social science becomes a "real science" when transactions are separated from the intentions of the individual actors. Those intentions occupy the same position as mythical accounts of natural phenomena: they offer reasons instead of causes. To study causes, we must observe behavior.

No one studied the economy in the premodern world because the idea of a social system had not yet been imagined. There were, of course, economic transactions, but they were seen as a part of ordinary life; that is, they were studied on the same terms in which they were transacted. One engages, for example, in a purchase because one wants to obtain something. Such transactions were part of the management of the home or business.[41] The economy is an invention of a social imaginary that has turned to system.

To most modern economists, it does not matter what reasons I had for buying or selling. Those reasons might be good or bad for oneself and others, but such moralizing with respect to individual transactions has no place in the analysis of system. Rather, what matters is the way in which particular transactions relate to each other in regular patterns—laws—that are constitutive of the whole. The basis of the economy is no longer the individual reasons for pursuing a single transaction, but the functional relationship of supply and demand. The transaction is relevant only as it relates to the curve that represents that function.

Not surprisingly, the idea of a social contract, which dominated early modern political theory, is approached from the double perspectives of project and system. There is no single answer to the question of whether the social contract is the first project a community must undertake to bring itself into existence or the transcendental condition—the immanent, systemic structure—of any actual community.[42] Do we negotiate a social contract among ourselves as our mutual project, or do we find ourselves already bound by the terms of a social contract as an immanent principle of order that necessarily attaches to our political condition? When Hobbes describes the terms of the social contract as following from the laws of our nature, he imagines a project of political creation and sets it implicitly, if not explicitly, against contemporaneous civil conflict. Rousseau's *Social Contract* also imagines a project of creating a new political order. In subsequent social contract theories, however, there is often surprisingly little actual contracting as the project of particular wills.[43] There is instead a good deal of theorizing about the systemic character of the political. Political order becomes an aspect or manifestation of a deeper, systemic order of sociability. The contemporary political theorist often speaks a language of social contract, but his work may be entirely theorizing system through variations on the prisoner's dilemma.[44]

The modern accounts of project and of system agree on the critical point that God has no place in the political covenant. Both accounts also agree that there is a necessary relationship between political order and justice. A political project relies upon a theory of justice, and conversely theories of justice are developed in response to the idea that politics can be a project. Thus, the age of revolution is also the age of normative political theory. Revolution condemns the status quo as unjust and formulates a plan to realize a more just state. Concretely, many of the political leaders of 1776 were deeply engaged by political theory. Many were lawyers; very few were ministers.[45] Absent an appeal to an idea of justice, revolution is simply unimaginable.

No less evident is the link between the rise of social science and theories of justice. The link of system to justice was already evident in my observation that the origins of modern ideas of system are in theodicy, which becomes an argument for the public value of private vices. Recent work has argued that modern economic thought arose as a response to Hobbes's view of sovereign authority.[46] Modern economics, on this view, was born out of a skepticism that absolute authority can secure either freedom or well-being for the citizen through a political project. In place of the project of the *Leviathan*, early economists argued that order will emerge naturally out of individual freedom. This is an idea of law without sovereignty or system without project. This same idea continues to fuel much conservative political thought in the United States today—at least in domestic political controversies. Deregulation is always on the agenda because of the belief that markets tend not only toward efficiency, but toward a just distribution: the successful have "earned" their success.

Political project and social system are both concerned with justice, but they are structurally inclined to theorize justice differently under modern, democratic circumstances. A project will incline toward issues of redistribution because political projects begin with popular dissatisfaction and the public must take ownership of the project. Systemic theories will incline toward a defense of property rights.[47] Property rights will ground a system of contract as the mechanism by which property is made to do the work of social ordering in the absence of political projects.[48] These different tendencies ground two different strains of modern constitutional discourse: one is organized around ideas of equality; the other is organized around ideas of property.

Project and system also take different attitudes toward the norm of legitimacy. Projects are not abstractions; they are not free-floating. A project belongs to a person, a community, or a people. It must be pursued as someone's plan, if it is to have any presence at all. All of us can imagine more just political orders, but until those ideas become someone's project, they are mere imaginings. Precisely because a political project appeals to a theory of justice, scholars are always in danger of thinking they are doing politics when offering innovative theories. Theory becomes politics, however, only when someone or some group takes it as their project. Projects, accordingly, point toward an idea of self-government—of self-authorship of law—as the ground of legitimacy. Of course, people are unlikely to take up a project they believe to be unjust, but justice can be contested in a legitimate system of self-government.

From the perspective of system, this idea of legitimacy as authorship of the project can make no appearance, for it depends upon a first-person point of view. It makes no sense to speak of authorship with respect to a systemic order, for systems are not the end of any particular subject's actions. To the theorist of system, the distinction of legitimacy from justice collapses: both point to the same immanent order. The system is legitimate, then, as long as it is not suffering from some pathology. As Alexander Pope argued, it is not to be remade by reason.

In a politics of projects, the question of legitimacy inevitably points toward issues of political participation. Must a political project be that of the people? Is there a special role for founders or other elites? What about judges or other government officials?[49] These questions raise issues of legitimacy that are distinct from claims of justice. Modern political projects always raise questions in both dimensions, justice and legitimacy. Justice was, for example, not an adequate excuse for colonialism. Life for white men in the British colonies of North America in the eighteenth century was arguably the freest in the world. That did not make the political order legitimate even for them. When the American revolutionaries claimed that Britain was treating them as slaves, they were not dissembling or being ironic. Rather, they were invoking ideas of legitimacy, not justice. The claim of legitimacy for the new regime remained secure—among white men— even when it became clear that the new constitutional order, which protected slavery, was arguably less just than that of the British, which abolished slavery.[50]

The paradigm of the political project came distinctly into view in the American and French Revolutions. From that moment forward, every existing political order has labored under the possibility of a call to revolution and thus to the radical reconstruction of the project.

Decolonization was one vibrant moment of the politics of projects, as was the recent Arab Spring, which reminds us that projects carry with them the possibility of failure.

Despite the growth of a political vernacular of the project, the paradigmatic political developments of the contemporary period are better described as systemic. Above all, we see this in the subordination of political order to the economic order—an idea expressed by Marxism in the last century, and by the appeal of neoliberalism today. A contemporary state's success is measured by the success of its economy. Because the economic system does not have political borders, political projects today are increasingly viewed and evaluated from the perspective of a global economy. Concretely, we see this in the dominance of economic institutions—for example, the World Bank or the International Monetary Fund—over state decision-making processes. We see it again in the pressure on European nation-states to subordinate their political projects to the managerial role of the European Union, which rests on the necessities of an economic system.

The clash of system and project is one way of understanding the recent crisis in the EU. We saw this first in Greece, which lost control of its political project as it was forced to subordinate itself to the systemic demands of a European and global economic order. Sovereignty, from this perspective, appears to be an increasingly anachronistic concept, for the boundaries of the political project do not correspond to those of the systemic order. Yet, we saw a resurgence of the politics of sovereign project in the British referendum that resulted in a decision to withdraw from the EU. British voters favoring withdrawal said that they desired "control"—a project virtue. They did not want to imagine the United Kingdom as only a part within a larger, systemic order. They wanted a politics of project, and they wanted that project to be their own.

The differing outcomes in the cases of Greece and the U.K. tell us that there is no single way to characterize the relationship of project and system today. Global neoliberalism may appear to dominate, but the politics of national projects has not disappeared.

When politicians claim they want "to make America great again," they too are appealing to project over system. The politics of national projects is not on a course of extinction. It seems, instead, to be rapidly reappearing in the West. Russia and China, too, are pursuing their own nationalist projects. All we can say with confidence is that the tensions between project and system are likely to continue to inform attitudes toward the political order for some time to come.[51]

two

AN AGE OF SUSPICION

In 1776, the ideas of project and system, which had always occupied the life-world and long occupied the theological tradition, took on a new importance. Politics became a project; the social became a system. Of course, the events of 1776, miraculous as they might seem, had histories. We can trace the political events that led to the American Revolution, just as we can trace the development of the idea of system in the years prior to the appearance of *The Wealth of Nations*. Yet, the events of 1776 focused the attention of successive generations; they serve as markers of paradigm shifts. Modernity became visible as a distinct period, with its own truths and its own problems. At the center of those problems was how to think simultaneously of politics as project and system.[1]

After 1776, revolution is a political option that casts a shadow on politics everywhere.[2] If revolution is imagined as a possibility, then politics is a project. Revolution is simply the logic of the project carried to its political endpoint: the state is a malleable site of institutional and legal construction, and we can always start over with a new constitution.[3] To this idea of project, the Marxists and Social Darwinists, as well as a wide variety of political scientists and legal formalists, responded with claims of system. For them, the truth of politics is revealed only to the systemic perspective that discloses the immanent order of historical development, economic markets, or legal arrangements. Revolution invokes a project of the popular sovereign, system points to an order of governance of a population. The nineteenth century is the era of democratic belief in the popular sovereign; it is also the era of statistical measure of populations.

After *The Wealth of Nations*, we live with the idea that ordinary understandings of our relationships to others are an incomplete account of the social order of which we are a part. The understandings that guide our everyday activities appear now as only partial; they must be corrected by an account from a systemic perspective.[4] That perspective was once occupied by theological reflections on providence; it now requires the expertise of the social scientist. Not surprisingly, initially the expertise most relevant to government was economic, but over time multiple forms of analysis of the social made contributions.[5] Among those disciplines was the science of law. Lawyers became a new form of social workers: they make therapeutic interventions to repair the system. Over the course of the century, constitutional interpretation, in particular, became a site for endless conflict between project and system perspectives. This is not an argument with which we are done.

After 1776, the distinction between appearance and structure must be acknowledged with respect to every dimension of the social, from private matters of family to public matters of elections. I may see my family as a project, but that same family figures as an element in national and global demography; I may contribute to a candidate who I think will work to implement my idea of justice, but that same campaign figures as an element in a system of political economy that can be analyzed by graphing statistical relationships among multiple factors ranging from interest groups, to ethnicity, to advertising dollars. We live with a sense that we are no longer at the center of the truth of our own lives. Access to that truth requires disciplinary expertise. By the end of the nineteenth century, law is one such discipline.

The sense of modernity as an age of suspicion arises from these fundamental shifts in the social and political imaginaries. Project and system create a twofold suspicion of ourselves and of our political arrangements. The idea of project requires that we adopt an attitude of reform and recognize the possibility of radical reform—revolution. We come to politics with a suspicion that our political order is failing to meet the ends for which it was constructed. The Declaration of Independence announces such a suspicion as a first principle of all political order when it recognizes "the right of the people to alter or abolish" a government that fails to secure citizen rights and well-being. Because every project suffers slippage between its idea and its implementation, a politics of projects is a politics of endless reform.[6] The visible signs of project failure are everywhere: injustice and inequality. Imagining politics as a democratic project, we hold ourselves accountable for these failures. As citizens, it is our responsibility to further the project.

The attitude of system raises the suspicion that our ordinary beliefs and practices are nothing more than surface appearances, as likely to mislead as they are to reveal. We are always in danger of being captured by our own perceptions. Descartes worried that perception may be nothing more than an illusion created by an evil demon. The demon has gone the way of the invisible hand: both are discarded as remnants of theological belief. Nevertheless, Descartes' worry that perception is an illusion is now an integral part of our understanding of the social. Just as an ethos of the project fears that we are failing to take responsibility for the law, an ethos of system worries that we know neither why we are acting as we are nor what the consequences of our actions might be. We may believe we are acting freely as rational agents, but we know not what we do. Our well-intentioned actions may only make matters worse. Consider, for example, the movement to address rising crime by increasing rates of incarceration. Might it actually have led to increases in the crime rate? We cannot know absent a systemic analysis.[7] Or consider treating national debt as a project failure—a failure to exercise the virtue of living within one's means. Do such "good" intentions actually lead to more economic failure and more debt?[8] Only a systemic analysis can identify the consequences. Private virtues, when seen systemically, may produce public vices.

Not only do project and system each generate paradigmatic suspicions, but juxtaposing project and system generates still more suspicions. Each perspective tends to undermine the other. Consider, for example, property. To gain wealth through acquisition of property appears, in the first instance, as an individual project guided by an idea of personal and familial well-being. I measure success not just by accumulation but by the kind of life property supports. Property, however, is also a system of wealth distribution that may perpetuate longstanding injustices and create new ones. Acquiring property, am I securing my own family's well-being or injuring others? Do we approach property by asking who has succeeded in their projects or by asking about the structural characteristics of its distribution? Neither approach can proceed innocent of the other. Neither represents the truth of the matter.

The two events of 1776 focused the mind—one in the direction of political practice, the other in the direction of social theory. These changes in the imagination of practice and theory were of boundless reach. By the time the idea of the project had fully worked its way through the social imaginary, the leading value of modernity had become autonomy: all of us must make our lives, as well as our communities, a project.[9] We should never settle for that which we inherit; rather, we must make our lives our own. Similarly, the idea of system expands through the entire range of the social. The systemic approach to economic phenomena may have been first, but the nineteenth-century differentiation of the social sciences follows rapidly: sociology, anthropology, linguistics, law, and psychology. Later still, the process of differentiation of the social continues with positive political theory, international relations theory, and behavioral economics. By the time this revolution in the analysis of the social is through, we are speaking of nudges, heuristics, externalities, and systemic biases. This is the language of regulation, not that of the project: systems are administered or managed, projects are created.[10]

What was not clear in 1776 is certainly clear today: there is a deep tension between the perspectives of project and system. To take responsibility under the idea of project is to work under an ideal of autonomy; to take responsibility under the idea of system is to work under an ideal of management. Take up the perspective of economics and one becomes skeptical about the possibility of changing behavior through political projects; take up the perspective of project and economics is likely to appear as an ideological defense of the status quo. Is responsibility for the self and the polity a matter of autonomy or management?

We understand how these conceptual tools are used only by looking at their actual use, for there is no single answer to this tension of project and system. One way to characterize modernity is as a condition under which no matter which perspective we choose, we will be subject to criticism from the other perspective. If that is the case, modernity is a condition in which theory and practice can never be brought into a stable alignment.

Some Texts: More, Jefferson, Smith, and Tocqueville

That modern political practice and modern social science both appear dramatically in the same year would not be particularly remarkable if the two events were related as practice to theory. But the American Revolution is not an application of the new social science, and that social science does not arise from a consideration of the new political practices of the American Revolution. While the leaders of the Revolution were theoretically informed, the political science upon which they relied was for the most part the traditional political theory of rights and institutions, not the newly emerging social sciences.[11] They had a penchant for adopting classical names as pseudonyms, for they saw themselves in this tradition.[12] And while the new social science of economics was directed at a form of political theory, that form was the idea of sovereignty associated with Hobbes. The conjunction of a practice of revolutionary, democratic political projects and the rise of modern economics launched the still-pressing question of the relationship of equality to liberty.[13]

To get a sense of the transformations of 1776, it will help to begin with an earlier text and end with a later text. I start with Sir Thomas More's *Utopia*, first published in 1516, well before the emergence of the modern ideas of political project and a science of the social. With some foresight of the personal danger that can arise from suggesting too much change to a powerful ruler, More published on the Continent, not in England. After *Utopia*, I consider directly the central texts of 1776, the Declaration of Independence and *The Wealth of Nations*. I end this section with a consideration of Alexis de Tocqueville's

Democracy in America, the first volume of which was published in 1835. Tocqueville's work illustrates how deeply the idea of a social system had already penetrated into the European analysis of the political.

Thomas More, Utopia

Utopia's outlook on the political has more in common with Plato's *Republic* than with modern political theory. In form and manner, More follows the *Republic*. In form, *Utopia* too reports a single evening's conversation. Plato's Socrates, who never leaves Athens, is replaced by More's Raphael, who has traveled the entire world. The effect, however, is much the same, for Raphael is recounting his memory of a place he has visited on the other side of the globe. More is offering a geographical representation of Plato's metaphysical claim to a memory of the Ideas seen before birth. Plato's un-Christian metaphysics of memory is replaced by a mythical account of a voyage of discovery. Like Plato, More offers "a city in speech" in which there is no private property and in which the well-being of the whole depends upon a sense among everyone, including the rulers, that their interests lie in advancing the commonwealth.[14] Political well-being is not the aggregation of individual interests formed apart from the community, but a common end to which all citizens must devote themselves: "no man has any property, all men zealously pursue the good of the public. . . ."[15] Individuals may have different roles, but they have common goals.

Like Plato, More sees no way in which his vision of an ideal political order can become a reality, except by gaining the attention of a ruler who is already in power. It is not a plan for a project of construction of political order by and through prepolitical individuals—a social contract. More's work resembles the wisdom literature of the Jewish rabbinic tradition. It is practical in the sense that it is not a theoretical inquiry pursued for its own sake. But its actual use in practice turns on whether the advice is followed, which is not the same thing as whether the exposition is persuasive. Someone might be persuaded by More's imaginative account of a well-run city, but still find himself unable to act.

More confronts a paradox of application. He suggests that a ruler give up his wealth, privileges, and property. Why, however, would any ruler follow this advice, given that it runs counter to the ruler's apparent interest in using the state as a means to his own ends? Of current regimes, More writes: "I can have no other notion of all the other governments that I see or know, than that they are a conspiracy of the rich, who on pretense of managing the public only pursue their private ends. . . ."[16] Paradoxically, a ruler would be interested in following More's advice of renouncing his apparent interests only if he had already been educated and trained in More's Utopia. Precisely because Raphael cannot imagine a sympathetic ruler, he chooses to stay out of politics entirely. He offers his account in a private conversation, not as direct advice to a ruler.

More, accordingly, confronts the same quandary as Plato: the well-ordered state is the necessary condition of its own existence.[17] The well-being of a state depends upon the character of its rulers, but the laws and practices of the state are what produce that character. The well-ordered state may reproduce itself once it is brought into being, but its creation is a puzzle. There is no reasonable prospect of its starting—short of the accident that a philosopher happens to be born into power.[18] Thus, the first chapter of *Utopia* is concerned precisely with the reluctance of Raphael even to offer his advice to a European ruler. In that direction, he argues, lies only danger to himself from the selfish interests at court. There is no reasonable prospect of successful reform of the state. Better, as Plato put it, to keep one's head down and seek shelter behind a stone wall.[19] More himself will become proof of the accuracy of this concern.

Turning to the utopian state that More describes, we see that it must make up for the absence of private property, and thus of market transactions, by government planning, on the one hand, and the inculcation of virtuous habits, on the other. An idea of the family displaces that of the market: "[A]ccording to [each town's] plenty or scarcity, they supply, or are supplied from one another; so that indeed the whole island is, as it were, one family."[20] This order is maintained by habits of virtuous behavior, which, in turn, rest on appropriate beliefs in divine reward.

"They have but few laws," but unwritten regulations guide behavior everywhere.[21] Thus, days are divided into periods of work, meals, and leisure, while leisure is directed toward educational activity. No one wastes time; waste is connected to private ownership. Everyone is provided for according to his or her needs and abilities—an idea that has a long future. There is no local use for gold or currency, but these do figure in foreign policy, for even Utopia must deal with other states in the conditions under which it finds them. Accordingly, the Utopians have an active program of foreign aid, and they do not hesitate to use their wealth to avoid conflict. When conflict does arise, they use that wealth to pay mercenaries. The citizens of Utopia are to be disturbed as little as possible.

Just as gold and wealth are evaluated from the perspective of their possible contribution to the public welfare, so too are beliefs. Describing the Utopians' core ethical belief to be that the happiness of man is pleasure, More emphatically decouples private property from pleasure.[22] The pleasure he has in mind is not that of bodily sensation: "But of all pleasures, they esteem those to be most valuable that lie in the mind; the chief of which arises out of true virtue. . . ."[23] It is man's nature to live virtuously, which means to live according to the direction of reason. On this view, pleasure arises from right beliefs about God and society: "we should consider ourselves as bound by the ties of good-nature and humanity to use our utmost endeavours to help forward the happiness of all other persons. . . ."[24]

Management for the public good extends to religious belief. Belief in an afterlife of reward is a necessary condition, More says, of pursuit of virtue in this life. "These are their religious principles, that the soul of man is immortal, and that God of His goodness has designed that it should be happy; and that He has therefore appointed rewards for good and virtuous actions, and punishments for vice, to be distributed after this life."[25] This principle is passed on by their tradition, but it is also, according to the Utopians, established independently by reason alone—a position that will be taken up by Kant.

At various points, More aligns this politics of reason with the teachings of Christ: both describe possible worlds, even if they are unlikely to be realized in this world. Much in his account sounds familiar—even if still aspirational—today: the belief in education for everyone, a concern for the least well-off, a criminal justice principle of lenity, a foreign policy of friendship and peaceful coexistence, a practice of religious tolerance, an understanding that the purpose of the state is to advance the common good, and an alignment of public office with merit. This state could, in some other world, be the object of a political project.

Like Christ's message, however, the doctrine of *Utopia* does not easily translate into a step-by-step program of reform. Early on, Raphael rejects the argument that a philosopher should temper his advice in order to achieve whatever reforms are practicable given the politics he actually confronts. One cannot be a little bit in the "kingdom of heaven," and one cannot be a little bit in the kingdom of reason. One does not approach the character of a state that has neither money nor private property by reducing the amount of money in circulation. One cannot practically limit the amount of private property, because private property of any amount fosters a certain character type that will always want more.[26] From where, then, could such limits come?

Despite these intimations of modernity, *Utopia* is not a modern book. The idea that politics can be a project of some sort is, of course, suggested by describing a utopian order that could be the object of deliberate action. In this sense, *Utopia* offers a plan. But this is hardly our modern idea of politics as a project to be pursued by a political community. This is clear when we ask, whose project is it? More remains under the grip of the Platonic idea that reason enters political order through the philosopher advising a ruler. He has no concept of a community shaping itself through a common project. More's model of the philosopher's rule will persist right through Kant's essay *Perpetual Peace*. Kant too can see no way of aligning politics and reason except by the philosopher advising a ruler.[27] The philosopher can theorize a just state. The authority of the ruler, however, remains external to the philosophical project. The narrative is to persuade the person who already has authority, while the substance is to advance a philosophically established truth. That conjunction remains no less a fiction for More than it was for Socrates. For both, it was a dangerous fiction.

Plato grasped the accidental and extremely unlikely character of convergence of rulers and philosophers. Plato had hopes for Dionysius of Syracuse, but was disappointed. Kant imagined Frederick II of Prussia might be such a ruler. Did More imagine Henry VIII in this role? Philosophers are no better at judging the character of rulers than anyone else. But, then, why should they be?

Even if philosophers were more successful at assessing kingly character, this idea of a virtuous practice still understands politics to operate in the dimension of what the *Federalist Papers* called "accident."[28] The well-being of the polity depends upon the accident that potentially good rulers will find good advisors willing to risk their own lives on a political undertaking that is not even their own. History tells us that this is a slim chance indeed. More ends up dead; his fictional character, Raphael, knows better than even to try. Utopia remains a mythical place beyond the oceans.

Despite the alignment of nature and reason, More's *Utopia* is not imagined as a polity that comes about "naturally." There is no promise that acting according to one's true nature will in fact lead to the social good and a utopian order. Unlike the natural order of other "social animals," a well-ordered, natural polity does not come about absent the intent of actors directed by an ideal plan. Everyone in Utopia is to practice the same natural virtues, but natural virtues require "unnatural" effort in order to be effective. Instead of nature as a system with an immanent principle of order, we find an appeal to the religious belief that God will reward virtuous behavior after death. The afterlife, however, is not a political space. A well-ordered polity continues to depend on a faith outside of politics, just as its origins rely on an authority that it cannot create.

For More, nature—at least human nature—will not take care of itself. What is called nature is a normative order discerned by reason and demanding action that may not seem natural at all: it demands the pursuit of virtue, not immediate pleasures. That the pursuit of virtue can lead to pleasure remains in God's hands. In other words, for man, the nexus of virtue and pleasure remains a matter of faith. The model of politics here is neither that of project nor that of system, but that of mediated virtue. It is the structure of Christian belief become political.[29] The philosopher steps into the place of the priest, offering mediation between God and fallen man.

A successful politics depends upon the virtue of the ruler. That virtue has an extrapolitical source: the ruler must fear God and have faith in the afterlife. Even a virtuous ruler, however, cannot direct his political practice himself. Rather, his character opens him to the influence of the philosopher. The philosopher knows what should be done, but has no capacity to do it. The ruler has that capacity, but does not know how best to use it. Theory and practice have split apart. Political success depends upon the accident of them coming together in the relationship between particular individuals—rulers and philosophers. The revolution of 1776 will put an end to this vision of politics.

The Declaration: Public Order as Project

For More, thinking about a radical alternative to the existing state required an exercise in myth making. To actually match the real to the ideal was just barely imaginable, which meant it depended upon chance events, not a plan of action. The question was how a philosopher could possibly hope to move a ruler to adopt this project—a question to which there was no practical answer outside of myth and the possibilities represented by an endless duration.[30] In endless time, anything is possible.

That More, a devout Christian, has no better answer to the problem of practice than did Plato may be surprising. Christian ideas of sin and of a history incapable of redeeming itself had come to occupy the ground of what had been Plato's political pessimism, itself grounded in his experience of Socrates' execution by democratic Athens. *Utopia*'s account of a perfect politics stands beside the New Testament accounts of Christ's life: the truth has been revealed, but there is an open question of whether fallen man is capable of taking it up. For More, truth does not provide a privileged point of entry into actual politics. Indeed, it may be just the opposite: More's own effort to speak truth to power follows the Socratic pattern of sacrifice.[31]

This way of imagining political history within the broad context of man's fall was thoroughly abandoned by 1776. The Declaration of Independence starts with a completely different call on history:

> When in the Course of human events, it becomes necessary for one people to dissolve the political bands which have connected them with another, and to assume among the powers of the earth, the separate and equal station to which the Laws of Nature and of Nature's God entitle them, a decent respect to the opinions of mankind requires that they should declare the causes which impel them to the separation.

These words are so familiar as to seem almost banal, but fully to understand their modern character requires close examination.

First, history is understood as course of human events, not of divine events. History is not the field upon which God shows Himself. Nor is there a divine measure of these events. History is a course of human events in the sense that the responsible actors are individuals, who together constitute a people. Their concern is not directed at a God who shows his pleasure or displeasure with a people's behavior, but rather at the opinions of mankind.[32] The Declaration is offered as one people speaking to other peoples, who will form opinions based on the explanation offered. These others are imagined as open to persuasion by reasonable argument. The justifications offered speak neither of partisan interests nor of religious beliefs, but rather of moral claims of universal purport. Thus, citizens must act with a "decent respect" for the opinions of mankind. Those opinions are plural because there is no simple community of all men constituted by their worship of the same God. There are instead multiple peoples constructing their own histories.

Second, while God is neither actor nor audience, he is not completely out of mind. He appears now in the conjunction "the Laws of Nature and of Nature's God." The conjunction captures the ambiguity of Deist sentiment on the source of law, both natural and moral. Perhaps the oldest question of moral theory is whether justice is grounded in divine command or divine command is grounded in justice.[33] Does God's will define justice, or is that will guided by justice? The Enlightenment form of this question asks whether reason alone, without revelation, can discover the moral law. The Declaration imagines a neat conjunction of the two: reason and revelation lead to the same point. They are laws *of nature* and *of nature's God*. Presumably, we could start at either point and reach the other.[34] We don't quite know whether God's role in this conjunction is only that of creator—laws must come from somewhere—or of normative authority—law binds because it is God's. We don't know because there is no need to know once history has become a human affair. For that reason, immediately after this ambiguous invocation of God, the Declaration turns to the importance of public opinion. Public opinion matters because it is the forum in which the political project will be judged; it is the space within which claims of nature's law will have to be defended.

Third, this normative political order of reason and revelation already imagines collective subjects—that is, peoples—as actors. Norms do not run only to individuals; the political is not simply an aggregation of individuals, each subject to universal, moral demands. Political norms run to political groups, that is, to peoples. In the Declaration, history has a natural normative order, but it does not operate independently of peoples taking responsibility for themselves. Doing so, they act on a world stage before other peoples, who must be persuaded to see the justice of the revolutionary act. That politics is not morality becomes clear as the Declaration goes on to accuse the king of interference with American control of slaves.

Fourth, the God of the Declaration, while banished to the margins, remains a creator God, not an eschatological God. Men are endowed by "their Creator with certain inalienable rights." There is no mention of God's judgment. There is a formal acknowledgment of "divine providence" at the conclusion, but this is given no operative weight. Not one of the complaints against king and Parliament listed in the Declaration touches on religious command or practice. Rather, they are political complaints that run to the operation of law, the responsiveness of government, and the claim to representation. The complaints concern the abuse of power; they are not claims of religious violation or accusations of sinful behavior. The Revolution has no theological basis apart from the natural rights of individuals and peoples.

The Declaration, accordingly, sets forth the imaginary space within which politics appears as a collective project on a human scale.[35] History is no longer to turn on the accidental conjunction of a ruler's character and the presence of a philosopher among his advisors. The whole of political history is now seen through the lens of a popular project. Governments do not arise by nature; rather, they are chosen by the people. Thus, governments "derive their just powers from the consent of the governed." This is not just a matter of theory, but an active principle of history. The people "institute" government to secure their "inalienable rights." These governments remain subject to popular review:

> whenever any Form of Government becomes destructive of these ends, it is the Right of the People to alter or to abolish it, and to institute new Government, laying its foundation on such principles and organizing its powers in such form, as to them shall seem most likely to affect their Safety and Happiness.

History is a series of such active interventions—projects—in which the people alter, abolish, and institute governments and policies of governance, that is, laws. In all of this, they are directed by their own judgment; they act with an eye to "their Safety and Happiness."

Even a successful governmental structure cannot last forever, for circumstances change, rendering existing laws and institutions

problematic. Institutions that once worked eventually become coun-
terproductive. Accordingly, "any Form of Government" can become "destructive of these ends." When that happens, the people
have the right to "institute new Government." Whether they do so
depends upon an assessment of the practical risk involved in any such
project. The urgency of reform must be measured against the likeli-
hood of success and the burdens of transformation—what I called
effectiveness in the last chapter. That is, the demand for justice must
be tempered by the virtues of prudence. It is entirely common to
make matters worse through a new intervention. Thus, the Declaration notes that people are often more willing to suffer injustice
than to take on the risk of action. They settle for a second-best constitutional design. At some point, however, the calculation shifts
toward action. The people have then been persuaded to take up a
new project. The decision and the reasons are their own.

A politics of projects has the existential quality of being *experimental* because no one can know with certainty what outcome will follow.
For More, time represented the possibility of reform. For the Founders,
time represented the inevitability of decline. Thus, the people may
have been persuaded to act, but they may come to regret their decision. They are likely to have to adopt modifications to their original
idea of the project. This is hardly a new idea. God's project of creation
took on an experimental quality once a subject with a free will was
brought into being.[36] Even God must exercise prudence in his projects
of creation. Perhaps this is why he agrees to enter a covenant with
Noah under which he will no longer entertain the possibility of total
destruction. Prudence dictates that it is better to work with what one
has than to start over, when what one has are free agents.

Most of the Declaration is a list of very concrete particulars. The
litany of complaints points to the polycentric character of history.
The list includes multiple failures; there is no single cause of pathology. For this reason, there is no single answer that theory can identify
as the cure for all political pathologies, even when the analysis of
pathology appeals to natural law.[37] Because men are free, they have

different concerns and respond to different reasons. If history is their product, it cannot have a single direction. Politics, even successful politics, is a matter of persuasion, not deduction.

Citizens and politicians must act on their best judgment and await the result. In American history, the first projects of political construction were more or less failures: the Continental Congress did not manage the Revolutionary War well; the Articles of Confederation failed to manage the peace. Even the Constitution failed in its first form: a bare seventy-five years later, the country was at war with itself. Substantial constitutional amendment was required.[38] The risk of failure simply cannot be eliminated from a politics of projects. Nevertheless, an enlightened people must take responsibility for their own institutions as their own projects.

The responsibility of the people does not mean they can do whatever they like. They are constrained in two directions. First, there is the law of nature. A people has no more right to act unjustly than does a king. Thus, the pursuit of political projects requires an analysis of the laws of nature—"inalienable rights"—which are constraints on choices made in pursuit of "Safety and Happiness." For this reason, an age of political projects must also be an age of political theory. This is not because philosophers should be kings or because rule is a form of discourse—the early and late expressions of the same confusion of power and theory. Rather, it is because projects require ideas as their origin and end.

Second, there is the political psychology of institutions. If political theory's first role is to identify rights that must be respected, its second role is to suggest institutional means of achieving the ends of government within the constraint of rights. About the design, there cannot be the same certainty as about the rights. There are no "inalienable institutions." With respect to issues of institutional design, prudence tempers theory with practical judgment. Theorizing institutional design requires consideration of ideas of the second best, for it is in the nature of the human material—that is, of the stuff of politics—that we can never shape it wholly to meet our diverse ends. Compromises must be made.

Part of the reason people are not entirely malleable is that a politics of projects never really starts from scratch. To imagine starting from scratch is to turn to myth. Hobbes offers one such myth in his description of the state of nature; Rousseau another. Even in those myths, family precedes the state. In fact, we always find ourselves under some political order and operating with some political expectations, even in the midst of a revolution. Not all government institutions were overthrown in the American Revolution, and of course habits and expectations of governance remained.[39] Political projects come late to the formation of political character, which itself comes late to individual character and interests. If political projects seek to make citizen character too a matter for revolutionary reconstruction, they can easily find themselves on a course toward totalitarianism.[40] Move too far toward an ideal vision, and one ends up eliminating private property and collectivizing the family—ideals that informed Plato, More, Stalin, and Mao. The last two actually exercised power in pursuit of a totalizing political project; their lack of prudence brought disaster.

Conservative virtues must, accordingly, be balanced against the project virtue of achieving a set of ideal ends. The idea of a political project does not tell us how to strike the balance between ideals and risks, between justice and prudence, between action and patience. Just the opposite: imagining politics as a project, these are the sort of issues of effectiveness we confront. Neither does removing God and insisting that politics is a project of a particular political community acting on a world stage remove this normative ambiguity. That ambiguity is precisely why the project of politics cannot rely only on theoretical expertise, but requires virtues of character as well.

There is one final point to emphasize about the Declaration: its double role as performative utterance and justification.[41] The Declaration itself breaks the tie with the British Crown when it declares the community an independent nation.[42] In this sense, it is also a declaration of war. For the British, this is a civil war—a rebellion to be put down. If the revolution were to fail, that is all it would ever be. The project can succeed only if there is victory at war. The revolutionary war will come to be seen as realizing its end in the Constitution. The war becomes part of this larger project of constitutional creation; it is the beginning but not the end.

Thinking of the project as beginning with war points toward the international context within which every political project moves forward. The justification offered to third parties—that is, to foreign nations—is simultaneously an effort to persuade them to support the new nation.[43] The political project accordingly goes forward not just within the multiple dimensions of a free people pursuing their varied interests, but also among other nations freely exercising their own judgments and pursuing their own projects. America, for example, owes the success of its revolutionary project in substantial part to French intervention and assistance. The war was their project as well: a project with quite a different end than our Constitution.

Whatever we might think about the possibility of a politics of war and peace taking the form of a national project, there is no similar claim in the Declaration that the political order among nations is also a project. Whose project would it be, after all? National history— the history of a project—occurs, then, within a history of global order that cannot itself be easily modeled on the idea of a single project. The political project of the nation always has reference to and depends upon the larger order of nations, which is itself beyond the possibility of ordering through a project—at least for another 100 years. To the degree that a separate global order was imagined at the beginning of the nineteenth century, it was a systemic order expressed in the law of nations. The domestic project of constitutional construction was related to the legal order of the law of nations as project to system. Understood in this way, this relationship of the two legal orders served as a modern iteration of system offering a theodicy to project.[44]

Adam Smith, The Wealth of Nations

Opening a recent edition of the *London Review of Books*, one finds this sentence in a description of the beliefs of the twentieth-century

Austrian school of economics: "The economy was a self-generating, self-correcting system which owed nothing to government or to conscious design, and at its best depended on the unfettered play of the energies and appetites of men."[45] While the Austrian school has no monopoly on the science of economics, this description captures the power of the model of system and the direction in which it heads. A system is "self-generating [and] self-correcting." It is not the result of an external force imposing order; rather, it is immanent and spontaneous. A system, moreover, is not ephemeral; it maintains itself against disturbance.[46]

The author of the review is quick to point out that Adam Smith was not himself adverse to all government action on the economy. Smith, for example, believed that a progressive income tax is an appropriate way for government to raise funds. In 1776, economic analysis was not offered as a general argument against government regulation. Rather, it was to provide a basis for more enlightened regulation. Most immediately, economic analysis suggested eliminating many of the archaic forms of intervention in the economy—for example, the granting of monopolies.

Smith did not understand himself as "an economist" and certainly did not limit his analysis to matters that we consider subjects of economic expertise today. He ranged broadly over the entire social order—from education to religious belief. He tended to view all these matters from the same perspective that he used in his study of the economy proper: a combination of individual psychology and systemic order. *The Wealth of Nations* draws upon, and follows from, his earlier work, *The Theory of Moral Sentiments*.[47] This broader reach makes Smith a point of origin for the social sciences well beyond the particular concerns of economics. One might best describe Smith's ambition as that of founding a science of the social upon which enlightened government regulatory interventions could be based.[48]

Smith's ambition to see the social as a system places his work in tension with the contemporaneous expression of project in the Declaration. Both begin from a vision of man's fundamental nature. For the project, this is man "endowed with certain unalienable rights." For the system, this is the "propensity in human nature . . . to truck, barter, and exchange one thing for another."[49]

In the Declaration, unalienable rights are the just measure of government, because their realization is the end for which governments are created. As final causes, they do not operate of themselves. A political project must adopt these rights as ends; it must seek to realize them through law. This "must" is entirely normative: the project must adopt these ends, if it is to be just and legitimate. For the project, human nature operates in the first instance not as fact, but as norm.

Smith appeals to human nature not as the final, but as the efficient cause of the social order. He explicitly rejects the idea that the social order depends upon a vision of final causes. It is not the product of anyone's wisdom, because it is not a project at all. No one—at least no market participant—adopts the economy as his or her project. Individuals truck and barter for whatever particular ends they have in view. Together, these individual transactions form a systemic order— the economy. The system is produced by the individual actions, but it is not their end. Although Smith denies that man has a natural quality of sociability, the social is naturalized, for it arises of its own, that is, without artificial intent. Man comes in and through history to what other species have by nature: a systemic, social order. This idea of order is not that of the Declaration, which located the force of historical development in popular political projects.

One way to understand the difference between project and system is to ask about the location of reason. For the Declaration, the practice of politics is directed by the reason of those who design and then seek to implement the institutional order. They make the law on the basis of what they think to be a science of politics, which includes ideas about rights and institutions. In a democracy, the role of "maker" is generalized to the entire citizenry, all of whom must guide their behavior according to the principles of political science. This is particularly true at certain moments, for example, that of debating and adopting a constitution or constitutional amendments.[50] Yet, even in ordinary politics, the project view requires citizens to include among their reasons some concern for constructing and maintaining a just political order. For a citizen to say that the political order is not his or her concern would represent a failure of character that could lead to a failure of the project.

For Smith, on the other hand, reason is located in the phenomena of the social, not in the intentions of the actor. An order of reason is realized in the social quite independently of intention. Reason is not in the social world in the way that reason is in a machine—a product of the intentions of its maker. Rather, reason is in the economy in the same way that it is in the structure of a functioning organism: in the arrangement of parts to whole, with every organ playing a function in relation to every other. This order is objective in the sense that it is discovered, not established, by a scientific inquiry. Of course, just as knowing the laws of biology may help us to achieve more productive farming, knowing the laws of the economy may help to improve the efficient use of resources. To what degree systemic knowledge allows us to make the economy itself a project remains an open question—as suggested by the description of the Austrian school above. All agree that systems—social or biological—can suffer pathologies that are the objects of repair.

We see the contrast in approaches to the location of reason when we consider the nature of contractual origins in the two imaginaries of 1776. Behind the Declaration is an idea of the social contract as the origin of political order. Thus, governments "derive their just powers from the consent of the governed." Citizens will enter into that contract only if it respects their unalienable rights. They must be persuaded to agree. Agreeing, they take on a common project that is the source of order.

In contrast, for Smith the original contract is not a modern, secular form of the Old Testament covenant. It is not a social contract at all, but a contract of exchange. People will always come together to truck and bargain to advance their own interests. They measure those contracts not against some idea of unalienable rights, but against their actual preferences. They exchange some of what they have for something that they want, making both parties to the exchange better off. No value attaches to these items of exchange in the abstract. Their value is determined at the moment of exchange. Thus, there is no natural or essential price.

Both of these images of origins are individualistic: the state and the society arise from the coming together of individuals, not the other way around. One proceeds from reason and the other from interests. One believes that the social contract is founded on justice; the other believes that justice has little to do with the origins of the social. We don't measure biological order by justice, and Smith approaches the social as if its systemic order constituted man's environment. Thus, while *The Wealth of Nations* is deeply concerned with the nature of distribution—among individuals, families, regions, nations—it has little concern with justice. The question is never "Is the distribution just?," but always "How does wealth come into being and what will be the consequences of any accumulation?"

Smith puts labor at the foundation of his analysis: the capacity to labor, and thus to commit ourselves to labor, is what each of us has by nature. It is, accordingly, the source of wealth. This is power, not right. Smith does not approach labor from the perspective of the things made—the world that man creates. Rather, he sees labor as a quantum of energy that can be put to work. Man's labor places him in the world, just as other animals relate to the world through their labor. But while other animals direct their labor naturally toward maintenance of their social order, man's labor has no natural end. There is nothing we are born to do. Order comes later, with the development of an economy.

The energy of labor flows through man's capacity to truck, barter, and exchange. Unlike that of other animals, man's labor is not bound to instinctual activities. He can invest his labor in one place rather than another. He will make these investments on the basis of agreements to exchange with others. This ability to truck and barter is a function of man's capacity for speech. For Smith, the first use of speech is to contract, that is, it is to enter into an exchange. It is to set a price, not to make a claim of right.

Reading Smith, one is struck by the way in which he imagines a sort of underlying physics of the social. Labor is the source of energy; it is the elementary input that animates the entire system. Smith treats it as if it were a fluid that will naturally flow of its own direction.[51] Thus, he makes constant reference to conditions of "perfect liberty," meaning the absence of any impediments to individuals determining how to direct their labor in order to maximize their returns. Blockage of the flow can emerge from many sources, including government policies—for example, authorization of monopolies or limiting entry into a field.

Classical economics' focus on flow is captured symbolically in its representation of particular transactions as continuous functions graphed as curves. More broadly, nineteenth-century science, which extends from Smith to Freud, is dominated by the imagination of flows. It is profoundly "hydraulic."[52] This is true even of that most important of nineteenth-century scientists, Darwin, who makes of species reproduction a natural flow subject to blockages in the form of environmental change. Loosely, we can characterize the earlier science of the seventeenth and eighteenth centuries as laboring under the image of the unit: the elements of matter that are subject to Newton's laws. Twentieth-century science will displace the image of hydraulics with that of a field of interacting forces.[53] The mercantilism that precedes Smith depended upon an idea of aggregation of material elements—particularly gold. The move in contemporary economics toward information reflects the turn to an idea of a network of interacting forces and away from an idea of flow. Mercantilism relied on government projects of tariffs, protectionism, and trade. Ideas of flow and field support forms of systemic reasoning to identify immanent laws of system.[54]

Smith's idea of perfect liberty straddles the divide between the positive and the normative. For the most part, Smith thinks of his work as offering a positive representation of the economic system. He is not, for example, concerned about the interests of any particular individual, about winners and losers in particular transactions. He expresses no view about whether any individual or class would be better off with perfect liberty. Perfect liberty operates in a way analogous to pure space in Newtonian physics. Hypothesizing conditions of perfect liberty, the economist can identify the laws of the economic system. Once identified, those laws can be seen at work in ordinary life.

Smith's analysis of the mechanics of truck, barter, and exchange offers an internal perspective on systemic virtues: a system works well when its immanent, natural laws operate without hindrance. This idea of the internal virtues of the system can then be brought to bear to analyze actual situations. Today, we might say that the internal norm of an economic system is efficiency, which is realized when blockages of perfect liberty are removed.[55] Sometimes we choose not to remove those blockages because they are doing other normative work. The internal norms of the discipline of economics are not the only norms at stake in the working of an economy. We may be quite willing, under some circumstances, to sacrifice efficiency for the sake of justice—for example, with respect to distribution.

Smith begins his work with an analysis of a pin factory—an account that enters deep into the inventory of the modern imaginary. His point is to show how the division of labor dramatically increases the quantity and quality of production. One man alone could make only a few pins a day, and probably of poor quality. When the process of production is divided such that each step becomes the responsibility of a specialist who forms his labor precisely to match the task and devotes his ingenuity to a task with which he is entirely familiar, production and quality soar. That increased output is wealth.

As pins become better and cheaper to produce, more expensive production processes will be driven out of the market. Supply will continue to increase as long as there is demand. Every pin producer will try to produce more at a cheaper rate than his competitor. The energy flows are almost palpable in the account as workers, capitalists, merchants, transporters all direct their labor toward the end of meeting consumer demand for pins. Each contributor is subject to the dynamic of the division of labor because that is the natural flow of labor under conditions of truck, barter, and exchange.

New production methods will draw in new investments of stock, labor, and land. The owners of these elements will compete among themselves in their claims on the wealth produced by the totality of the manufacturing enterprise. Smith analyzes the factors that will determine the outcome of this competition under conditions of less than perfect liberty, but he can do so only because he has already imagined what would happen under perfect liberty. Economics can do no better than formulate generalities or probabilities, rather than precise predictions, for every factor that enters into economic consideration is embedded in contexts that work against perfect liberty. These can be habits and customs, imperfect information, personal relationships, or errors in judgment—as well as positive laws that limit use of the land, competition among firms, or organization among workers. The laws of the social sciences are, therefore, statistical regularities; they are not descriptions of causal necessity.

The pin factory shows us something else important about the nature of systemic analysis: it moves in both a microscopic and a macroscopic dimension. Thus, the division of labor plays itself out in the structure of production within the factory. About every activity of production, we can always ask whether the division of labor can repeat itself. In theory, there is no stopping this process of division until we get to the single movement across a continuous span of time. This is the point at which human production becomes mechanical production, which means it is the point at which the machine can replace the person. Labor, for this reason, is always threatening to undermine itself; it does so all the more as it approaches conditions of perfect liberty. This is another way of making the point that systemic order is not justice. Only external blockage prevents movement all the way to the end of the continuum of the division of labor—an end that may be the end of labor itself, or at least the destruction of the laboring class. For this reason, perfect economic liberty, while a systemic norm, is not necessarily a morally defendable, political norm.

Just as the analysis of the division of labor descends the order of production, the analysis of demand—a sort of hydraulic pull—forces us to ascend from the pin factory to a macroscopic view of the entire system. To understand the point of equilibrium between production and demand, one has to look at the alternatives for investment as well as the alternatives to pins. The demand for pins depends upon how pins figure in the larger system of the social—the uses of pins, which include both necessities and luxuries. Smith tells us we must look very broadly, for every good sits in relation to everything else. Pins might be displaced by zippers or buttons, but they might also be displaced by cheaper pins coming from abroad. Styles of clothing may change, as may the way in which clothing is produced. Pins also depend upon metal production, but the cost of metals reflects supply and demand well beyond the control of the pin manufacturer. Similarly, whether it is worth investing one's capital in the machinery of pin production, as well as whether it is worth devoting one's land to pin factories, depends upon everything else that might be done with these resources.

For all these reasons, a pin manufacturer is not in control of his destiny. He may have the most praiseworthy of reasons to devote himself to a project of pin making. He may do everything right, given the available information. Yet, he may find himself bankrupt for reasons that he could neither foresee nor prevent. From the system point of view, nothing has gone wrong if his economic failure has been caused by the free flow of resources—land, stock, labor—or by a change of taste such that there is no longer a demand for his pins. System virtues do not necessarily work to the advantage of men of good character, for character has no exchange value in itself.

Natural systems extend indefinitely in both the micro and the macro directions. Our investigation of the division of functions within the organism knows no limit in its reach toward the microscopic; our investigation of the environment knows no limits in its reach toward the universe. To describe this, we might say that life flows. In *The Wealth of Nations*, labor flows and the consequence is systemic order in every direction. Smith builds the entire systemic order of the social from this propensity of labor to flow and to move through the mechanism of truck, barter, and exchange. Accordingly, the order he analyzes arises of itself. It is "not originally the effect of any human wisdom which foresees and intends that general opulence to which it gives occasion."[56] This opulence is no one's project; it is rather the result of a "self-generating, self-correcting system. . . ."[57]

If order arises spontaneously from human interactions, what are the implications for law? To the extent Smith talks about law, it is positive law as blockage of perfect liberty. Different interest groups will try to use law to their advantage. This will have systemic effects on the flows of labor and investment, as they move around these barriers. Yet, Smith poses a deeper question for the nineteenth-century understanding of law. Does law itself arise from and express systemic order? Is the reason of law in us as creators of a project, or in a system that is immanent in our practices? If the origin of the economic system, with its lawful regularity, is individuals pursuing truck, barter, and exchange, might not other practices be the origin of a society's law? Does a social system produce the law it needs quite regardless of the projects of our political representatives? The nineteenth century offers one long legal debate over this issue of project versus system. This is a debate with which we are not yet done.

Tocqueville, Democracy in America

Tocqueville has been called the "first social scientist."[58] While that claim is implausible given the earlier rise of modern economics, he was the first continental social scientist to write in detail about American society. French social science of the early nineteenth century moved in a decidedly different direction from that of the British tradition of Smith and Bentham. French intellectuals had the burden of explaining the failure of the revolutionary political project. The emerging social scientists asked what it was about French society that made it unreceptive to the democratic ambitions of a revolutionary project.[59] Tocqueville brings that orientation to America, inventing comparative sociology in the process.

Of France, Tocqueville writes, "[T]he democratic revolution has taken place in the material of society without making the change in the laws, ideas, habits, and mores that would have been necessary to make this revolution useful."[60] As social scientist, he relocates the phenomenon of revolution: it is not performed on the body of society by a political project of negating and constructing law; rather, it occurs immanently within that body. The social scientist perceives the radical changes that have occurred spontaneously in society. He studies the changes in beliefs, attitudes, and practices. Understanding the character of the social, he can then measure formal structures and norms (laws and customs) against that character. A polity in which there is a mismatch between society, on the one hand, and its laws and institutions, on the other, is in an unstable situation. Governance becomes a practice of trying to bring about a harmonious relationship between society and state.

In America, Tocqueville finds the same "generating cause of laws and mores" as he sees in Europe. Those causes, he tells us, are so broad and sweeping that they describe the arc of Western history moving from social hierarchy to democratic equality. In America, the democratic principle "could grow in freedom, and advancing along with mores, develop peacefully in laws."[61] Thus, he hopes to find in America "what we ought to hope or fear from [democracy]."[62] America, to the social scientist, offers a sort of natural experiment in which the social determines its own superstructure of institutions, practices, and beliefs. American liberty functions with respect to the social in the same way as Smith's idea of "perfect liberty" functions with respect to market transactions. Indeed, Tocqueville's language closely parallels that of Smith even as he expands his idea of the social beyond markets to include the entire range of human relationships.

Tocqueville offers a vast range of observations and theories regarding America in the era of Jacksonian democracy. The details—whether accurate or not—are less important than the imaginative model of system that he brings to his enterprise. System coopts revolution, stripping it of its quality as a project. Tocqueville invokes the idea of revolution—"A great democratic revolution is taking place among us"—but it is no one's revolution. It is no one's project; it has no single locus. It has that Kantian quality of "purposefulness without a purpose."[63] Strikingly to an American ear, he writes that America "sees the results of the democratic revolution operating among us without having had the revolution itself."[64] The idea that America never had a revolution has a long subsequent history in European social thought.

America had political change but no revolution because America is from the first a democratic society. It has no aristocracy to eliminate. The first few chapters of Tocqueville's work are devoted to showing how the American settlers established an egalitarian society from the time of their arrival. The causes of their inclination toward equality lay in the circumstances of emigration as well as the character of those who emigrated. Geography plays its part—the very facts of distance, rough passage, and wilderness. More important, however, are the religious and political beliefs, economic status, and organizational inclinations of those who came.

From the beginning, the colonists confronted the necessity of cooperation. They hit upon institutional practices (communal and religious) that recognized and reinforced a fundamental equality among themselves. Thus, the leading principle of European history—equality—arrived in America. All of those archaic structures of class and political differentiation that resisted the realization of this principle failed to transit. The self-governing nature of the American town emerged immediately and continued right up through the Revolution and into the era of Jacksonian democracy. Americans have always governed themselves locally with relatively little intervention from higher levels of governmental organization. The center may pass laws, but there is no central authority to administer the laws locally.

If American democracy is essentially a story of the self-governing township, then the Revolution's claim to reconstruct politics as a wholly new project is vastly out of proportion to its actual role in American practices and beliefs. The Founders believed their project to be shaped by a science of politics, but when Tocqueville writes that a "new political science is needed for a world altogether new," he has in mind an entirely different idea of that science.[65] No longer the classically inflected science of republicanism, it is rather the new social science of which he is a leading practitioner. The science of politics, like natural science, is the possession of the expert investigator/ observer; it is not constituted in the sort of knowledge claims that inform the practices of a committed citizen.

Just as Tocqueville's idea of revolution is not that of a project, neither is it that of a wholly natural order. It is not revolution as in the "revolution of the planets": the continual return to starting points. Rather, history has a natural direction toward which it tends through free acts of human agency. It is moving toward the end of democratic equality: "It appears to me beyond doubt that sooner or later we shall arrive, like the Americans, at an almost complete equality of conditions."[66] Revolutions can become violent when this natural direction meets obstacles in the form of institutions and beliefs. Neither wholly natural nor wholly planned, democracy has the same character as Adam Smith's idea of the economy. This is the order of the social: an immanent principle of order that is realized through the actions of free agents, but is not itself the end for which they act.

Where Smith analyzed the social from the perspective of the individual's propensity to truck, barter, and trade, Tocqueville takes as his subject a far broader range of beliefs and actions. Economics becomes just one subject within the broader field of the social. It has no privileged place in the democratic movement of modernity. American democracy reaches into institutions ranging from churches, to political parties, to all manner of local associations; it reaches from town halls to state and national governance. It extends to the formation of public opinion through debate, media, and education. These are all systemically linked as elements in the realization of a democratic society.

Tocqueville begins with what seems an implicit acknowledgment of Smith's work, even as he broadens the idea of the systemic order of the social. The acknowledgment is in his parallel deployment of the idea of an invisible hand. Rather than moving markets toward efficient outcomes, however, this hand is moving history toward equality. Making explicit the reference behind the metaphor, Tocqueville describes this movement as a "providential fact." Just as every economic transaction, regardless of the intentions of the participants, advances the systemic quality of the market, political practices are moving toward equality:

> Everywhere the various incidents in the lives of people are seen to turn to the profit of democracy; all men have aided it by their efforts: those who had in view cooperating for its success and those who did not dream of serving it; those who fought for it and even those who declared themselves its enemies; all have been driven pell-mell on the same track, and all have worked in common, some despite themselves, others without knowing it, as blind instruments in the hands of God.[67]

This is the systemic order that the social scientist perceives behind the exertions of individuals. The social scientist alone is not blind, for he sees "the hands of God." The order he reveals makes use of, but is not the object of, individual intentions. Systemic explanation, for the social scientist, moves in an entirely different dimension from that of individual intention.

The movement toward equality is "an irresistible revolution," relentlessly destructive of all that would stand in its way. It is, Tocqueville writes, "still advancing today amid the ruins it has made."[68] This is, for him, a fact as certain as the revolutions of the planets. An order that has an objectivity independent of our particular wills can only be explained, he believes, as the intent of God. The analogy to natural system is quite exact. The hand of God has become wholly and completely invisible, but still it must be working, for we see the consequences of its action. Thus, we do not need "special revelation" to understand the system of the heavens; nor do we need special revelation to understand the system of the social. Because the systemic exposition of the social reveals God's hand, Tocqueville offers his account in a spirit of a "sort of religious terror." Reason and revelation are never far apart in the systemic explorations of modern science deep into the nineteenth century.

The invisible hand offers an imaginative bridge from project to system, for all these thinkers. The pattern that began with Christian faith in providence repeats itself in economics and now social science more broadly. The system must be God's project, even if we have nothing more to say about God's intentions. With this belief in place, society can become an object of study apart from the intentions of individual actors. We also see again the move toward theodicy. The systemic view shows us the virtues of negation and destruction in markets and politics.

As with nature and the economy, we can already anticipate the quiet abandonment of the bridge from revelation to reason, from God's project to social system. The social can get along without God, once his hand has become invisible. The origins of order remain a mystery for systemic analysis; we simply stop asking the question. A question that has no answer, that produces only a metaphor of invisibility, is one that serves no epistemic purpose. Expelled from science, the providential character of the fact of system becomes a matter of personal faith.[69]

Accordingly, despite Tocqueville's explicit linking of revelation to reason, of God's project to the social system, his discussion of actual religious beliefs and practices in America does not take up this idea at all. What interests him most is that the clergy all support the separation of religion from politics. They support civil freedom as preservative of their own practices and institutions. When Tocqueville turns to actual religious beliefs, his primary concern is the inculcation of Christian morality, including Christian beliefs about family. In America, "Christianity . . . reigns without obstacles, on the admission of all; the result is . . . that everything is certain and fixed in the moral world, although the political world seems to be abandoned to the discussion and attempts of men."[70] Religious morality can thereby provide a necessary limit to the democratic imagination. It provides some assurance that a political democracy will pursue order not anarchy. Absent religious beliefs, political attempts—that is, projects—might lose all sense of limits.

Tocqueville was fascinated by the way in which the first colonies enacted their laws democratically, but nevertheless remained within the boundaries of Christian faith. Democracy in America does not free men from faith, but provides a space for the realization of religious beliefs. The story is otherwise in Europe, where the Church supported archaic forms of social hierarchy and thereby become the object of political attack. Tocqueville sees this continuing conjunction of civil freedom and moral authority as paradigmatic of the relationship of church to state in America: formally separate, but in fact deeply intertwined in the citizen's character. "Next to each religion is a political opinion that is joined to it by affinity."[71] Tocqueville, in sum, is interested in the systemic, democratic implications of religious practice and belief. He has no interest in developing the theological implications of his own claim to see God's invisible hand.

This displacement of the site of religious significance from the providential view of history to the institutional molding of character illustrates the formal point that system is not the end of any project. The invisible hand moves without the deliberate assistance of particular actors; belief in the presence of that hand is not a necessary condition of the realization of the modern principle of equality.

That system is not dependent upon project does not mean that we can simply let ourselves be carried along by the providential direction of history.[72] This is no more true of the social order than of the economic order; both arise from human agency. It is not enough to say—indeed, it is impossible to say—that we will simply let the invisible hand make our choices for us. That is to confuse first-person and third-person accounts. The proposition makes no sense; it expresses a category mistake. In Kant's terms, human subjectivity is no less practical than epistemic. System is not independent of action; it is the order of action seen from a particular point of view.

The systemic view of the economy can inform a regulatory regime of internalizing externalities, facilitating the availability of information, enforcing contracts, and managing the money supply. These are all in aid of markets, which tend toward a "natural" state only with a good deal of assistance. As Tocqueville moves the locus of the invisible hand toward a broader system of the social, other sorts of managerial tasks come into view. One may not be able to direct providence, but well-informed actors—experts—can make the democratic, social revolution less disruptive than it might otherwise be. Or that at least is the promise. "Therefore it is not only to satisfy a curiosity, otherwise legitimate, that I have examined America; I wanted to find lessons there from which we could profit."[73] God may have a plan for us, but we still must decide among actual choices in the present. We can do that more or less well.

As a matter of political theory, Tocqueville works in the same anti-Hobbesian tradition as Adam Smith. Both take as their target Hobbes's belief that political order requires the creation of a sovereign authority that, once created, operates independently of citizens. For Hobbes, citizens have to invest the totality of their political will in the sovereign. Political order requires citizens to see the sovereign as representative, by which Hobbes meant that citizens have to see themselves as the authors of the sovereign's actions.[74] The sovereign's project must, accordingly, remain their project. Smith and Tocqueville believe this to be a fundamental misconception of the origins and nature of political order. That order arises not from the alienation of citizen will, but through citizen's interactions with each other. Order is not the product of anyone's particular acts—even the acts of a sovereign. It arises from the systemic relationships that spontaneously arise among citizens. The political virtues are, accordingly, prudential and largely negative. We need only be ourselves for political order to flourish. Grand projects are likely to be swept aside by the invisible hand, which, if not exactly the hand of God, nevertheless destroys all that gets in its way.

PART 2

The Constitutionalism of Project

Modern American law, not just constitution making, has about it a persistent element of the project. This arises not just from the preference for written, positive law over unwritten common law, but also from the association of law with the judge's point of view. The internal point of view of the judge, as he decides a case, is that of project. No judge ever writes an opinion that says the law cannot be stated apart from the facts of the case.[1] The judge's role is first to discern the legal rule at some level of generality and then to apply it to a set of facts. This is how he imagines himself; it is what we generally expect of him.[2] He cannot say he has an "intuition" that a particular outcome is best.[3] He cannot appeal to his own character or capacity for judgment; he does not say, "Trust me." He does not look to the strength or virtue of the particular parties; he does not ask which one would profit most from a decision in its favor. He does not ask himself what would be best, all things considered.[4] We expect the judge to identify with the project of applying the law, when we speak of judicial character and the virtues of a judge. Of course, few judges would describe their project as one of making the law: the rule they apply has its origin elsewhere. The judge might say his project is a continuation of that democratic project of law creation.

This judicial self-understanding shows itself in the judicial opinion, the structure of which follows the logic of the project. The applicable rule of law must be imagined as preceding the circumstances of the case.[5] Only when both facts and law have been set forth independently of each other does the opinion apply the latter to the former.[6] Judges persist in this belief in the projectlike character of their work even as scholars argue that judges are interpreting a complex combination of facts and norms, rather than pursuing a project of rule application.[7] As the scholar's theory of public order moves away from the model of project, a gap will develop between the internal and the external point of view. Eventually, that gap between theory and practice, between scholars and judges, will become a chasm.[8]

Treating law application as a project, the judge operates at a high level of abstraction with respect to the facts of a case. The parties are stripped of their individual characteristics; they become representatives of kinds of claimants. We don't care about their feelings, their friends and relatives, their life stories. Personal biography matters in life's experience, but not in the judicial opinion, which often fails even to speak of parties by name: they become "plaintiffs" or "appellants." There are claims and defenses; there are not rich personal narratives. Because opinions have as their goal neither history nor investigatory reporting, efforts to use the courts to expose past wrongdoings may lead to quite unsatisfactory ends. Internationally, in matters of transitional justice, the role of "truth and reconciliation commissions" is quite different from that of courts adjudicating claims against rights abusers.[9]

Traditionally, equity stood opposed to the idea of the judge pursuing a project of law application. Equitable judgments were inseparable from the facts of the case, which meant that the authority of the judgment depended upon who made the decision, not on the character of the rule applied.[10] Equity stood to law as God's mercy stands to his justice. But equity has long since collapsed into law, and there is no law of the singular.[11] Remnants of equity remain in the pardon power, which neither applies a rule nor is subject to judicial review.[12] Exercise of the pardon power comes without executive explanation, while appellate courts write opinions. They do so in order to set forth the rule that determines the outcome of the case.[13]

The common law, I have argued, is a model of system. Yet, I have also suggested that even common-law judges think of their own decision making as a project of law application. Does this render the distinction of project from system of no relevance? Does it simply collapse? Not at all. First, the legal order is not exhausted in what judges do. Those committed to the systemic order of the law do not take up projects of constitutional creation. Second, the distinction affects the ideas of civic and legal virtue maintained by ordinary citizens as well. The idea of system suggests that citizens need not turn from self-interest to public interest when they turn to politics. The system will create a public good out of private interest. Third, it will affect the method and sources of legal interpretation. Is there a place for abstract principles of political theory in the interpretation of law? Fourth, it will affect how judges understand the relative roles of precedent and original intention. A common-law judge is likely to stick close to the facts, avoid abstract theory, and believe that she is bound by precedent. The belief that precedents move in a particular direction over time may support the judge's confidence in her work, but she will not think it any part of *her project* to anticipate that end.

Just as common-law judges, who believe an unwritten law is immanent in practice, are likely to stick close to the particular facts of the case, American judges of the first part of the nineteenth century reproduced at the micro level the same imagination of law that informed the project of constitutional construction.[14] There is a direct line from the constitutional draftsman imagining a project of law creation to the judge imagining a project of law application, for both understand their task as carrying out a project of reason. Both are bound by the same abstract principles of political order, because they are the principles of reason itself. This was exactly where Chief Justice John Marshall located the origins of judicial review. Thus, he aligned the Supreme Court's role with the view of "all those who have framed written Constitutions."[15]

The idea of law as a project of reason provided, in the early nineteenth century, a sort of master paradigm upon which adjudication, administration, and constitutional construction all converged.[16] This is the practical, political meaning of the Enlightenment.[17] It is why we associate the practice of the Enlightenment with law, both morally and politically. No longer writing for a monarch—as in Thomas More's *Utopia*—the theorist is writing for himself as the paradigmatic citizen of an imagined project. In this way, *The Federalist Papers* could become a leading work in political theory, a part of political practice, and a resource for the courts.[18] The citizen of the democratic political project labors under a similar obligation to imagine himself as a man of enlarged theoretical views, a site of the popular sovereign engaged in the project of law construction, and a subject who applies the law to himself and others in his ordinary dealings.

In this part, I explore the social imaginary of law as project in the early part of the nineteenth century. Theory can help us to understand the elements of this imaginative form, but in the end the inquiry cannot be other than an interpretation of exemplary practices and beliefs. While the imaginative form of the legal project has by no means been lost to us, it no longer has the same dominance in our thinking about law.[19] That is no longer possible after the development of the social sciences, which treat law as a systemic phenomenon realizing immanent principles of order in and through history. Nevertheless, once described, the imagination of law as project is readily recognizable within our own experience.

The generation of American revolutionaries imagined history as a narrative of intentional political projects that succeed or fail. They imagined that future histories of their era would offer accounts of their decisions and actions; they were careful to keep a record of those intentions.[1] Leaders in this era tended to be lawyers, taking over from sectarian ministers: people of one sort of text (law) displaced people of another sort of text (Bible). The legal texts were to be drafted by enlightened political actors who understood the principles of political science.

This generation thought that the political order of the future would be a consequence of their deliberate actions. The most important of those acts were those that resulted in the production of written texts that both expressed and constituted a new political order. That politics could be ordered through the construction of a text was itself a radical idea.

Even before the actual Declaration of Independence, these leaders were engaged in projects of constitutional construction.[2] The Revolution furthered this wave of state constitution writing.[3] Not surprisingly, the decision to draft a constitution for the collective states—what became the Articles of Confederation—was made at the same moment as the decision to draft a Declaration of Independence.[4] Revolution and constitution have always been linked in the American imaginary: violence to text, and text to order.

An Enlightenment Political Project

Americans take for granted this link of writing to political identity, but it is a thoroughly modern idea. Prior to this, movements for radical political change focused on changing leaders and changing religious denominations—not on drafting new legal texts. Of course, political leadership is not likely to remain the same across a radical change of texts, but individuals are secondary. America has founders, but no founding families. Leadership has a certain accidental quality; it is determined by chance circumstances of time and place.[5] What endures is the text and the order that it creates. Thus, the new beginning is marked by the reorganization of political life around a new text.

Imagining public order to be a function of a text produced by a collective political project marks a new political era. Not just political identity but the quality of political life is thought to depend upon a well-drafted text. Done poorly, as in the Articles of Confederation, there will be neither community nor efficiency. Done well, as in the Constitution, America becomes a model for statehood everywhere. To do it well, for this generation, meant to base the project on the principles demonstrated in the study of politics—that is, on political science.

The idea of revolution remains so deeply linked to text that we are still likely to deny that a political revolution has taken place in the absence of the construction of a new constitutional text.[6] Political violence that does not produce a text loses the right to call itself a revolution.[7] The violence, in that case, is more likely to be described as crime, civil disturbance, or civil war. We don't say that the Southern states had a revolution; we say that they lost a civil war. If mass disturbance leads only to a change of power holders, but not to a change in legal texts, it is described as a coup—not a revolution.

The British colonial practice of chartering colonies no doubt was partly responsible for this textualizing of politics. Distance meant the absence of the sovereign, and a writing was one way of representing that absent authority. To make present an absent sovereign by establishing an order of law will remain an important aspect of American constitutionalism. The colonial charter established a form of government; different charters created different institutional structures.[8] Charters established the boundaries of colonial legislative practices, or what we would now call self-rule. Charters also established boundaries in a literal, territorial sense. An order of law requires a bounded community.

The charter represented a sovereign act by which bordered territory was linked to legal order. In this, charters followed the pattern of title: a property title links a historical narrative—we "trace title"—to a territorial representation—we map boundaries. The charter, like a title, simultaneously represented and created authority. In a new, unexplored—that is, uncharted—land, the origin of law depended on the construction of an order of representation in this double respect of law and map. This linkage of legal order and space is still conveyed in the multiple meanings of jurisdiction. Constitution making and mapping go hand in hand in the American experience. This was true not just in the colonies, but in the continual expansion of the nation as new states were added—each with its own constitution.[9]

The linkage of political order to a writing reflected as well broader intellectual changes that were already working their way through British political practices and political theory.[10] The Plymouth Colony, for example, famously grounded itself not just with a royal charter, but with a common writing: the Mayflower Compact.[11] We immediately see displayed the tension between the royal charter—a legal document—as a source of colonial authority and the practice of self-government, which will characterize colonial politics. The charter established jurisdiction—these people, in this place—but the Compact realized a practice of self-government. The relationship of legal authority to self-government remains the central problematic of American political experience.

Of central importance in this turn to founding texts was not only the fact that they were written, but also that they were to be the result of projects grounded in reason. British politics had already begun to take this turn, particularly with the Glorious Revolution and the production of a Bill of Rights. The project of constitution writing draws on all of these ideas of sovereign chartering, self-government, and the application of reason in and through law.[12] It draws as well on a philosophical tradition that begins with Hobbes's idea that reason effectively determines the content of the social contract.

Before a revolutionary politics of the project emerged, the self had already become a project. The textualization of that project of self-construction was marked by the circulation of moral tracts, written sermons, self-help guides, and autobiographical testimony.[13] Most important, this project conception of the self was at the center of new philosophical work.[14] From Descartes on, philosophy took the self not just as an object for reflection, but as an object for construction. It put belief and practice on trial, with the aim of setting the rules for the self. Simultaneously with the American Revolution, Kant was inventing a modern moral philosophy grounded in the idea that the autonomous self must give the law to itself; it must write the constitution for the self. Such a writing—Kant's categorical imperative—is to reflect the form of reason. Less philosophical, but even more representative, is Benjamin Franklin. He is a printer—that is, a producer of texts—who makes himself a project, even as he is both a world-renowned scientist—that is, a "natural philosopher"—and a leading figure in the political project of revolution and constitution. Franklin represents the unity of science, politics, and self under the idea of text as project.

The most important texts of the American political projects are constitutions. These texts mattered not just for the sort of reasons that Benedict Anderson has identified: common texts produced a common sense of community among their readers.[15] Anderson's point is that readers were linked to each other through these common representations, even when they did not know each other and could not be in each other's presence. Legal texts do function in this way, alongside the novels and newspapers that he describes. Because Anderson is concerned primarily with the emergence of an imagined community identity out of otherwise unconnected subjects, he does not pay much attention to the multiple ways in which the social imaginary constructs narratives of order. It mattered that in the early decades of the United States these texts were embedded in a social imaginary of project. The community organized around the reading of these texts thought of itself as their author. Identity was mediated through this idea of authoring as much as through the idea of reading. Nothing similar can be said of the newspapers and novels that Anderson focuses on. With respect to such texts, we are a community of readers, not authors.

A constitution is a text that asserts the rise of a new legal project. This project was set against the common law, of which no one was the author. Classically, the common law was imagined as existing from time immemorial, while a constitution as an authored text has a distinct beginning. A constitutional project is similarly not a continuation of past legislative practices. British legislation had worked against the background of the common law. Legislative texts are exceptional interventions in the law, while a constitution constitutes the normal order of law. To the common-law understanding, legislation never quite qualifies as law.[16] It is too close to politics and thus lacks the neutrality, objectivity, and reasonableness of law. A constitution bridges the gap between politics and law. It is politics as self-authorship.

Americans, then, are to read the constitutional text as the product of their common project of shaping political order on the basis of reason. They are to imagine themselves as the authors. Reading the text, they are to know themselves as "We the People" whose texts these are. Revolutionaries became founders, and founders became framers. The American Constitution is a text, a set of institutions, and a political identity. What united all of these was the idea of a project.

The American project of legal self-authorship parallels the turn in political theory to accounts of the state of nature. Hobbes, Locke, and Rousseau all offer variations on this theme. Nature is imagined as prepolitical, for politics begins only with the project that is the social contract. It begins, that is, with a writing by which men take responsibility for themselves. The social contract is the first political project because prior to its achievement there is no politics. Men are not naturally political; they make themselves so. Politics, accordingly, begins with the artificial construction of order: we must form ourselves into a political order of our own design. Because that design can be better or worse, political theorists argue about the terms of the social contract.[17] Political origins, then, coincide with a political writing, and that writing is a project of self-ordering.

The Declaration of Independence adopts this point of view when it proclaims not only a right, but a duty to "institute new Government"—a political project—when the existing political order fails to respect rights.[18] A failed political order is effectively a return to the state of nature. According to the Declaration, the king has become a tyrant and his subjects are a conquered people whom he treats as if they were slaves.[19] Revolution, by projecting the constitutional moment into the future, identifies the existing political order as nothing but the state of nature in which the strongest rule. Thus, the existing colonial order is not politics at all; it is, rather, nature showing itself in human affairs.

The order of nature is determined by violence; there is only ruler and slave. For Hobbes, the prepolitical order is neither contract nor property. In war, neither is secure, for war is a return to the state of nature.[20] Whatever man's natural sociability, it is not enough to create order absent the political project. That project requires the subject to take responsibility for himself by claiming his "unalienable rights." This is another way of saying that man's moral stature demands that he be a citizen. This is a demand for self-formation: individuals must claim this for themselves by creating the political order. This is the revolutionary ethos of the late eighteenth century.

To distinguish in this way between an order of nature and an order of rights is to locate self and community in the space of projects, for the movement from nature to politics is the course of a project: constructing the social contract. This also tells us the status of unalienable rights: prior to the project, they exist only as abstractions available to theory. They are like Kant's moral law: available as an object of theoretical cognition, but effective only when applied to the self through an act of will.[21]

Revolution, accordingly, is not simply a new start; it is a collective project of taking responsibility for one's own humanity under the standard of unalienable rights.[22] Because these rights are thought to have an objective truth, the political project is not aesthetic creation. It is not art, but applied political science. It does not look so much to past examples—as artists study examples of the beautiful—but to the theory of rights and the science of institutions. Man's unnatural nature requires that he construct himself under the correct idea of what he should be. Man must give up his merely natural life to take on a new birth as a rights-bearing citizen. Thus, revolutionary politics and constitution making is one site for the modern project of self-transcendence through self-construction.

In both its American and French versions, the political project is identified with the work of reason: the political order must be constructed by the application of reason to law and political institutions. For example, William Rawle begins his 1825 work on the American Constitution with the following definition: "By a constitution, we mean the principles on which a government is formed and conducted."[23] A government is *formed*, and those who form it must look to principles. Such a project requires reasonable citizens, that is, citizens who will form their own behavior according to the same principles that inform the polity.

The politics/nature distinction carries with it the psychological distinction of reason from the lower faculties of the soul. Revolutionary politics inevitably becomes a highly moralized endeavor, for it is thought to depend upon reasonable character. In France, this leads to the Terror led by Robespierre, who cultivated an aura of the most virtuous of the revolutionary leaders.[24] In the United States, revolutionary virtue is cultivated in the image of George Washington—also an incorruptible figure. The link of moral character to reason, and of both to politics, is the object of Thomas Paine's writings in America and France.[25] The man of reason is the revolutionary, who must become the author of law. In the constitutional project, we can never separate citizen from polity: both are constructed simultaneously.

Revolutionary politics was continuous with Enlightenment political and moral philosophy. It was philosophy become practice, for virtue is understood as pure, practical reason. Reason appears first in the identification of ends (the rights of man) and second in the construction of means (the science of government). It was, for example, a principle of late eighteenth-century political science that a failure to keep separate the three branches of government would lead to the abuse of citizen rights.[26] The appeal to reason meant that the good man, the good citizen, and the philosopher—the one who cultivates reason—were all imagined to intersect. They still do behind Rawls's veil of ignorance.[27] It also meant that a failure of reason in any one dimension would infect the others as well. The belief in this possibility of a convergence of reason and politics was strikingly optimistic compared, for example, to Thomas More's skepticism about the fate of those who would speak truth to power.[28]

America is seen from Europe and sees itself as the promise of Enlightenment turned toward the political. That promise is to be realized in a project of law.[29] This revolutionary belief in the power of reason in politics of projects was hardly universal. It was contested as a matter of theory and of fact. Joseph de Maistre, for example, attacked the French revolutionaries for their prideful effort to displace God as the source of order in human affairs.[30] In place of the revolutionary privileging of reason over interest, he placed faith over both. Perhaps the most effective and enduring critique of a politics of projects based on abstract reason was that of Edmund Burke.[31]

On Burke's view, political order is not something that can be built according to a rational plan—not because we are in God's hands, but because politics is an intergenerational affair that grows through countless small decisions and a process of trial and error. Citizens act in a politically responsible manner not when they appeal to abstract reason to construct a new Leviathan, but when they preserve and pass on an inherited order. This does not make reform impossible, for a political system is not a natural order. It is constituted by habits and expectations, by institutions and laws. Reform, however, must work within these established patterns, not attempting to remake them wholesale. Political order is not the product of a social contract to be rewritten whenever someone or some group claims to have a better idea. Rather, it is "a partnership not only between those who are living, but between those who are living, those who are dead, and those who are to be born."[32] Those committed to the project of reason would, of course, respond that we speak for these absent participants when we speak with the voice of reason.[33]

Burke could support the American revolutionaries because of what he perceived as their moderation: the Americans began by demanding that they be accorded the full rights of Englishmen. He thought the policy of the British government misguided and therefore capable of reform. The French Revolution, in contrast, he believed to be founded on the misconception that politics can be a project of creation. "The very idea of the fabrication of a new government is enough to fill us with disgust and horror."[34] However much Americans may have appreciated Burke's support, they tended toward a more radical reading of their own Revolution. For them, it too was the "fabrication of a new government."

Given the general sense of failure of the Articles of Confederation—the first writing of a new project—there was certainly an opportunity for a Burkean response of caution.[35] Instead, the Framers offered a new project that seized for itself the status of successor to the Revolution. The Articles become a footnote in American history, while Revolution and Constitution are inextricably linked. The Burkean critical attitude, however, will reenter American political thought in the middle of the Civil War, when Sidney George Fisher criticizes the American Constitution as a poorly constructed project precisely because it does not allow for the moderate but continuous operation of reform characteristic of the British unwritten constitution.[36]

Constitutional politics as a project of reason remains the dominant form of American narrative right until the Civil War. This may partially explain the failure of Americans to develop a strong idea of the social—civil society—as a public order recalcitrant to deliberate projects of political formation. French sociologists thought of civil society as that which resisted the radical project of the French Revolution. While Tocqueville saw continuity between American politics and its civil society, Americans tended to see only a political project that defined its own borders. Thus, the Bill of Rights was an expression of self-limitation: fundamental rights are part of the project of law creation. For that reason, they are not protected from the possibility of amendment.

The political tends to fill the entire space of the public in the American social imaginary because it is the project of the sovereign people who imagine themselves to be unlimited. Thus, the Marshall Court early on insists that where the Constitution has created a power, its potential reach is without external limits. Such power can be only self-limiting.[37] This naturally unlimited power of the popular sovereign is self-limiting because America's ideological conservatism tends to restrain the actual reach of government. This produces that exceptional American phenomenon of a conservative revolutionary project.[38]

The alternative to public projects is not thought of as civil society, but rather as private life. The scope of the private, however, is itself the result of a political decision, for the constitutional project always defines itself. Americans still think, for example, of churches and corporations as occupying the space of the private, not as constituting civil society. No matter how socially engaged, a church is thought of as private, not public. Corporations too, no matter how big, are thought of as private. Without an idea of civil society, Americans have trouble understanding corporations or religions as deploying power capable of challenging the political itself.[39]

By the middle of the nineteenth century in Europe, the social is not the alternative to a politics of projects, but has itself become the object of revolutionary reconstruction. European revolutionary efforts of the nineteenth century become ever more radical as they aim for the reconstruction of civil society. By the early twentieth century, the revolutionary project has become one of complete social transformation. Political leaders of the total revolutions of the late nineteenth and twentieth centuries are not so much framers of political projects as they are vanguards at the leading edge of history. They simultaneously lay claim to a new science of the social—for example, Marxism or fascism—and to the charismatic quality needed to proselytize a totalizing social movement. Because the social sciences purport to be universal, revolutionaries can become international figures. These new sciences of the social are distinctly not the science of republican political projects to which the American Framers had referred.[40]

Of course, the American political project of the early nineteenth century was not conceived in opposition to the yet-to-be European politics of the social transformation. At its revolutionary beginning, American political order is imagined in contrast to the British, including the central role the British assigned to the common law. The common law expressed the organization of legal practice as it emerged from "time immemorial."[41] The expression "time immemorial" pointed to the obscurity of origins—an obscurity that attaches to the origins of every system.[42] In contrast, the American popular sovereign acted to create law in actual historical time: revolution before constitution.

The American reversal of the imagined relationship of sovereign to common law captures the central meaning of revolution as a project of law. The sovereign people are imagined as the author of the Constitution; the people precede the law as the maker precedes the made. Famously, Justice Holmes claimed that in America the sovereign always precedes law: "The common law is not a brooding omnipresence in the sky, but the articulate voice of some sovereign or quasi sovereign that can be identified."[43]

The idea of two distinct approaches to legal order—an American and a British model—had become a commonplace by the latter part of the nineteenth century. Gladstone captured the contrasting views of law as project and as system in a most complementary manner: "[A]s the British Constitution is the most subtle organism which has proceeded from the womb and the long gestation of progressive history, so the American Constitution is, so far as I can see, the most wonderful work ever struck off at a given time by the brain and purpose of man."[44] Project and system, he is saying, are different, yet both aim to achieve the same end. One suspects he perceives a common Anglo-American nature in both.

Gladstone's observation is actually a bit dated, for system was already competing with project in American constitutional thought by the time he wrote.[45] Thus, just a few decades later, Justice Holmes sees more similarity than difference: "the provisions of the Constitution are not mathematical formulas having their essence in their form; they are organic, living institutions transplanted from English soil. Their significance is vital, not formal; it is to be gathered not simply by taking the words and a dictionary, but by considering their origin and the line of their growth."[46] In suggesting that the American project has its origins in the British system, Holmes is reading back into the founding the larger history of the nineteenth century, which did indeed trace a movement from project to system in the understanding of the American constitutional order.[47]

The American Project of Constitutional Construction

We get a sense of what it meant to the revolutionary generation to imagine the constitutional order as a project from the opening page of *The Federalist.*

> AFTER an unequivocal experience of the inefficacy of the subsisting federal government, you are called upon to deliberate on a new Constitution for the United States of America. . . . It has been frequently remarked that it seems to have been reserved to the people of this country, by their conduct and example, to decide the important question, whether societies of men are really capable or not of establishing good government from reflection and choice, or whether they are forever destined to depend for their political constitutions on accident and force.[48]

To establish good government "from reflection and choice" is to pursue politics as a project. The alternative is imagined not as system with an immanent order, but as a product of "accident and force"—a characterization suggesting the state of nature. The political project begins with reflection: an idea, principle, or norm must be found to be persuasive. Reflection suggests reasoned deliberation;

collective reflection suggests reciprocal efforts to persuade matched by openness to persuasion. Both theory and experience contribute to deliberation: considerations of what is best in the abstract and what has proved best in practice are the elements of persuasion. This is how a practical science differs from a theoretical science. It is a commonplace that what is right in theory may fail in practice. Exceptional circumstances can arise. The deeper point, however, is that there are always multiple ways to realize abstract principles. A practical science differs from an abstract science precisely in the consideration that must be given to circumstances. Principle alone won't determine what to do in the particular case, when the best in theory may not be available.

Reflection must be followed by choice, for choice is the movement from abstract possibility to particular actuality. We choose to realize one possibility over others. Reflection may lead us to identify the right principle, but without the commitment to act nothing new will happen. Politics is not just a matter of arguing with each other; it is not just a matter of writing books or pamphlets. Something must get done, and that requires an exercise of the will: choice. Unlike for God, man's projects require work—choices—beyond speech.

Together, reflection and choice constitute a project, the end of which is to "establish" order. Done well, the result will be "good government." Done poorly, the project will provide only "the inefficacy of . . . government." In this approach, *The Federalist* deploys the basic terms of social contract theory: citizens must use their reason and exercise their wills to constitute a political project. Doing so, they exit the state of nature.

The Federalist is a work of persuasion appearing in the popular press. It is persuasive, in part, because it models a politics of collective projects, reflecting upon and offering a justification for each element of the proposed constitution.[49] The new political order is to be a project of civil engineering carried out on a nationwide scale. Embedded in the actual political debate of 1787, the work assumes the point of view of the citizen who imagines himself a participant in the project of constitutional construction. It is the perspective of "We the People" acting "to form a more perfect Union."

Any individual project can succeed or fail for an indefinite number of reasons—from inadequate reflection to bad luck. However, the American political project, according to *The Federalist*, places at issue not just a particular project, but the very possibility of a politics of projects. Here will be decided whether politics anywhere can be a matter of reflection and choice. After the success of the Revolution, the ex-colonies offer a natural experiment on the possibility of a successful political project. If this cannot be accomplished here, it cannot be done. Everywhere else, there are more impediments in the form of established interests and institutions. The importance of the moment is underlined by the perception of the failure of the Articles of Confederation ("the subsisting federal government"). That was a poorly designed project, for it had neither the right theory of federalism nor proper institutional design.[50] Its problems might be attributed to its origins early in the war for independence and early in the process of constitutional deliberation. By 1787, the states are no longer burdened by wartime circumstances. They are free to pursue a new project—or at least as free as any people will ever be to take up such a project.

A project raises issues of accountability alongside those of design: whose project is it? *The Federalist* states clearly that the project is that of "the people of this country." They are responsible for "establishing good government." Whatever may have been true in the past, now the people must choose for themselves. That the choice is theirs renders government legitimate, but it does not in itself render it reasonable or just. Can they exercise their will ("choice") in a manner that accords with reason ("reflection")? Can legitimacy, justice, and efficacy coincide in a democratic state? This is the deep question of a politics of legal projects in the New World. More than that, it is the question for politics everywhere in the modern age.

From the perspective of project, we come into the world as if by accident. We do not reflect upon and choose our family, our station, or our nation. Political changes, too, have been the consequence of "accident and force"—wars, coups, threats of violence, and acts of corruption. The question posed to Americans in 1787—and through them to all mankind—is whether politics can take the form of a successful democratic project. If the arguments offered in *The Federalist* persuade the citizen-readers, then politics can be a project. The work, accordingly, shows us how a political project internalizes theory: a theory of politics is not just about political order; it can itself be the object of political choice.

The Federalist, as an effort to persuade citizens to choose the proposed constitution, offers an *ex ante* perspective on a project. Although addressed specifically to the people of New York, there is no need to distinguish the arguments appropriate there from anywhere else. They are, after all, arguments that appeal to the reasonable character of citizens: the project extends as broadly as the reach of its arguments. For this reason, there is no suggestion of the question of authorship that will come to dominate constitutional argument in the first half of the nineteenth century: Is the Constitution a project of the people of the entire nation as a singular popular sovereign, or is it the project of the peoples of each of the sovereign states acting severally? Because the argument is imagined as one that appeals to reason rather than to interests, and because it addresses individual citizens, there is no conceptual space for this distinction to emerge.

From the *ex post* perspective, this question of "who" operates both as an issue of political identity—expressing character and loyalty—and as a matter of principle. From its resolution will flow answers to a wide range of questions about the proper construction of the text. We see this view expressed quite concisely by Justice Henry Baldwin in his 1837 book on the Constitution. Baldwin's primary concern is to support the claim that the Constitution was the product of the peoples of the individual states acting severally to create a federal government. This argument is relevant, in his view, not just as a matter of political identity, but as one of constitutional construction. To explain its importance, he offers a paradigmatic expression of the

Constitution as project. Speaking of cases in which the Supreme Court holds a state law unconstitutional, he writes:

> In such cases, it is particularly necessary to recur to safe principles, to sustain them, and when sustained, to make them the tests of the arguments to be examined; these principles are few and simple, and though somewhat obscured by too much refinement upon them, can be easily ascertained by the same mode in which we find the principles of other machines, a reference to the first moving power which gives impulse to government.[51]

Baldwin asserts that by understanding the Constitution as a grant—or what I would call a "project"—of the "people of the several states," he is able to answer "all questions arising under it." To make his argument, he moves very widely in political history, legal history, common-law practice, colonial organization, and the rhetoric of publicists, statesmen, and lawyers. The point of all these references, however, is to answer the much-contested question of whose project the Constitution is.[52]

Baldwin was no doubt responding to the views of his colleague Justice Story. In his 1830 work *Commentaries on the Constitution*, Story had offered a rather more lawyerly set of arguments in order to establish the opposite answer: the Constitution was the project of the collective American people acting as sovereign. His argument begins from the text: "[T]hat which would seem conclusive on the subject . . . is, the very language of the constitution itself."[53] He moves on from there—again in a lawyerly fashion—to examine the objects or ends for which the Constitution was constructed. This is an inquiry into the history of the Constitution's formation and the inferences supported by the structure it creates. These are read as evidence of authorship: whose project is this?

Story, like many others—including Baldwin—uses the language of a "complicated machine" or a "beautiful fabric" to convey his sense of the Constitution as a made object—the end result of a popular project.[54] Chief Justice Marshall used this same language of a "fabric" to connect the legal project to political theory as a tool for constitutional construction.[55] A machine begins from an abstract design. The more complex the machine, the more it relies on a well-developed theory. Yet Story expressed skepticism toward the usefulness of theory: "It is not, then, by artificial reasoning founded upon theory, but upon a careful survey of the language of the constitution itself, that we are to interpret its powers and its obligations."[56] One suspects that Story's skepticism is a consequence of his belief that those arguing for a compact-view of the Constitution, with its privileging of the place of the states, rely heavily on political theory, as if it follows as a matter of logic that the states would only have agreed to a confederation.

Consequently, Story, as compared to Marshall, has a less theory-driven understanding of the nature of the project. He sees its formation resulting from political compromises as much as from political philosophy: "many of [the constitution's] provisions were matters of compromise of opposing interests and opinions."[57] In the project of constitutional construction, reflection on principles was tempered by choice, and choice had to take into account that citizens are not, and never will be, wholly reasonable. We are not a nation of philosophers. Citizens come to the project with interests as well as opinions. Just to the degree that one emphasizes that the form of the project is not the result of an abstract science of politics alone, the normative ground shifts from reason to choice. The project is normatively compelling because it is *ours*, not because it is true. From the perspective of *ex post* interpretation of the law, the idea of project supports a diversity of methodologies, for both reason and will are elements of the project.

Despite their differences, Baldwin and Story both illustrate the responsibilities of the judge who imagines himself situated within an ongoing political project. That role differs from the *ex ante* perspective of *The Federalist*. Now, one set of choices has already been made. The great machine has started up. Those exercising power within this political order are responsible for maintaining the ongoing project. They must stick to the plan; they must make it their own.

In practice, the critical test of commitment to the project is a willingness to reject proposed actions one believes would be good for the community, all things considered, but which, nevertheless, fall outside of the plan. Amendments to the project require a return to something like the extraordinary politics of the founding. Thus, both Baldwin and Story contrast their own work of constitutional construction with the possibility of amendment under Article V.[58]

Today, we associate articulation of the *ex post* position with judicial review: a court asks whether legislation is constitutional, not whether it is best overall for the community. In the first decades of the nineteenth century, this concern for policing the boundaries of the project was not unique to the courts. It was, for example, equally evident in presidential exercises of the veto.[59] This was famously played out in the controversies over the First and Second Banks of the United States. Washington agreed to sign the bill chartering the First Bank only after he was convinced by Hamilton, over the arguments of Jefferson and Madison, that the bank was constitutional. Madison, as president, admitted to a change of mind on the bank's constitutionality. In 1816, he signed the bill creating the Second Bank. Some twenty years later, President Jackson vetoed the recharter of the Second Bank, believing the legislation to be unconstitutional.[60] Jefferson faced a parallel problem—and a crisis of political conscience—when confronted with the opportunity for the Louisiana Purchase.[61]

Less famous, but even more revealing than the disputes over the bank or the purchase of the Louisiana Territory, were the vetoes by Presidents Madison and Monroe of internal improvements legislation. Both presidents acknowledged the need for programs of internal improvements, but both thought them beyond federal power. Their response was to argue for a constitutional amendment that would provide the needed authority.[62] A court, of course, can make no such suggestion; amending the project is a matter of politics, not law. The calls for amendment from Madison and Monroe, however, suggest what we could not know from reading only judicial opinions: amendment in the early nineteenth century was imagined as a real possibility. There was not yet a sense that the sovereign people could no longer be called upon to act. After all, twelve amendments had been passed by 1804. The project was that of the people not just as an abstract principle to be used in interpretive controversies, but as a palpable political possibility. The construction of the project was imagined as not yet closed; politics was not just under law, but could reemerge as a higher authority to law.

This suggests that the early Court may not have imagined its judgments as quite so final as they appear today. The collective people were still felt to be a political presence. If that is so, we may be engaging in anachronism when we speak of the Court's unique role "to say what the law is." The early Court shared with the other branches a common idea of a constitutionalism of project: judicial review was just one example of this imagination.[63]

In *Marbury v. Madison*, decided in 1803, Chief Justice Marshall presents the most famous judicial account of the Constitution as project:

> That the people have an original right to establish for their future government such principles as, in their opinion, shall most conduce to their own happiness is the basis on which the whole American fabric has been erected. The exercise of this original right is a very great exertion; nor can it nor ought it to be frequently repeated. The principles, therefore, so established are deemed fundamental. And as the authority from which they proceed, is supreme, and can seldom act, they are designed to be permanent. . . .
>
> Certainly all those who have framed written Constitutions contemplate them as forming the fundamental and paramount law of the nation, and consequently the theory of every such government must be that an act of the Legislature repugnant to the Constitution is void.[64]

This statement could have been written by any of the early presidents. Judicial review was not, in this sense, controversial. Controversial were claims about the consequences for the other branches of the Court's judgment—a controversy that does not really arise into public view until *Dred Scott*.

Marshall identifies in this passage all of the elements of a project of constitutional governance. There is an actor ("the people"), a set of abstract norms ("such principles"), and a product that is the result of the people's exertion (the "American fabric" of institutions and laws). Together, these support a theory of the Court's role: to declare unconstitutional any legislation that falls outside of the parameters of the project. Marshall declares this theory of the judicial role to be "essentially attached to a written Constitution. . . ."[65] That claim is false. Rather, this role follows when we imagine the text to be the result of a popular, political project.

To understand the Constitution as a project does not tell us what the law is or should be; it does not even tell us exactly whose project it is or what principles informed its construction. The idea of project only introduces an organizing narrative: the people's "great exertion." Going forward, contestation will arise over each of the elements necessary to that narrative: the nature of the people, the principles they identified, and the fabric they created. Of course, courts everywhere have problems of determining the facts and stating the law. These are problems in America as well, but they are not the distinct issues that arise for political institutions, including courts, confronting and sustaining a politics of projects. We can identify three such distinct points of controversy in the first half of the nineteenth century.

First, newly appearing citizens must adopt the political project as their own. Absent citizen identification, the project will appear as an external force asserting a right to govern, that is, it will appear illegitimate. The dead hand of the past does not naturally appear as our own. This introduces the problem of the formation of the character of a citizenry willing to sustain the constitutional project as its own. Text and character are intertwined in American life from the beginning.

Second, a project rests on norms identified at a level of generality greater than any particular set of facts. The rule of law as a project is not just good judgment with respect to particulars; it is applied theory, which means that it invites argument over the content of that theory. This element of reflection sets off a search for the appropriate methodology by which to identify the norms of this project. This introduces the problem of interpretation, or what was then more properly called "construction" of the law. The element of reflection that figures in the *ex ante* perspective becomes that of construction in the *ex post* perspective.[66] American political life remains, for this reason, remarkably bound to theory. Still today, law professors don't just write works on doctrine, as they do elsewhere. Instead, they are constantly claiming to state what the law is by appealing to a theory of what the law should be.[67]

Third, there are problems with identification of that which Marshall calls "the fabric" or that which is given shape by the project. What is it that the project has produced and must continue to produce? Most directly, that fabric is the formation of the people themselves: the people impose law upon themselves. The image is straight out of Hobbes's *Leviathan*, with its famous frontispiece, and the reason is the same: the political order is a formation of representation. This is why so much of our constitutional law is about the principles of institutional structure: for example, separation of powers, federalism, and checks and balances. These are the fabric of which Marshall speaks and about which so many others write, appealing to the metaphor of a "machine." That machine is nothing other than a project of self-formation of the people. Each of these institutions grounds its legitimacy on a claim to represent we the people.

Sovereignty may be singular and indivisible, but representative institutions are endlessly variable and divisible. They are artificial, meaning they are the product of a political project. The people, then, are both the cause and the effect of the constitutional project. As cause, they are the singular, sovereign author. As effect, they constitute the fabric of plural institutions. Acting upon themselves, they are their own project. The idea here is of biblical dimension, the people are the uncaused cause of order. This is the way in which popular sovereignty appears from the perspective of project.

When Plato thought about the problem of making a new political order, he quickly ran into the paradox of citizen character. A just political order requires citizens willing to act for the public good, but where are virtuous citizens to come from? Character is formed by institutions, including laws that educate the youth and create expectations of adults. Good citizens are not generally born that way; they are made that way by the state. If political virtue is the product of a just state, then it cannot be a condition of that state's coming into existence. A failing state may create the opportunity for revolution, but in a poorly governed state there may not be many citizens prepared to seize that opportunity. Or, those that do act may simply recreate the same forms of pathological governance under new leadership. Literally, they know no better. We are entirely familiar with this problem today, as failed states often seem caught in a cycle of violent political change followed by the continuation of the same political pathologies under new leadership.

The Declaration of Independence reflects something of the paradox of new beginnings when it states: "mankind are more disposed to suffer, while evils are sufferable, than to right themselves by abolishing the forms to which they are accustomed." Poor governance may breed passivity, if not corruption. There must be a decision to act for the public good, but no theoretical account can be offered of when or how that decision will be reached. History is not logic. Revolutions cannot be predicted, which is precisely why we describe them as free acts.[1]

Those who decide to act cannot know with certainty where they are going or if they will succeed. They have a complaint before they have a plan, a plea for redress before an idea of revolution—let alone a constitutional scheme. Thus, the American revolutionaries believed, at first, that they were claiming only respect for their existing rights as Englishmen. Before there was a Declaration of Independence, there was a claim of right directed to the king and against Parliament.[2]

The litany of complaints in the Declaration describes acts of British intervention in colonial governance and abuse of authority. These complaints did not trigger the paradox of citizen character, for the Americans were claiming only that which they thought was already theirs by right under existing political arrangements. They were making an appeal to law—the same law that had framed their character as citizens. Not surprisingly, many of the leaders were lawyers and many were wealthy. Washington and Jefferson were among the wealthiest men—slaveholders both—in the colonies.[3] Leadership did not generally arise from the lower classes, for the wealthy have the most at stake when existing rights are abused.[4]

John Adams, looking back years later, claimed that the real revolution had occurred before the violent Revolution even started.[5] But this was hardly the way it appeared at the time. Prior to 1775, when the fighting began, there was very little talk of independence; only of claims to existing rights.[6] Adams's assertion was based on his observation of the rise of vigorous local self-government before 1776. He anachronistically identifies that rise with the subsequent revolutionary break. Self-government, however, was a part of the colonial system. The colonies had locally elected provincial assemblies with limited legislative power. Even more important, in Adams's New England, they governed their own townships through collective participation in town meetings.[7] The town meeting was the legislative body of the town. This was direct, not representative. This was hardly a revolutionary practice, however.[8]

Americans, in short, did not initially set out to become other than they were. They did not proclaim a new age requiring new men. Unlike the French revolutionaries, Americans did not attack religion, did not attempt to establish a new cult of reason, did not claim a need for extraordinary virtue, did not set out to upset the social/economic order, did not reject their local institutions of government, and did not unleash terror as an instrument of political purification. They wanted to be fully what they thought themselves already to be: self-governing. Revolution came only after they failed to convince British authorities to reform practices of colonial governance.

Because revolution emerged from within a politics of protest and reform, it called upon existing beliefs about, and practices of, virtuous character. No one better modeled these virtues than George Washington, who could accordingly move smoothly from colonial landowner with aspirations for a British military appointment, to military leader of the Revolution, to president.[9] Washington is simultaneously a figure of continuity within change. His self-conscious personal narrative is that of a modern Cincinnatus who takes up public service reluctantly, episodically, and strictly for the good of his country.

The Legal Project and Citizen Character

The circumstances of the Revolution may have made it possible to avoid the Platonic problem of the paradox of the foundation, but the problem of character emerged dramatically with the postfounding generation.[10] Washington, in his Farewell Address, is acutely aware of the need to align psychological motivation (character) and political order. Citizens must be personally invested in the new political order, if it is to last. They must see the public interest as also their private interest, which does not mean seeing the public as a way to advance individual, market interests. They must be willing to give up self-interest for the public good. This requires persons of a certain character.

Washington speaks directly to the connection of interests and character:

> The unity of government which constitutes you one people is also now dear to you. . . . But as it is easy to foresee that, from different causes and from different quarters, much pains will be taken, many artifices employed to weaken in your minds the conviction of this truth; as this is the point in your political fortress against which the batteries of internal and external enemies will be most constantly and actively

(though often covertly and insidiously) directed, it is of infinite moment that you should properly estimate the immense value of your national union to your collective and individual happiness; that you should cherish a cordial, habitual, and immovable attachment to it; accustoming yourselves to think and speak of it as of the palladium of your political safety and prosperity; watching for its preservation with jealous anxiety; discountenancing whatever may suggest even a suspicion that it can in any event be abandoned; and indignantly frowning upon the first dawning of every attempt to alienate any portion of our country from the rest, or to enfeeble the sacred ties which now link together the various parts.

For this you have every inducement of sympathy and interest. Citizens, by birth or choice, of a common country, that country has a right to concentrate your affections. The name of American, which belongs to you in your national capacity, must always exalt the just pride of patriotism more than any appellation derived from local discriminations. With slight shades of difference, you have the same religion, manners, habits, and political principles. You have in a common cause fought and triumphed together; the independence and liberty you possess are the work of joint counsels, and joint efforts of common dangers, sufferings, and successes.[11]

Washington follows Montesquieu in his belief that republics, more than any other form of government, require virtuous citizens.[12] The constitutional project depends upon a virtuous citizenry all the way down. Virtuous citizens direct their activities to further the national project. That, in turn, depends upon "sympathy and interest" for the national union by which each person comes to see him- or herself as an American. Thus, while the principles of the project may be a function of reason, the commitment to the project is a matter of character. Principles without character are no better than reflection without choice.

Washington's strategy is to show the alignment of the public body and the individual citizen: "with slight shades of difference," all citizens are the same. Whatever those slight personal differences, they are as nothing given the "infinite moment," "immense values," and "sacred ties" of national unity. He presents law and war as elements of the same political project, requiring the same willingness to sacrifice. Thus, he begins his address by speaking of the personal "sacrifice" that serving as president has been for him. Like him, citizens must act on the public good even when it conflicts with their immediate self-interest. As we would say today, there can be no free-riding if the project is to succeed.

Like *The Federalist*, Washington's address is an effort to create through persuasion the very object it describes. Showing himself to be an exemplar of citizenship is a rhetorical strategy for Washington. So are speaking of the "sacred ties" that bind together the parts of the nation and reminding citizens of their common religion. Several decades later, Lincoln, too, will link the sacred ties of nationhood and private faith in calling explicitly for a civil religion of "reverence for the constitution and laws. . . ."[13] For Washington, however, the values of the state and religious faith remain separate. The new state may have an infinite value, but Washington still relies upon traditional religion as the source of politically necessary character formation. He cannot yet imagine a self-sustaining civil religion, even as he becomes one of the founding saints of this new religion.

Washington seems aware of the paradox of citizenship. He sees a continuous need for character formation both prior to and apart from taking up the political task. The new state cannot rely only upon the traditional political virtues of the colonial Englishman; it must rely upon the virtues produced by religious belief and practice. Thus, of religious practice, Washington says:

> Of all the dispositions and habits which lead to political prosperity, religion and morality are indispensable supports. In vain would that man claim the tribute of patriotism, who should labor to subvert these great pillars of human happiness, these firmest props of the duties of men and citizens. The mere politician, equally with the pious man, ought to respect and to cherish them. A volume could not trace all their connections with private and public felicity. Let it simply be asked: Where is the security for property, for reputation, for life, if the sense of religious obligation desert the oaths which are the instru-

ments of investigation in courts of justice? And let us with caution indulge the supposition that morality can be maintained without religion. Whatever may be conceded to the influence of refined education on minds of peculiar structure, reason and experience both forbid us to expect that national morality can prevail in exclusion of religious principle.[14]

Washington's admonitions in support of traditional religious belief for those without "refined education" no doubt reflect his own class position, as well as his unease over the attack on the Church in the French Revolution. It is also a commonplace of late Enlightenment thought that for most people morality could not survive absent faith in God and in the eternal consequences of his judgments. Kant said exactly this at virtually the same time as Washington's remarks.[15] Religion, Washington believes, may be a matter of private faith, but faith shows itself in character, and "virtue or morality is a necessary spring of popular government."[16]

Picking up a metaphor that will also be used by Chief Justice Marshall in *Marbury*, and that becomes common in nineteenth-century writings, Washington speaks of virtue as "the foundation of the fabric."[17] Fabric is a telling metaphor just at the start of industrial production of cotton goods. The metaphor aligns the invention of new forms of governance—a constitution—with the invention of new machines of production. The American project takes this double form of public and private innovation in the early nineteenth century. Both forms require a virtuous character, that is, the virtues of citizen and worker.[18] Ordinary citizens/workers must believe that their interests are aligned with those of the political and economic leadership.[19] In both cases, this requires that a substantial portion of the population—slaves—simply disappear from public view. No one speaks of slaves and slave labor as a part of the American fabric—political and economic—but of course they were central. Their support depended not upon virtue, but upon coercion.[20]

According to Washington, the project of state building requires citizens whose character exhibits an enlarged point of view. For the educated, the identification of the political project with reason is

enough to support their commitment. For them, the political project is an aspect of the larger project of the Enlightenment. For those
less educated, however, the connection of private interest to public
virtue relies on religion. Reason can step into the place of religion
because there is still a background belief that reason and revelation
converge on the same normative order: God's creation.[21] The char-
acterological effect of reason is not—at this moment—to create skepticism, but rather to overcome self-interest.

For both the elite and the commoner, law and character are so
deeply intertwined as to be inseparable. The character formation at
stake is not simply a matter of maintaining the traditional virtues:
prudence, courage, modesty, and reasonableness. Those private virtues must be harnessed to a political character that maintains a love
of law and identifies with the people whose law it is. There is no hint
here of the systemic view that imagines the public good arising
naturally out of private interests. We are not yet in a political world
of "private vices, public goods." Public goods require virtuous
characters.

The revolutionaries figuratively killed their king, removing the
father figure to whom many had been bound by ties of love. The
American political project thus poses the question of unity without
the father. Washington speaks in terms that Freud will echo 100 years
later: can the patricidal brothers resist the divisive forces that will
arise among them? Washington responds with a further intimation
of Freud: success depends upon an internalization of law (conscience)
in place of what had been commanded in the father's name. Character must re-form itself by subordinating itself to a law that is no longer experienced as external demand, but as self-realization. The law
will make us all Americans. Religion is understood as a means to this
end. Politics is no longer subordinated to God's plan; rather, religion
is valued because it contributes to the political project.[22] This political function of religion will be very much at the center of Tocqueville's
attention a few decades later.[23]

Washington hopes to surround the law with the moral weight of a
taboo. Americans quickly come to identify the source of law's author-

ity with a new imaginative construction: We the People. To violate the law will be seen as a sin against the truth of oneself as part of the collective, sovereign subject whose project law is. Washington still appeals to a prepolitical commonality—including religion, habits, and a reciprocity of sectional interests—to describe this new collective subject. Soon enough, it will stand on its own. "In America," Thomas Paine proclaimed, "the law is king."[24] He spoke with an Enlightenment faith in reason. In fact, he just missed the mark: in America, the people as author of the law are king. They reign, but they do not govern, for when they are present the law loses its force and the conditions of revolution return.

By 1838, when Lincoln speaks of the public character of private virtue in his famous Lyceum address, he demonstrates an entirely different attitude toward traditional, sectarian faith. He no longer believes that political character needs a prepolitical supplement from religious training. When the pulpit appears in Lincoln's speech, the minister delivers a homily on reverence for law: he too has become a citizen. Importantly, the minister's homily is not delivered under the direction of the state; he is not told what to say. There is no such need. Lincoln is speaking of a democratic faith, not an authoritarian project.

This shift from a dependence on a faith outside of politics to a faith in politics marks the start of a move away from a politics of projects to one of system—a move that will become more pronounced during the Civil War and will be fully realized in the latter part of the nineteenth century. Lincoln, in 1838, already sees a need for the state to continually reproduce the conditions of its own existence. Reverence for law fills that need. That capacity for reproduction is an essential characteristic of an organism, which is the paradigm of a natural system. The American political order is beginning to be thought of not just as a machine or a fabric, but also as a living organism. The machine has taken life, which is to say that it not only sustains itself, but does so according to an immanent principle of order.

If we ask what character trait made possible the American state as a political project of democratic self-authorship, the answer is a willingness to accept a legal text as a rule of action. What sort of a people put so much weight on the written word, as if politics were first and foremost a matter of getting the text right? A nation of philosophers might be persuaded by the theory of the social contract, but as Washington warns, those of "refined education" will be few in number. Those citizens who lacked such an education were, nevertheless, accustomed to reading a text as a synecdoche of divine creation. The Bible is not just a narrative of God's project; it is itself a central part of that project. We come to that text with reverence not just because of what it represents, but because of what it is. Its representative quality is inseparable from its authorship; it is a remnant of divine presence.

Project and text are linked at the imagined origin. Both the Bible and the Constitution are imagined as founding texts. Americans identify writing a text with creating a polity; they identify defending that text with maintaining the state. America is not something apart from that text, such that the text can be called to account. Thus, any law or practice inconsistent with the text is a false appearance. It is, as the Court will later say, only "action under color of law," which is not law at all. That false appearance of law is the object of judicial review. Such a law is not ours; it is not something we have done. The Court's role is to eliminate the aberration. There is something of the Puritan inheritance in all of this. The Puritan colonies were text-based communities. They maintained a reverence for text well before We the People became the author of our founding text.[25]

In the early decades, claims about citizen character reflect the virtues of a practice of writing: authorship and readership. Washington captures this idea: "This government, the offspring of our own choice . . . adopted upon full investigation and mature deliberation . . . has a just claim to your confidence and support."[26] If problems with the project arise, Washington emphasizes the need to take up again the role of author. "If, in the opinion of the People, the distribution or modification of the constitutional powers be in any particular wrong, let it be corrected by an amendment in the way which the

Constitution designates."[27] The text is to be produced by reason and read with reverence. Only then can we see ourselves as members of the popular sovereign who authored this text.

The view that the success of the republic depends on private virtues of public value—whether of the Washingtonian or Lincolnian variety—will be challenged by the rise of commercial interests and the belief that America should be imagined as a commercial republic. That political order can rest on conflicting private interests is an idea that can persuade only those who have taken up a systemic point of view far more radical than Lincoln's appeal to a reverence for law and to organic metaphors. These new theorists of the systemic quality of the political will see political order as analogous to (if not the same as) economic order. Those committed to an idea of project are likely to see the emergence of this character type as a failure to maintain the fabric of the republican polity. System not only follows project, it undermines it.

Project: Rule and Abstraction

When we adopt a project, we identify a norm, principle, or idea that we intend to realize within the limits of our circumstances. This way of imagining what we are doing is entirely ordinary. The ancient Greeks spoke of movement from being to becoming: ideas need to be brought into the world of space and time. The first myths of creation are always narratives of a god's project, for the most accessible narrative of how order came into the world is that it was put there through the intentional act of a subject striving to realize an idea. Contemporary creationists are the primitives among us.

A project can be entirely mundane. We form an idea of a table or a house. We may draw a blueprint, specifying and elaborating the idea. Then, we shape materials to match the abstract scheme. Sometimes, the work of the project is in the shaping of institutions: we might imagine an ideal plan for educational institutions or for the offices of government. Sometimes, we don't just have projects, but make ourselves a project. In that case, we will hold ourselves to account and measure our success against an abstract norm.

Imagining a project, then, is not simply imagining the creation of something new. Aesthetic creation does that, but it is not a project because there is no separation between the idea and its instantiation in the work of art. The artist works out what it is that he is doing in the doing itself. She may start with an idea, but find that she creates something quite different from what she originally imagined. In that case, we don't say that she failed. Rather, we ask the same questions that we ask of all aesthetic creation: Is it beautiful, provocative, inspiring, or imaginative? When we judge a painting to be beautiful, we are not measuring it against an abstract idea, but that is just what we are doing when we judge a project to be successful. When we disagree about whether a work of art is beautiful, we are not disagreeing about the proper idea against which to measure it. As Kant says, judgments of beauty are not judgments of perfection.[28] Judgments about projects, however, are. A project can appeal to science and theory because of this separation of idea from product.

The appropriate epistemic attitude toward the work of art is interpretative.[29] We tend to use the term "interpretation" broadly, but in considering the nature of a project it is important to be precise. Interpretation refers to the meaning of an event, act, or work. Interpreting a work of art, we don't ask—or don't only ask—what idea the artist had in mind before she began production. The work is always richer than any such idea, which is one reason why artists are often not very good at interpreting the meaning of their own work. Indeed, it is possible that an interpretation we judge to be excellent might be totally at odds with the artist's own conception of what she intended to make. A project, however, exists in the relationship of ideas to realization—a relationship mediated by the productive agent.

Interpretation interrogates relationships among representations. It explores the networks of meaning within which a particular representation operates. An interpretation becomes better as it becomes richer; it becomes richer as we make analogies and distinctions that allow us to travel further along these webs of signification.[30] Because interpretation operates within these "webs," there is no single, right interpretation. Indeed, we expect every interpretive effort to be different—even when conducted by the same subject. For this reason, no two works of art are the same.

We don't interpret facts; rather, we offer causal accounts that can be right or wrong. Consistency of accounts is now what we expect. Interpretation speaks of reasons, not causes; it offers a narrative as an account of free action. We interpret political history; we don't interpret a prehuman history, even though we have diverse theories about it. Similarly, we don't interpret abstract concepts or norms, including justice. We offer theories of justice, although it is perfectly plausible to say that we are interpreting a society's practices of justice. Interpretation begins when freedom begins—that is, an explanation of a free act is always an interpretation.

These distinctions are important when we turn to the epistemic attitudes characteristic of a project, including the political project of authoring law. This project, I have argued, begins from abstract principles of justice that are elements of a political science that links norms to institutions. Theoretical disagreement in the case of science, including political science, is not interpretive disagreement. The question we ask in the face of such disagreement is, who is right? We don't, for example, say that everyone is entitled to their own interpretation of the norm of justice. Rather, we pursue an argument to determine which idea we believe to be correct. That argument may not resolve the matter, but disagreement is common in the sciences. If we thought it irresolvable in principle, we would not think we were involved in a scientific inquiry.

Of course, my argument that law in the early nineteenth century was imagined as the result of a project is itself an interpretive claim about a set of practices and beliefs. Just as we can write a history of a science as an interpretation of cultural practices and beliefs, we can write a history of legal practices and beliefs—indeed, I am doing so. For those within the social imaginary at issue, however, law is not interpreted as a project; it simply is a project.[31]

Questions inevitably arise about the meaning of our laws. As long as that text is imagined as the result of a project, to answer those questions requires identification of the idea or ideas that the project sought to realize. Those ideas are not themselves objects of interpretation, even as they might be objects of contestation. Imagining the American Constitution as a project, we more appropriately speak of the "construction," rather than the interpretation, of the text. "Construction" carries an implicit sense of the project. Chief Justice Marshall, we will see, uses this language, as do numerous nineteenth-century commentators.[32]

Approaching law as project would not be possible absent a belief that there is a political science from which the project can proceed. If this science is to support the work of a democratic project of law creation, then it must be generally accessible. Accessible means both capable of being comprehended and capable of compelling agreement. We must believe that there is a general convergence on a single science of law. Just as there is only one science of chemistry, there can be only one science of democratic constitutionalism. If we could not agree on the content of this science, then we could not believe that law can be the product of a project. Of course, that does not mean that there is only one way to write a constitution, any more than the fact that there is one physics means there is just one way to construct a bridge. The idea, for example, of legislative authority won't tell us how many seats such an assembly should have. In pure science there are no projects, only deductions and proofs.

A belief in political science is necessary if we are to imagine constitutional construction as a project that is not simply a negotiation among competing parties. That belief describes an aspect of the social imaginary within which the Founders operated. We find, for example, a compact expression of these views in an essay by Thomas Cooper from 1787, in which he sets forth the necessary principles for the "foundation of civil government." This setting forth of a scientific foundation is a Hobbesian political science of first principles, even if the content is different. Having set forth a series of propositions derived from the fundamental idea of consent of the governed, Cooper concludes:

> the preceding propositions have been deduced abstractedly from the consideration of any particular society, and appear to hold universally true concerning society itself. . . . Hence whether a man is about to enter for the first time as a member of any political community; or whether . . . he finds himself already a member of such a community, his rights are still the same. . . . [33]

Cooper wrote this at the moment of founding, but the idea of a project is no less relevant when judges or others are asked to construct the meaning of the legal text. Judges acting with a project understanding will ask what proposition—principle, norm, or concept—grounds the text as the product of a popular project. Cooper illustrates this form of reasoning in a commentary on the Constitution that he writes some forty years later. Responding to the constitutional controversies of the day, he offers for their resolution the same abstract principles and deductive logic that he deployed in his earlier work. Interestingly, he publishes the two essays together in a single volume, for they are two perspectives on the same project.

Cooper believes that statesmen and judges are differently situated with respect to the fundamental principles of the project. Courts may be bound by legal technicalities, including *stare decisis*, while statesmen can look directly to the founding principles. He suggests that the same project may appear differently to those differently situated within it. Constructive disagreement does not necessarily undermine the project.[34]

Cooper also believes that recourse to the people under the amendment power remains possible, and that they can resolve conflicting construction. That possibility of continuing recourse is itself a principle used in constructing the existing text. The project remains ready to hand to the people; the founding is not a past event. This is a common belief among early nineteenth-century presidents and justices.

We find a detached example of how the imagination of project informs constitutional construction during the first part of the nineteenth century, in Chief Justice Marshall's famous opinion *McCulloch v. Maryland.* To judge the constitutionality of the charter of the Second Bank of the United States, as well as the power of the states to tax a federally chartered bank, Marshall offers a "fair construction of the whole instrument [the Constitution]."[35] Such a construction begins from the principles of political science that informed the project. Among the relevant principles Marshall set forth are the following:

- "If any one proposition could command the universal assent of mankind, we might expect it would be this—that the Government of the Union, though limited in its powers, is Supreme within its sphere of action."[36]
- "It is not denied that the powers given to the Government imply the ordinary means of execution."[37]
- "This great principle is that the Constitution and the laws made in pursuance thereof are supreme; that they control the Constitution and laws of the respective States, and cannot be controlled by them. From this, which may be almost termed an axiom, other propositions are deduced as corollaries. . . . These propositions, as abstract truths, would perhaps never be controverted."[38]
- "It is of the very essence of supremacy to remove all obstacles to its action within its own sphere, and so to modify every power vested in subordinate governments as to exempt its own operations from their own influence. This effect need not be stated in terms. It is so involved in the declaration of supremacy, so necessarily implied in it, that the expression of it could not make it more certain. We must, therefore, keep it in view while construing the Constitution."[39]

Marshall continues the inquiry by looking for "intelligible standards" to apply "to the circumstances of the case." He cites no precedents.[40]

He does not argue from the evolution of practice, apart from noting that the long acceptance of the bank "ought not to be lightly disregarded."[41] These principles count because they assert the ideal, abstract order upon which the Constitution was constructed. They did not emerge gradually as the Constitution was put to work. They are the principles that inform the plan temporally and conceptually.

The best description of Marshall's argument is as a construction of the Constitution in light of the principles of political theory that necessarily informed the project of creating that text. As I explained earlier, there is convergence of text and institutions: the project of writing the text is the project of forming the institutions.[42] Marshall identifies a series of fundamental principles from which other propositions are derived by deductive reasoning—or at least what purports to be deductive. The occasion for appeal to these principles was historical, but the rules themselves are not products of history. They are simply the principles of political science relevant to the legal issues of the case at hand. This way of reasoning may still seem natural to us, but there is nothing necessary about imagining the Constitution as the product of a project based on a comprehensive, principled, science of political order. We make no such assumption when, for example, we interpret a contract or explain what it is that an individual has done.[43]

On Marshall's view of the constitutional project, there is no need to match the circumstances of the case to the intentions of particular Framers. A project is an intentional act, but Marshall understands the relevant intention to be that of the people, not that of the delegates. There is an unexpressed connection between the appeal to abstract principles and the location of intention in the sovereign people. The people, like God before them, will the general principles of order, not the particular applications.[44] Thus, in the *Dartmouth College* case, Marshall acknowledges that the particular situation the Court confronts—legislative change to a charitable institution with an original charter from the Crown—was not itself considered by the Framers: "It is more than possible that the preservation of rights of this description was not particularly in the view of the framers of the Constitution."[45] This, however, is of no significance once the rule for which the textual clause stands has been constructed: "[A]lthough a . . . case may not, in itself, be of sufficient magnitude to induce a rule, yet it must be governed by the rule, when established."[46] The Court's role is to continue the project by identifying the right rule, which means to properly derive it conceptually.

The paradigm of project is a way of organizing thought and action at different levels of generality. The constitutional text is imagined as the product of a project: that of drafting and the adopting the Constitution. The individual case is imagined as a project: that of applying the constitutional norm to the facts at issue.[47] Marshall's easy movement between text and abstract norms suggests that rather than two distinct projects operating at different levels of generality, constitutionalism can be seen as a single project moving from abstract norms to particular facts. The norms are always accessible to shape—that is, judge—the particular circumstances.

Application of the rule to the facts, even imagined as a continuation of single project, introduces problems of a different order from those that arise in constructing the constitutional text. A new attention to particular facts is required. In *Marbury*, Marshall distinguishes the legal rule from facts in execution of the project. He writes, in considering the question of which executive officers are amenable to judicial orders, that "there must be some rule of law to guide the court in the exercise of its jurisdiction. In some instances there may be difficulty in applying the rule to particular cases; but there cannot, it is believed, be much difficulty in laying down the rule."[48] If such a difficulty were to be admitted, the very idea of law as project would begin to collapse, for there would be no norm by which to construct or measure.

A necessary condition of a project is the belief that the rule or norm can be stated separately from and prior to its application. That rule, then, serves as an ideal measure of the work of the project. If the project succeeds, there will be a convergence of the ideal and the product, beginning with the legal text. Marshall expresses this convergence rather precisely in *Fletcher v. Peck*:

> It is, then the unanimous opinion of the Court that, in this case, the estate having passed into the hands of a purchaser for a valuable consideration, without notice, the State of Georgia was restrained, *either by general principles* which are common to our free institutions *or by the particular provisions* of the Constitution of the United States, from passing a law whereby the estate of the plaintiff in the premises so purchased could be constitutionally and legally impaired and rendered null and void.[49]

Marshall can be indifferent to the distinction between theory and text because the project imagines their convergence: the text is to express the "general principles."

We might have theoretical disagreements over the content of the idea put to work in the project. If the disagreement is deep and sustained, then we don't agree on the nature of the project. The best example of such a theoretical disagreement in American constitutional history is apparent in *McCulloch*: the state of Maryland argues that the Constitution emerged from acts of the sovereign states, while the defenders of the bank argue that the Constitution is the product of the people themselves. For the former, the leading principle of the Constitution is an ideal of federal order in which the states remain principals and the national government their agent. The Court decides for the latter, asserting the autonomy of the national government as against the states. This conflict over the source of authority to pursue the project is critical to the construction of the text. Because different parties continue to disagree over this basic principle, it becomes increasingly difficult to argue that Americans in the antebellum period are pursuing the same project.[50] Each constructs the law differently in light of their differing commitments to the ideal locus of sovereignty. That is not a conflict that can be worked out by interpreting legal artifacts, despite Justice Story's best efforts.[51] Rather, it goes to the very nature of the project.

The separation of idea from its realization means that we can consider and debate an idea prior to or apart from its realization. The
rights of man and the logic of institutions are objects of study before
they are projects of drafting. We cannot really speak of revolution
before the rise of modern political theory—a connection rather precisely expressed in the Declaration of Independence's linkage of
the political project to the unalienable rights of citizens. Similarly,
the French National Assembly in 1789 issued the Declaration of the
Rights of Man and Citizen, which states in its second paragraph,
"The aim of all political association is the preservation of the natural and imprescriptible rights of man. These rights are liberty, property, security and resistance to oppression."[52]

Modern revolution imagines itself as a new beginning precisely
because its ground is in ideas, not history. It enacts an idea of freedom as the capacity to have projects, which means to direct one's behavior according to a belief in the truth of ideas: the rights of man
and the science of political institutions. This is not the only idea of
freedom; it may not be the best idea of freedom.[53] It is, however, the
idea of freedom that has powered modern revolutions as constitutional projects.

Because a project links idea to facts through the mediation of an
agent, it is a uniquely human activity. Without the capacity for abstraction, animals can have order, but they cannot have projects. In
Hannah Arendt's terms, they labor, but they do not work.[54] There is
no sense to calling them free: we can train them, but not persuade
them. From the fact that man is capable of projects, however, it does
not follow that he will approach politics as a project. Only with modernity does the idea that politics can be a project—even a democratic project—arise. A political order framed, for example, by the
idea of the king's two bodies is not a project.[55] The political subject
was not to measure the legitimacy of monarchical rule against an abstract ideal of justice. A king might rule well or poorly, but that did
not make him more or less a king. His authority did not refer to an
abstract rule; it ran directly to him. His power was personal and particular. Citizens were subjects owing personal obedience to a ruler.

To be ruled poorly was like suffering from a natural disaster; it was not an invitation for re-forming the political order.

The Declaration of Independence rejects this idea of kingly power, subjecting George III to an abstract measure of just rule. Failing to respect unalienable rights, the king no longer exercises legitimate power. He is subject to a theory of politics that is to ground a new idea of law. Similarly, Louis XVI, now Citizen Louis Capet, is tried before he is executed. The trial acts out the separation of the law from the personhood of the king. In both cases, the source of the law is now the people. The people are sovereign; the law is their project. This means, in part, that they get to speak in place of the king. More important, it means that they create law by taking up a project informed by science, which is not something the sacred monarch did or needed to do.

In placing the project at the foundation, modern democracy differs from the democracies of ancient Greece. Classically, democracy was a rule of decision. It answered the question of who gets to decide, not who writes the law. Modern democracy is inseparable from modern political science, because law has become a project. As long as democracy is aligned with the legal project, it has answered the old fear that democracy produces anarchy, which in turn leads to tyranny. Democracy as project not only allows a role for courts; it can put judicial review at the center of its own self-conception. *Marbury* is as important to the American idea of democracy as the election of Jefferson in 1800. American democracy is as much at stake in the Court's pursuit of the rule of law as in elections.

When we learn about a project, we learn the rules or norms that define the character of the project. If we did not know, for example, what executive or legislative powers were in the abstract, what sense could we make of a constitution that assigns those powers to newly constructed institutions? How we learn the norms does not bear on the status of those norms within the project. Political theory might claim its principles are self-evident. Or it might proceed inductively by examining history in order to discern the norms of governance—rights and institutions—that will lead to public welfare and security.[56]

A politics of projects begins with the recognition of the ideas, principles, and norms—from whatever sources—that are to guide intentional acts of creation.

How much agreement there must be on *the content* of the ideas that inform a project is an open question. Absent any agreement, it would make no sense to say we had a common project. Even when we agree on the principle, we may disagree on its application.[57] Some projects do not allow detailed specification of an abstract norm—a rule, rather than a standard—because the materials upon which they work are too varied and unpredictable. We might, for example, agree that courts are to be independent, but disagree about whether that norm requires life tenure or only a long term of office. Political projects are likely to include substantial discretion in their execution, which is why the idea of project often appears in a negative assertion: some proposed law or act is identified as inconsistent with the project. This is the idea of judicial review, which reviews but does not initiate action to carry out the project. It matters whether one is taking the *ex ante* or *ex post* perspective. An ideal of judicial independence may not direct us to an exact institutional structure of the judiciary, but appeal to that ideal will inform a court's construction of the legal text when controversy over that institutional structure arises.

Consider parents taking up together what they imagine to be the project of raising children. They may agree on norms at some level of generality—for example, to inculcate virtues of character, to encourage individual achievement, to teach self-reliance, to ensure the child's health and well-being. They may also find that they disagree when they try to be more specific. Or they may find that what they thought was self-reliance in the abstract turns out to be a poor idea of the self-reliance of which their children are capable. If they often find their abstract norms to be of little value, they may come to think that child raising is not a project at all. In that case, they may find that they agree on what is to be done in the particular case, even as they disagree on abstractions. The same sorts of disagreements operate in politics. By the middle of the nineteenth century, many judges and theorists came to question whether a politics ordered by law was properly imagined as a project. They turned to a new model of order: system.

The project's need for articulation of a legal rule at a level of abstraction greater than that of ordering a particular set of facts explains a paradox noted by Roberto Unger.[58] He observes that most statutes emerge from hard bargaining among interest groups pursuing their own ends—often at the expense of others. Nevertheless, when a court sets forth the meaning of the law, the judge does not speak of what the private interests achieved in the bargain. A court does not interpret a law by speaking of the lobbyists' ambitions; it does not interpret a law by looking to campaign contributions made to the relevant political actors. Rather, a court interprets the law as an expression of a reasonable public policy. The law sets forth a general norm; it does not set out the terms of a bargain.[59] It sets out the law as if it were a part of the project of reason.[60] The rule must be capable of being stated independently of any set of facts. A law that cannot be interpreted as anything more than a bargain among interest groups is, as a matter of doctrine, unconstitutional.[61]

One might respond that if a contract between parties can be their joint project, then the legislative product can be understood as nothing more than an outcome reached through bargaining among interest groups. That bargain would reflect the relative power of different groups. The rule for courts, on this view, should be the result of that bargain, just as it is when a court is asked to resolve a contract dispute.[62] An entire branch of legal studies—law and economics—tends to think this way about legislation. These scholars believe that the fact that legislators are elected provides sufficient democratic warrant for this idea of the nature of the legislative norm. Yet, this theory entirely fails to capture our judicial practice of saying what the law is; it fails again in ignoring the imaginative narrative of law as the people's project. That project would fail were it perceived as irrational or as injuring some for the benefit of others. A democratic project will converge on the idea of an order of reason. The people and reason are two forms of expression of the general nature of the legal project.[63] They relate to each other as thinking to the content of thought. The law and economics scholar is offering an analysis of causes to explain how the law came into existence, while judges are offering narratives of reasons.

Of course, agreement on principles can never give a complete account of the content of a particular legal order. A people as a historical formation will have contingent commitments and practices. A people is not governed only by abstract reason, even in the form of political science. Even if there were a common commitment to a legal project under the ideal of a science of politics, constitutional practices would differ across nations and history. A constitutional text elaborates reason as it has been revealed in the experience of *this* people as a collective agent. Thus, the opinion of a court offers us a reading of the law as an expression of a norm of public policy that simultaneously appeals to the universality of reason and to the actual history of this community.[64] This is what makes the law *our* project, even as we imagine it to be universal. It is one iteration of the universal.[65] This distinguishes adjudication from abstract theory, on the one hand, and from arbitration, on the other. Setting forth the law is neither an exercise of pure theory nor of compromise among conflicting groups.[66] The legal project always sees a convergence of "the rights of man and of citizens."

When we argue, for example, about the meaning of free speech under the First Amendment, we might consider the nature of unalienable rights, the sources of political legitimacy, the dangers of government abuse, and the need for the progressive development of knowledge. In each instance, we are considering how a practice of free speech fits into larger ideas of democratic self-government. We are trying to understand the right theory of free speech.[67] We might also inquire into original intentions, but this too must be cast as intentionality with respect to a general theory of free speech. It would not help us to know only that the Framers had a particular set of problems in mind.[68] Those problems must be understood to stand for something more general. The same will be true when we turn to an examination of relevant precedents. They too must stand for ideas.

Multiple sources of possibly relevant ideas means multiple positions are possible. Imagining law as a project shapes the way in which we disagree; it does not resolve disagreement for us.

The project character of law and the need to formulate an abstract norm hardly mean that the construction of text is independent of practical concerns. Political science is practical not just because theory must be applied, but because it must take into account possible pathologies of governance, interests of citizens, and the dangers of power. These are matters for theory as much as for practice. The right rule is the one that can work under the actual conditions of political order. Those conditions will be different in different places and at different times, but they are never absent. No politics can be a practice of pure, practical reason.

An argument that looks to facts is not the same as one that is bound to facts. A legal rule that can appeal to nothing more than particular facts is an argument from faction. If we can say only that a law takes from A and gives to B, or that it rewards the farm lobby for its campaign support, or that it grants a monopoly to a relative of the party leader, then we are no longer describing a project of governance by law. Instead, we are describing transactions among those who possess the power to make law. Those are not likely to be just transactions. Even an authoritarian regime may govern through the form of law, but that is no longer rule by law. It is no longer a democratic project of constitutionalism.

One final comparison to the simple project of building a house can help to draw all this together. A blueprint might call for a particular room—a kitchen—in a particular location. Implicit in that call is a reference not just to the entirety of the house, but to an indefinite amount of knowledge concerning engineering, architecture, energy, the sociology of family, the preparation of food, as well as government regulation and the history of similar efforts. Were a controversy to arise over the construction of the kitchen—what exactly does the project demand?—all of these implicit, epistemic supports would be available to ground different arguments. Not all would be at issue in the resolution of every controversy, but any might be. So it is with the project of the construction of law. If we were to come to think that no sense could be made of legal norms as general propositions, that all judging is "result-oriented," we would also come to think that the modern ambition of the legal project is a false ideal. We would, in that case, stop reading opinions and look only to the outcome of the vote among the judges. We would not ask what the law is, but what the judge will do.[69]

Project: Text and Representation

Projects occupy the space between an abstract norm, concept, or principle and its realization. A project is the work of realizing an idea in some material. The carpenter forms wood, an educator forms minds, but what is it that bears the political project of constitutionalism? In the first instance, the political project authors a law, but a law is not just a text. A text that counts as law is performative, that is, it simultaneously represents and accomplishes a change in the world. The law is a new normative ordering. If it is not received in this way, it is a mere imagining, that is, a fiction.

The material of legislative projects includes the diverse objects of regulation in the modern state. These include economic transactions, public institutions and agencies, as well as the procedures that shape the multiple processes through which we resolve public and private disputes. These legislative projects parallel the endless projects we give to ourselves in daily life, for example, starting a business, organizing a family, or contributing to a community. Legislative projects shape the way in which we act toward others and, therefore, the possibilities for mutual, reciprocal commitments: we join together to invent and accomplish these projects. We look to the legal norm to understand what it is we are to do and how we are to respond to the actions of others.[70] The norms give form to the inchoate shape of these particular relationships.

To think of constitutionalism as a project also requires that we imagine some material that is to be given shape in and through the realization of an idea. The constitutional text performs a change in our common world, but what is the material in which that reordering occurs? What is ordered or given form by constitutional law?

Hobbes begins modern political theory with an answer to this question. To construct the Leviathan is to take up the project of giving form to representation—that is, representation is the material of the political project of self-government. Because people can be represented, a democratic political project of law is a possibility. Hobbes's social contract specifies the fundamental terms according to which a people should give shape to a political project of representation. That project begins with a theory of the *laws* of nature, which reason derives from the fundamental *right* of nature. That right is "the liberty each man hath to use his own power, as he will himself, for the preservation of his own nature. . . ."[71] The laws of nature set forth the basic terms upon which individuals should agree to deal with each other in order to persevere and advance this fundamental right. They should agree because these laws are principles provided by reason itself; they are derived from an incontrovertible ground. The terms Hobbes derives specify the establishment of a sovereign authority whose acts are imagined as "authored" by each citizen because all have consented to be represented by the individual or individuals who are sovereign.

Modern constitutionalism is the project of specifying the nature, power, and limits of representative institutions. Contra Hobbes, Rousseau rejected the idea of political representation. The popular sovereign, he insisted, acts directly or not at all.[72] Rousseau imagined a democratic politics of direct participation. When the people act, they must always act directly, without any mediating, representative structures.[73] Indeed, Rousseau argued that individual citizens should not even to speak to each other before they vote.

Both Rousseau and Hobbes theorized the possibility of a government in which the citizens give the law to themselves. Hobbes, however, relied on representation and thus imagined politics as project defined by a science. For Hobbes, representation was a condition of the popular sovereignty acting at all, for it was only brought into being in and through the representation. For Rousseau, efforts to represent the popular sovereign effectively killed it.

Rousseau relied on direct, citizen instantiation of the sovereign power and thus rejected a politics of projects. Absent the idea of a project with abstract norms that must themselves be justified on reflection, Rousseau's sovereign can never err: there is no measure of the direct actions of the popular sovereign because it is a matter of will, not reason.[74] Just the same claim had been made for the sacral monarch. Rousseau becomes the philosopher of the French Revolution, which never makes it to a stable constitution; Hobbes becomes the philosopher of constitutional order.

Rousseau believed there will always be a gap between representatives and citizens. Spontaneity marks sovereign presence. This spontaneity is incompatible with a political project of representation. For Rousseau, accordingly, a free politics must be one of unlimited possibility. Anything less would subject the people to laws that they had not given themselves or to laws which they would no longer give to themselves. A politics of spontaneity that cannot take the form of projects is, however, always in danger of pursuing a course of destruction, as every institution can appear to be—and indeed is—a constraint on freedom. A revolution that rejects the project of constitutionalism can easily turn to terror.

America's project of constitutionalism follows Hobbes on representation, rather than Rousseau on sovereign presence. The constitutional project gives shape to institutions of representation; these are the American "fabric." As William Rawle puts it in 1825, "It has been reserved for modern times and for this side of the Atlantic, fully to appreciate and soundly to apply the principle of representation in government."[75] To represent is to have the authority to speak for another. The represented will see him- or herself in the actions of the representative. Because the representative acts in the place of the represented, he can make commitments for them. Thus, representation is a kind of agency: the representative acts with the authority of the principal. Political representation is a form of collective agency. When political representation works, citizens imagine the collective, including themselves, as authoring the laws enacted by the representatives. At that moment, self-government and the rule of law coincide.

Hobbes imagines every individual in the community assigning the power of representation to a single agent—the sovereign—such that the agent's acts are taken as the acts of everyone. We are collectively and individually the author of the sovereign's acts. American representative institutions do not speak in the Hobbesian language of sovereignty; they speak instead of sovereignty remaining with the people. Yet these political institutions operate with the Hobbesian idea that they write law on the authority of the people. The people are to be seen as the author of the law. These institutions are not the sovereign; rather, they represent sovereignty. They exercise the sovereign powers of law creation and deciding on war and peace, but only as representatives. This merger of "not being," while "acting as," is the status of representatives. This is the American version of the ancient idea that the sovereign rules but does not govern.[76] The power is that of the sovereign people (they are author), but the order is that of representative institutions. The relationship of the popular sovereign to government is mediated through the mechanics of representation.

Accordingly, the constitutional project of creating enduring representative institutions is imagined quite literally as the work of "We the People of the United States," who "do ordain and establish" "to form a more perfect Union." Of course, even in this constitutional work, the people can act only through representatives as agents. They were represented by particular individuals at Philadelphia. More interesting still, they were represented by a prior generation of citizens: those who actually participated in the ratification of the Constitution. If those predecessors are not seen as representatives, there is no compelling reason for believing the current generation to be bound by their project. Just as Hobbes theorized, the people see themselves as a single collective agent only through their representatives, which means through the project that the representative accomplishes under their authority.[77] That is a belief that must endure or be replaced by some equally compelling narrative of the legitimacy of law. Direct presence is a limit-case, which in American politics is the meaning of the Revolution.

That American constitutionalism is a project of constructing institutions of representation is a central idea of *McCulloch*. There, the Court must fix the boundary between the powers of the national government and those of the states. The "intelligible standard" upon which Chief Justice Marshall settles arises from a theory of representation:

> The people of all the States have created the General Government. . . . The people of all the States, and the States themselves, are represented in Congress and, by their representatives, exercise this power. When they tax the chartered institutions of the States, they tax their constituents, and these taxes must be uniform. But when a State taxes the operations of the government of the United States, it acts upon institutions created, not by their own constituents, but by people over whom they claim no control. It acts upon the measures of a government created by others as well as themselves, for the benefit of others in common with themselves. The difference is that which always exists . . . between the action of the whole on a part, and the action of a part on the whole.[78]

The people's project is to create a representation of themselves that can exercise "their power." Their representatives then act under the authority of the people in creating legislation. That legislation is legitimate because it acts upon "their constituents"; it acts upon those who are responsible for its very existence.

The constitutional project illustrates the Hobbesian thought that sometimes we have no other access to the represented than through a representative. A lawyer might represent an institution: for example, a corporation or a trust. We cannot, in such a case, bypass the representative and deal directly with the represented. We might think that way of God: he is represented, not directly present, on earth. Yet, even then the distinction between represented and representative does not collapse. The priest is not himself God. People may come to reject the priest's claim of representation, even though they continue to believe in God. In that case, they will turn to another representative. We might say something similar about the sovereign people and their political representatives. As long as the project continues, we have no access to the people apart from their representatives. Conversely, appeals to the sovereign people outside of representative institutions are a sign of the collapse of the common project. We might in that case move from a Hobbesian to a Rousseauian idea of free politics. Even then, in defining the boundaries of the political community—that is, establishing who is a part of the popular sovereign—we are likely to rely on those very representative institutions that have now collapsed.

When a craftsman builds a table, a house, or a bridge, he has in mind an idea that the project is to realize. That idea is the formal cause: it defines his work as one thing rather than another. It is not the case, however, that the table represents its maker. The table succeeds or fails, but it does not represent anything. The table endures long after we have lost any knowledge of its maker. When Plato thought about politics as a project, his effort failed at just this point. He could imagine an intelligible, abstract plan—what he called "a city in words."[79] That plan called for a differentiation in the functions and the training of citizens. Different citizens had different roles that together constituted the well-being of the city. However, Plato had no way to imagine how citizens might see themselves in the whole of the political project. Each had to be content with the limited position he or she was assigned. But why would a citizen be content with a subordinated position in which he was ruled by others? Factions and then civil war would arise out of the ordinary psychology of human interests and ambitions.[80]

Rousseau had the same worry when he thought about political projects. Everywhere, he said, man finds himself "in chains."[81] That was not so much a statement about good or bad government, but about whose project government is. No one should be content to be an element in someone else's political project. When the American colonists thought they were figures in a parliamentary project that was not their own, they called their condition "slavery." It didn't matter that they enjoyed substantial freedom and wealth. They were very well-off compared to other communities both inside the British Empire and outside; they exercised some powers of self-government. Nevertheless, they did not believe the political project by which they were ruled represented them; it was not their own.[82]

To avoid this imagined condition of political slavery, every citizen must be able to see himself as author of the political project. The closest Plato got to this idea was his offer of a mythical foundation of the state in the noble lie that all men, despite their different political stations, are brothers because they were born of the same mother-earth. He appeals, in other words, to the natural unity of the family, for he does not have available to him an idea of common representation. Even Plato knew this appeal to family in place of politics was a strategy doomed to failure. It is not so far from the slaveholder's effort to naturalize hierarchy through claims of domesticity: a subject will accept subordination if he can be convinced it is what he deserves by nature. This strategy always fails in the end, for there is nothing natural about this idea of nature. Behind it, there is always the threat of coercion.

There can be no stable cure for this problem of the need for unity within a politically differentiated hierarchy until citizens come to understand the political project as the formation of institutions of representation.[83] Looking to the institutions of the state, the citizen is to see himself as their author. These institutions were made on his authority; their function is to represent him. Whatever position he has by law, it is one that he has given himself, for the state is only a representation of himself. It is the vehicle of his own agency. This is what he must believe, and this set of beliefs leads initially to a social imaginary of the project.

Under the American constitutional project, then, the people are everywhere represented, but they are actually present nowhere. When they are present, we are in a sort of extraconstitutional moment—the exception—which in the extreme case looks like revolution.[84] Law as representative of an absent sovereign is always looking back to its origins or anticipating a future reappearance of its principal, the sovereign people.[85] This looking beyond or through the law is what makes it our own, for what we see on the other side of law is ourselves.

The constitutional idea of the national government, accordingly, rests on a distinction between sovereignty and representation. This idea is deeply tied to the imagination of project, with its distinction of the maker (the people) from the made (the law). As the paradigm of project gives way to that of system, this idea of a sovereign will have less and less purchase. Ultimately, its disappearance will look like a global order of law—a system—that has no ground in any particular sovereign. That is law in the absence of project.

Because the people retain sovereignty, multiple forms of representation can be constructed without contradiction. In practice, these institutions may find their jurisdictions overlapping. That may cause practical difficulties, but there is nothing internally contradictory about the same subject being represented in multiple ways. I might, for example, be represented by more than one attorney or I might be represented by a parent, a pastor, an agent, a business partner, and a spouse. How all of these possibilities relate to each other—and to me—is a question of constructing their mandates, methods, and rules for resolving conflict. We may need some institution to adjudicate among them when their claims conflict. The same is true of political life: representative institutions can conflict even as they all rest on a claim to represent the same collective subject. Ordering these relationships is part of what is at issue in the constitutional project—consider, for example, the constitutional doctrines of separation of powers and federalism.

Institutions of political representation do not exist by nature; they come into being through political projects. The multiplicity of representative institutions allows for structural innovations. To construct these institutions requires a new science of politics. The principles of that science can be stated at a level of abstraction: checks and balances, federalism, direct and indirect elections, separation of church and state, protection of public-opinion formation, party competition, and administrative expertise are just some of these principles. Each of these principles can be implemented in any number of ways, and every choice will affect other possible choices. Representative institutions, accordingly, must first be formed and then maintained in an ongoing project of coordination.

The principles of the science will not tell you how often to have elections, what the boundaries of the electoral districts should be, whether judges should have life appointments, or what the procedural rules of a legislative body should be. Moving from the abstract principles of political science to an actual order of representation requires decisions on all of these issues. We make those decisions by thinking through how the principle of representation can best be realized in our own circumstances, which include the interests and expectations that citizens bring to politics.[86] People come to politics with already formed opinions, habits, and institutions. Some of these are malleable; some are firm commitments unlikely to shift in response to arguments.

A political project is not a matter of mechanical production; it requires persuasion of agents capable of reflection and choice. Constitutional negotiations will move across disagreements grounded in interests as well as those grounded in principle. We see an example of this sort of negotiation in the Framers' decision to grant two senators to each state regardless of size, even as they recognized a rule of equal representation of populations in the construction of the House. Yet another calculation of representation was used with respect to slaves. Political projects can include compromises that cannot be justified as a matter of theory. Those compromises can be so extreme as to threaten the principled character of the project. We might say, in that case, that they undermine the very idea that politics can be a project. For many Americans, this was the problem of slavery.[87] The slaves certainly did not see the project as theirs. For them, it was not a political project at all, but rather a continuation of a state of war. For all those citizens who could not see slavery as following from any principle, their political project had been coopted to do the work of the slave owners' war.

Because the people can be represented, self-government can take the form of a project. Thus, the Constitution does not imagine a spontaneously arising charismatic leader who represents the whole. It creates a president, who occupies a constructed role: the presidency. We measure the president's acts against the constitutional idea of a president, not against an idea of what would be good, all things considered. As a matter of law, the individual who occupies the office is never the measure of the office. We don't say President Reagan had powers that President Obama did not have, because he was somehow a "better" president—or vice versa. We don't recognize such an argument in law, even if it might be true as a matter of fact. The presidency governs, not the particular person who happens to be president. The same is true of senators, congressmen, and judges. The project is one of representative institutions; persons are recognized only as officeholders and citizens.

A constitutional project, then, gives form to institutions of representation. Those institutions are established in the space between the anarchic individualism of the state of nature and the spontaneous solidarity of the Rousseauian popular sovereign. Absent institutions of representation, this in-between space would literally collapse. For this reason, the work of the political project is never done: representative institutions are sustained only by the continuing belief that the people are their author. The first responsibility of all of our constitutional institutions of representation is to sustain this belief.[88] At least, this is their responsibility until the point at which the narrative of project is displaced by an alternative model of order, with its own necessary conditions of popular belief.

Because we cannot create representative institutions with the power to make law without also creating the possibility of abuse of that power, the work of the project is always demanding. Just as kings can become tyrants, representatives can become leaders of factions. Well-designed institutions may be less likely to lead to abuse, but they offer no guarantee. Responding to claims that the Constitution was insufficient to protect individual and minority rights, the first Congress added a Bill of Rights.[89] These rights then become elements of the same project, which is why the idea of rights in the United States is grounded in popular sovereignty. The source of these rights is not nature, but the people, who have included them in their project. Rights are not exogenous to a constitutional politics of projects; they too are authored by the people acting under the direction of a theory. Rights are the product of law, not an external restraint on law.[90]

This understanding of civil rights is quite distinct from the contemporary idea of human rights. The latter are set forth as claims independent of any particular political project. They are rights of everyone everywhere. They are formulated as elements of an abstract theory of politics. That theory is only just beginning to inform projects of transnational institutional construction. Whether those projects will succeed is an open question. For one thing, we cannot yet answer the question of whose project this is. It must be more than the project of NGOs, which make no claim to political representation.[91] Everything we know of modern politics suggests that claims of rights outside of a political project are not likely to offer much protection. Politics may begin with a theory, but it cannot end there. Theory must become project and the project must be claimed in the name of some collective agent.

The quality of representation in contemporary American politics is no doubt strained. So, then, is the idea that the Constitution puts forth a coherent project that is our own. Claims to represent the people are received skeptically.[92] Perhaps that has always been so— or at least since Jefferson and Marshall faced off after the election of 1800, leaving us *Marbury* in their wake. Marshall writes *Marbury* as if the people are present-to-hand in the representative character of law. They are there as the source of the Constitution: it is the people's opinion that is expressed in the constitutional texts; it was their effort that brought forth that text.[93] They are there again as the principal before whom the president is accountable in his political actions.[94] And they are there as those to whom the opinion of the Court is delivered. The opinion of the Court—a text—must represent the people to themselves. Thus, the Court too is a representative institution.[95] It succeeds when the people see through the judicial opinion to another text: the Constitution of which the people hold themselves to be the authors. What is nowhere to be seen in Marshall's representation of law is the factional politics of the 1800 election. Today, when we look at the Court, we may see nothing beyond factional politics. When we worry today that the Court has become "political," we do not mean that we see ourselves as the authors of their texts. Rather, we mean just the opposite: we worry that we have become objects of someone else's political project—just the problem that our Constitution was meant to address.

To capture in one final image what is at stake in a conception of law as project, consider the contrast with the traditional peace treaty—another important category of legal texts. Such treaties expressed the outcome of violence. They endured only as long as the balance of forces remained at the point of equilibrium that characterized the end of the fighting.[96] Whether to continue under the terms of the treaty was always an open question for sovereign decision. To renew a war was not wrong because it "broke the law." Rather, war was a sovereign prerogative.[97] Thus, the assertion that the treaty is "law" was not an answer to the question of what should be done. The peace treaty was the law of the singular; it was neither a rule nor a standard. It did not express an idea separate from the event that brought it into being. Just in this sense, peace belongs to the order of war, until it becomes a project of law.[98] To make it such a project was the end of the flurry of international law creation that followed the Second World War.

Accordingly, one way to think of the transition to a politics of modernity is as the transformation of the imagination of the paradigmatic legal text from peace treaty to constitution. Hobbes captures this change: the social contract is both the peace treaty ending the violence of the state of nature and a representation of a new political entity, the people. As the former, it must be continually reaffirmed by everyone; as the latter, it not only makes a legitimate claim on every citizen, it constructs the individual as citizen. If we come to think of elections as a sort of war between factions with the victor claiming the right to make law, we will have returned to the idea of law as a singular command, not as a rule. No longer a democratic project, law will be only a remnant of power.

The Constitutional Project from Marbury *to* Dred Scott

The method of judicial reasoning under the imagination of project is fully on display in *Marbury.* The Court's role is to maintain the constitutional project, which means to read the law as the product of that project. Marbury's claim to his commission as justice of the peace depends ultimately upon the meaning of the appointments and commissioning clauses of the Constitution. The Court's first move, accordingly, is to set forth the logic of these texts. So abstract is this discussion that it ends with a kind of apology: "These observations are premised solely for the purpose of rendering more intelligible those which apply more directly to the particular case under consideration."[99] Intelligibility is a matter of discerning the abstract principles that are the source of the legal text. The judge is to apply the principles to sustain the American fabric that is the product of this project.

The argument imagines that legal texts give expression to an order of reason. Thus, on the critical argument over the enforceability of a jurisdictional provision of the Judiciary Act of 1789, the Court appeals explicitly to an abstract science—a theory—of politics: "It seems only necessary to recognize certain principles, supposed to have been long and well established. . . ." These principles go to the nature of a text-based project of democratic constitutionalism: "[T]he theory of every such government must be, that an act of the legislature, repugnant to the constitution, is void." Any other view would, Marshall contends, render the entire project of creating a government through drafting a written constitution "absurd."[100]

Marshall is doing more than reflecting on a past project of law making. He is acting out the Court's role as a part of that project. "Those who apply the rule to particular cases," he says, "must of necessity expound and interpret that rule."[101] Failure to perform that judicial role would "subvert the very foundation of all written constitutions," for the legislature would then have "a practical and real omnipotence."[102] A legislature not bound by constitutional law would rule as if it were sovereign—quite the opposite of the project of democratic constitutionalism. Such a legislature might have projects, but it would not itself be a project of the sovereign people.

Striking in Marshall's jurisprudence is the way in which he places political theory at the center of his arguments about the meaning of the legal text.[103] He seems to reason that since the Framers' project was that of establishing a text on the basis of political science, then the way to identify the meaning of the text is to look to the relevant principles of that science. There is no distinction to be drawn between looking to the intention of the Framers and looking to political science, because these are two ways of describing a single project of law creation. Marshall knows all of this not as a theorist of law, but as a participant in the original—and continuing—project. He captures intuitively the overlay of the internal and external points of view characteristic of a project. He is a figure of continuity between the project of founding and that of maintaining the law. This is imagined as a single project occurring on multiple levels, from constitutional creation, to the application of law to facts.

Marshall's explicit appeal to abstract political theory as the method of judicial interpretation does not survive the passing of the Founders' generation. As I have described elsewhere, the interpretive techniques of the first half of the nineteenth century move from appeal to a science of politics, to appeal to a science of law—represented by Justice Story—to maintenance of the original intent (narrowly understood) of the Founders—represented by Chief Justice Taney.[104] The idea of law as the product of a project grounded in political science recedes over this period.[105]

Chief Justice Taney no longer believes that political science has any relevance to judicial determination of the meaning of the Constitution. If the Constitution can be said to remain a project for him, it is certainly not that of the citizens who receive the Court's judgments. The Court's role is to receive the law that the Founders left, as if it were a set of directives. The meaning of the law is located in the specific intent of the founders. There is no claim that those rules express principles of reason—political science—that bind all citizens equally to the project. There is no claim that the Founders were engaged in the application of a science of politics as opposed to the politics of self-interest. Thus, Taney writes in the infamous *Dred Scott* that it is the Court's role "to interpret the instrument [the Constitution] they [the Founders] have framed . . . according to its true intent and meaning *when it was adopted*."[106] The Court has nothing to say about the justice or injustice of the rules set forth by the text—a view no doubt driven by the defense of slavery.

Even for Taney, it may have strained credulity to offer a defense of the law of slavery as the product of a project grounded in political science. When Chief Justice Marshall had faced the problem of defending the legality of slavery several decades earlier, he had appealed not to the Founders' science of law, but to the role of violence and defeat in the law of nations.[107] That violence could produce the law of the peace treaty at best—that is, the law of victory and defeat. Not long after *Dred Scott*, the law of slavery will be determined by a new appeal to violence.

The Taney Court thinks of the Founders' project as an inheritance: the Court is the trustee of a national bequest. The judge's role is not to read text as a formation of principle; it is not to apply a science of politics. It is, rather, to obey the Founders' intentions. The bequest is no longer the theory-driven image of a project. The legitimacy of the enterprise of living under that constitutional order no longer depends on the place of theory in a project, but upon the self-identification of citizens as children of the Founding Fathers. This is not a project in the sense in which I have been elaborating it. A parent may think of his or her family as a project, but the child does not see it that way. The child does not reflect and choose; he has no theory of the family. He finds himself a part. I take up my father's project because of who he is and the very particular relationship in which I stand to him, not because of the principles and norms that inform that project.

For Taney, a court needs to know only the Founders' intentions with respect to the law they made. Obedience to a rule may remain, but the commonality of a free-standing project has been exhausted.

The paradigm of the project can no longer legitimate the enterprise, as is strikingly obvious in the reception of *Dred Scott*. Whatever the Founders may have thought about slavery, Taney is not articulating the norms of a project that all citizens can see as their own.[108] But why then should they be bound to a prior generation's intentions, when those intentions constitute a moral travesty?

The movement from Marshall to Taney—from principles of science to past intentions—reflects a process of development common to many institutions. Those who create the institutions do not see themselves as bound to a particular tradition. Indeed, they may have destroyed one set of traditions in order to begin anew. They reflect and choose; it is their project. Later generations can come to think of the institutions as something they inherit. They understand themselves to be differently situated from those whose project it was initially. Loyalty will come to compete with project; loyalty must overcome the impulse to begin again with a new project.[109]

The United States begins without definite borders and without a single national ethnicity, religion, or language. What citizens have in common is the idea that law can be a project in which the people construct themselves through reason applied to their arrangements of representation. The relationship of modern nationhood to texts has been explored before: newspapers, broadsheets, and novels all played a role in constructing a national social imaginary. So too did legal texts. Those texts created not just a common community of readers, but a community of citizens who believed the project of law to be both principled and their own. Competing ideas of law arise over the course of the nation's history, but this idea of project never disappears. Its influence can be traced not just in constitutional construction, but at different times and places, in the interpretation of statutes, regulations, and international law.[110]

From Political Project to Political System

No political undertaking had ever been so infused with theory as the construction of the American Constitution. In their own minds, the Framers acted on a world stage, expressing the very possibility of modernity.[111] As Enlightenment thinkers, the Framers believed in a science of politics that covered both rights and institutions. They thought they could prove to others the violation of their rights by Britain; they thought they possessed the scientific expertise to make a new constitution. The "scientists" they had in mind included Locke, Harrington, and Montesquieu, but also the classical political theorists. They were also part of that quite large group of secret Hobbesians.[112] They would not easily speak his name because of his defense of the British Crown, but they believed deeply in the project of representation, which is the Leviathan.

The Framers' combination of modern and classical theory places the constitutional project within the broadly humanist tradition.[113] Their project of applying the norms of political science to the institutions and practices of governance continued in the early jurisprudence of the Supreme Court. It gradually gave way to a narrower understanding of constitutionalism as the preservation of institutions and norms as they were understood by those who wrote and ratified the Constitution. As the idea of project weakened, it was increasingly disturbed by an idea of system, just as the humanist understanding of public life was disturbed by an increasingly commercial society.

The transformation to system as the master imaginative form will affect each of the dimensions in which I have traced the meaning of a constitutional project of law. First, from a systemic perspective, there is no such thing as the revolutionary clearing of the field for the construction of a new project. The political order, on this view, never appears to offer unlimited possibilities; there is no state of nature. Without a state of nature, there is no beginning before which there was no politics. The present is always a consequence of an already organized past. That past is beyond anybody's ability to control or plan. A project always has a beginning. A natural system displaces that idea of a beginning with an image of birth, which suggests the way in which new life is part of a larger cycle of coming and going.

Second, a systemic approach does not privilege text. On the project view, a legal writing is inseparable from a theory, but a systemic order is not the product of theory. A system is not the consequence of anyone's intentional action, which means that an idea does not precede the fact of the system.[114] The order of a system is immanent and it arises spontaneously. From the systemic perspective, theory occupies a position entirely outside of the legal order. Theory is the work of the observer, just as the scientist observes nature's order, rather than makes it. With that, the first- and third-person points of view split apart.

Third, project and system differ on the need for actors to direct their own behavior in ways that deliberately advance the idea of a constitutional order. A political project requires public-spiritedness; the ends of the project must be those of the actors. The project demands citizens whose character is open to direction toward the public good. Such a character will not develop on its own. Citizens must be educated in the right values. Because a system does not depend upon an intention directed at the whole, there is not the same worry about virtuous character. Metaphorically, a system relies upon an "invisible hand" directing outcomes behind the back of the actors. The systemic approach to political life believes that, just as with the economy, private vices can lead to public virtues.

Fourth, project and system imagine the work of the judge differently. Under the project view, the judge's responsibility is to mediate between abstract norms, on the one hand, and actual practices and institutions, on the other. He continues the project by applying the law to maintain the fabric of representation. When disputes arise over the meaning of legal norms, he looks to the ideas that inform the project of which the laws are the result. Questions of legal meaning are always pushing toward questions of fundamental political theory. To understand claims for freedom of speech, for example, the judge needs a theory of opinion formation in a democracy; to understand claims of presidential power, the judge needs a theory of executive functions. To sustain the project is to sustain this relationship of theory to practice. Contrariwise, the systemic judge eschews abstract theory. She appeals instead to precedents. The case law develops without an overt theory. The systemic view rejects any sharp distinction between common law and constitutional law. Indeed, there can no longer be a significant difference between the two, for each arises spontaneously and expresses an immanent order. Over the course of the latter half of the nineteenth century, there will, accordingly, be a convergence of constitutional and common law.

Fifth, the systemic judge is likely to be skeptical about the function of judicial review. To the degree that she embraces this function, she will see it as an appropriate response to social pathologies that have taken hold of the ordinary institutions of governance. Those pathologies prevent the natural self-correction of an evolving system. The systemic judge understands her remedial role as that of returning political institutions to their "natural" positions. She is likely to favor private law over public law, for the latter is subject to the ups and downs of politics, while the former is an autonomous order generally protected from political interventions. She is confident in political progress, not because she believes in the theoretical abilities of those who direct the political project, but because systems evolve. Political practices are no longer imagined as realizing a truth apart from themselves. Rather, they are themselves the site and source of political order. That immanent order is the real law, regardless of what any written texts may say.

Finally, the systemic judge has a faith that the law always maintains a sort of coherence—an internal logic—even though it is not the result of anyone's effort to realize a theory. Thus, there is no longer any need to internalize theory as an element of legal practice. Political and legal theories now become academic enterprises, producing fierce battles as to whether the role of theory is descriptive or normative.

After the Civil War, the American understanding of constitutional order moves away from project and toward system. In part, it was the tenor of the times, with the appearance of Darwin and the proliferation of the social sciences. In part, it was the horror of the war itself, which was viewed by many as a consequence of the failure of the

Founders' project. System has always supported theodicy, and Americans needed some way to think of the war other than as a tragic failure of their political project. The issue of project versus system endlessly proliferates in debates over American constitutional law to this day. This controversy is not one that can be settled. We can, however, come to a better understanding by tracing this fundamental shift in the social imaginary.

PART 3

System as the Order of Law

In his famous Lyceum speech of 1838, Lincoln reflects on the significance of the passing of the last of the Revolutionary War veterans.[1] They had held forth, to friends, family, and fellow citizens, the lived reality of the founding events—not just in the stories they told, but in their very presence. That link was quickly disappearing by 1838. Americans were well aware of the political and social consequences that can arise when the link to the past is broken: neither slaves nor Native Americans had access to their deep past.

Lincoln is on to something of deep significance as he reflects on the imaginative reorientation required when events pass from living memory to recorded history. If they are to survive, they must pass from first-person narratives to third-person accounts. We all know this phenomenon in our own lives as older family members pass on. Collectively, we experience the same thing today with the passing of the generation of veterans of the Second World War. That war must now be reconstructed from evidence; it is no longer present as a part of experience carried forward in ordinary conversation. If it is to remain significant to the community, it must be represented and taught. It can no longer be taken for granted; its value must be continually reconstructed. Sometimes that reconstruction is formal, as in a school curriculum; other times, it is informal, as in representations in films or popular histories.

In his speech, Lincoln notes that the Revolution had so far been known literally in the flesh—he speaks of the veterans' scars bearing testimony to the reality of those events. With the death of the veterans, however, the Revolution can be known only by texts that offer a representation. Slaves and Native Americans had no such texts. The particular texts Lincoln has in mind are those of the law. Law must come to take the place of the scar. Lincoln calls for a "reverence for law," introducing the idea of a national, civil religion. Veteran and Constitution remain bound together in the American imagination.[2]

Lincoln's rhetoric is full of biblical resonances. The Jews were to bear the scar of circumcision as the symbol of the legal text that is the covenant. The wound was an investment of the flesh in a sign; the scar is a sign of law. The permanence of the scar signifies the permanence of the text. Jews do not just follow the law; they bear the law on their bodies. Moreover, this scar tells the Jew who he is; it is a mark of his identity in the same way that the battle scar marked the identity of the veteran.[3] Jews are "the people of the book."[4] They know this corporally. The early Christians, believing that they lived at the edge of an eschatological moment, abandoned both law and scar. In politics, such a moment would be a revolution, when law and its meanings no longer hold.

In the Old Testament, there is no space between the body and the law, the individual and the covenantal community, or being and knowing. Even before the covenant with Moses, Cain had been marked (scarred) as a sign of God's command. The text written by God is never far from the body created by God: the scar is the intersection of the two. In these founding narratives of faith, text never stands far apart from reader, as if it were a proposal, an object for examination, or a mere representation. Just the opposite: representation here makes present what is absent—and what is absent is God. The text does not just found a project; it makes a claim. A scar is a text that cannot be abandoned; it is a representation that shows itself as a presence.[5] It is both a reminder and a remainder of the sacred. Most important, the scar signifies that life is owed to God and, conversely, that whatever meaning there is in our lives is a gift that we have not earned. The ritual circumcision of the infant represents the offering up on the child to God in an imitation of Abraham's offering of Isaac. He will be scarred and returned.

In *Marbury*, Chief Justice Marshall argued that the Constitution was committed to writing so that it would not be forgotten.[6] That is exactly the function of the scar, which is the wound become signifier. Both scar and legal text are a making present of an original act of creating. Lincoln holds forth this idea of the relationship of scar to law, of wound to text. The veteran's scar is a mark of the revolutionary presence of the popular sovereign. The death of the last of the veterans poses in a new way the problem of withdrawal of the sovereign: absent the living testimony of the veterans' scars, what or who speaks for the absent sovereign? Lincoln answers that the mark on the flesh is succeeded by the representation of law. This text makes present its author, the popular sovereign. To experience the absent sovereign through the text is the phenomenon of reverence, which is the object of Lincoln's preaching of a new, civil religion.

The veterans' scars had been reminders of the founding narrative of the Republic. In that narrative, the Revolution is the actual, direct presence of the popular sovereign. The Constitution, in turn, is the text the popular sovereign authors as it withdraws. First, the popular sovereign comes forth violently to negate an illegitimate legal order; then, it creates a representation of itself in a written constitution. This is not just the myth of the American founding: it has spread across the globe as the manner and method of popular sovereignty. Every revolution claims to be action by the popular sovereign; every revolution must end with the production of a legal text as the sovereign withdraws. Everywhere the scarred body of the revolutionary claims a certain privileged position; everywhere it is to be succeeded by law.

We saw this dynamic recently in the efforts of the Arab Spring. Most were judged failures precisely because they were not able to link a new constitutional text to a revolutionary claim of sovereign presence. Absent the successful production of a text, political violence— no matter how widespread—loses its claim to mark the presence of the popular sovereign. We know the popular sovereign only by the text that it leaves behind. Without a text, political violence is only criminal action or a failed sacrificial effort. About such acts of suffering, we might offer a moral narrative, but politics generally retains little memory of what might have been. In Egypt, after the return of the military, the ability to scar the body becomes again a sign of the power of the state as the instruments of state terror assert control over the bodies of those who would have been revolutionaries.

Lincoln's 1838 appeal to legal reverence suggests a rising anxiety over the understanding of the Constitution as the people's project. He sees already that the claim of a common project may not be enough to hold together the political community. The claim of popular sovereignty, Lincoln concludes, must be reconstructed for a postrevolutionary generation. Thus, alongside the temporal sequence of project—idea, intention, act—Lincoln suggests a set of symbolic equivalencies or reciprocities: scar to text, and revolution to constitution. This reciprocal transparency of revolution and constitution—we see each only in and through the other—is the reason that Lincoln, twenty-five years later in the Gettysburg Address, will date the origin of the constitutional order to the revolutionary Declaration of Independence: "four score and seven." Constitution must be already present at the founding: it is the form or *eidos* of revolution.[7] With Lincoln's appeal to organic metaphors—"conceived in liberty"—we are leaving a world of projects.

This rhetorical movement of the origin of the Constitution back to the moment of the Declaration is an appearance of the idea of systemic order. An organism, as I argued above, is a natural system. One of its distinctive features is that its mature form—its idea—is already present from the moment of conception. Paradigmatically, the acorn is already in-formed by the oak. So it is that the mature form of the nation—the Constitution—is already present at the nation's birth. By the end of the nineteenth century, the idea of organic growth will remain, but that growth no longer has a determinate beginning or a limited form. Systemic thought outgrows its origin in the idea of a singular birth. In its place, we find ideas of evolution. The Aristotelian conception of an *eidos* into which the organism grows becomes antiquated as forms too evolve. Thus, Darwin can write of "the origin of species," while for Aristotle species had neither origin nor end.

Lincoln's language of reverence speaks to more than respect for the law. We can respect the law of communities of which we are not a part. Respect can function as a universal moral demand: everyone deserves respect. Lincoln is not speaking of such a morality. Rather, he is calling for the formation of a political identity in which the individual citizen sees the truth of himself in the nation as a whole. The citizen is to experience the nation as a meaning that transcends all his finite interests; it is to be a truth that speaks to him directly and completely. Political reverence puts at issue the finite life of the citizen, for it affirms the possibility of self-transcendence in defense of the nation.

The possibility of sacrifice is the existential meaning of Lincoln's call for reverence for law. Just as the revolutionary soldier embodied the project of violent constitutional birth, the citizen soldier of succeeding generations expresses the capacity for self-maintenance of the living state. These are linked forms of sacrificial violence in a constitutional order; they trace the movement from project to system. The constitutional text has become a symbolic vehicle connecting the present citizen with the Founders. For both, the text is a matter of life and death—of the possibility of sacrifice.

Reverence rests on an experience of faith, not on a knowledge of the political science deployed in the constitutional project. Lincoln's appeal to reverence for law, then, signals a reimagining of the American political *project*. It must "come alive." Lincoln, in 1838, is still close enough to the national origin that the ethos of project, in the form of appeals to reason, largely informs his imagination, even as he turns to reverence.[8] The tension between reverence and reason reaches its full force in the Gettysburg Address, when he describes the nation as both "conceived" and "dedicated to a proposition." The former is the language of organic system, while the latter is that of an Enlightenment project. This mixed metaphor of system and project captures an enduring tension in the American political narrative.

The order of the organism is no one's project, least of all that of the organism itself. Organic order is not just an arrangement of parts, as in a machine; it is an order in which the whole informs the nature and the coming into being of the parts. Kant was deeply puzzled by how the organism does "violence" to time.[9] To anticipate the future ordinarily requires a representation. But how then can an organism anticipate its future such that its growth is directed by its end? Life just is this teleologically informed movement of system.[10] Yet, in what sense is a society alive?

In the post–Civil War era, the narrative of a political/legal project became increasingly unsettled. The general movement of American political and legal thought in the nineteenth century is toward a "living" constitution; it is a movement from project to system. Political order comes to be seen on the model of market order: it arises spontaneously out of individual transactions pursued for multiple, diverse ends. The problem for legal theory is to identify the immanent principles of order, that is, the systemic character of law that is working itself out in the history of the nation. If the nation is an organic whole, what is the natural form of this system?

The shift in the imagination of political order reflects a broad reconceptualization of history. History is no longer the site of disorderly becoming, as in classical thought, or of a post-Edenic fall, as in Christian thought. The meaninglessness of temporal change is not to be overcome by projects that are exogenous interventions—human or divine—based on abstract ideas. Rather, history itself becomes a source of order; it is self-organizing.[11] Social reproduction becomes the meaning of history. This idea takes one dramatic form in the romantic nationalism spawned in response to the project character of the French Revolution.[12] A nation, on this view, has no *eidos* apart from its own historical realization. It is not trying to become something other than that which it already is. This self-expression is all that gives meaning to political experience and is more than sufficient to ground a meaningful life of reverence.

Scientific accounts will now dismiss narratives that focus on actors with projects as merely anecdotal. Those narratives are seen as no less mythical than accounts that place God at the source of order. Thus, science breaks free of natural theology. The social sciences are directed at populations, not individuals. The new sciences will come to rely on statistics, not on intentions. After Darwin—and Marx—the agency of individual subjects becomes suspect, for there is no reason to think that individuals know how they figure in the larger systems of which they are a part. The cunning of reason is no longer an object of philosophical speculation, but becomes the object of social-scientific inquiry.

Not surprisingly, in the latter part of the nineteenth century, the significance of the founding events of Revolution and Constitution recede in the political and legal imagination. This is the end of the process that Lincoln saw beginning in 1838 with the passing of the revolutionary generation. By the turn of the century, there is a widespread acknowledgment of the anachronistic character of the written Constitution. This view is shared by progressives and conservatives.[13] A writing is no longer thought to remind citizens, as Marshall wrote, but rather to inhibit an otherwise natural process of growth. History must move on. A common critique now is that the eighteenth-century constitutional project failed to envision a legal order adequate to the social demands of modernity, which includes a rapidly changing commercial, technological, and social order.[14] How could it be otherwise, for projects are limited by the imagination and understanding of those whose projects they are? Systems know no such limits, for the reason of a system does not depend on the knowledge of any particular actor.

The question for late nineteenth-century thinkers was, accordingly, how to account for political order apart from the deliberate intentions informing projects. By the end of the century, there is an identification of the American legal order—including its constitutional order—with the common-law order. True, the common law is no longer understood in the way that Blackstone had imagined it, as principles extending back to "time immemorial." Nevertheless, this is a remarkable shift, given that Jefferson had won election to the presidency in 1800 by attacking the federal courts for applying a national common law. In his view, the Revolution had broken the national connection to that body of law.[15] The common law, he argued, was not a part of the American revolutionary project. The states had not agreed to extend any such authority to the federal courts.

By the end of the century, the written law is viewed with a new skepticism by those who purport to be legal experts. To them, its project character made it a matter of politics, from which law had to be distinguished. The Constitution had once been politics become law—the representation of the great national political project. After the Civil War, political projects—including projects of writing law—are seen as partisan affairs, while law is something beyond ordinary politics. Politics is a sort of surface play driven by the short-term conflicts between interest groups and politicians. The sciences of the social, including the science of law, must pierce this play of political appearances to reveal the immanent order. The science of law, accordingly, focuses now on the common law—not statutes and not constitutional text.[16] A science of legal formalism dominates the new American law schools. There is a striking absence of courses on constitutional law in the curriculums of those schools. That legal text is just too political to be studied as law.[17] By 1897, when Oliver Wendell Holmes delivers his famous lecture "The Path of the Law," there is hardly a word in it about the Constitution.[18]

As the idea of common-law constitutionalism develops in the late nineteenth century, it moves away from that reverence for law upon which Lincoln thought an organic constitutionalism depended. Lincoln's frame of reference had been biblical; by the end of the century, the frame of reference has become Darwinian. Immanent principles of order in a Darwinian world do not stand in need of a virtuous political psychology. This new idea of order needs neither traditional religious reverence—as Washington thought—nor that reverence for law characteristic of a civil religion—as Lincoln thought. Immanent principles of order can work through the bad man, as well as through the good.[19] This is exactly what we see in markets. Reverence for the Constitution—as for the Founders—will, accordingly, recede over the course of the century, before returning in the twentieth century to support a new politics of sacrifice.[20] When constitutional reverence does return, it will rest less upon an idea of organic system than upon an idea of representation. The text will again be seen as a making present of the absent popular sovereign. With this shift, Lincoln will be recovered as the nation's leading rhetorician. Indeed, he will be reconstructed as the nation's paradigmatic citizen: he who sacrifices for the Constitution.

five

SYSTEM AND THE THEORY OF THE COMMON LAW: FROM BLACKSTONE TO HOLMES

By the end of the nineteenth century, the idea of system displaced that of project as the organizing idea of the constitutional order. The constitutional project had a definite beginning: the Revolution. From the systemic perspective, however, the very idea of a beginning is an error. It confuses the appearance of deliberate intentions with the reality of immanent order. The expert social scientist learns to look through such appearances in the same way that a doctor must look beyond the report of symptoms and an economist must look beyond the intentions of sellers and buyers. In nineteenth-century legal theory, the deeper reality perceived by the social scientist begins with the common law as it had evolved in the Anglo-American world. As Francis Wharton put it in 1884, "From the development of jurisprudence . . . in the New World as well as in the Old, we must infer that law is an emanation from the people to the sovereign, and not a command imposed by the sovereign on the people."[1]

Because it is a category mistake to ask to whom we should ascribe authorship of a system, this conceptual turn raises the puzzle of the relationship of law to sovereignty. An Anglo-American common law is not exactly the product of a project of the sovereign—popular or otherwise—of either nation. Where, we might ask, are the sovereign people in the account of constitutional law as system? Can we make sense of the idea of popular sovereignty within the systemic world-view?[2] But if not, what grounds the legitimacy of law once it is no longer the people's project? The new science of law, accordingly, will have a deep political problem explaining the nature of law's legitimacy in a democratic polity.[3] Indeed, the relationship of claims of legal expertise to democratic consent will become the defining problem of late twentieth-century constitutional theory. This will be true both domestically, where it takes the form of the countermajoritarian difficulty, and internationally, where it takes the form of American exceptionalism.[4]

Interestingly in light of these puzzles of domestic political legitimacy, late nineteenth-century legal theory had little problem deploying the idea of legal system as a ground for colonizing efforts abroad.[5] Claims for law became claims for civilization.[6] Less developed countries were seen as less civilized; to bring to them the possibility of law was to help them to become more civilized. To bring this possibility was like bringing medicine: political health and physical health are both virtues of system. To resist civilization was to act against the best interests of one's own community. On such reasoning, American imperialism could understand itself as a successor to—if not still part of—the Christian mission of saving souls. Just as there could be no external saving of souls, but only the creation of the conditions under which indigenous people could realize the possibility of saving their own souls, legal theorists, too, thought that imperialism could only create the conditions under which a society could realize for itself—through the growth of custom—the immanent order of law.[7] To imagine that law could be given as a gift would be to imagine law as a project. The American civilizing mission, however, was not a project, but a remedial intervention to allow the growth of system.

Uniting all forms of systemic theorizing is the idea of order without purpose, order that arises without external intervention by an agent. To say it is order without purpose is not, however, to say it is without direction. While Darwin carefully denied that evolution was a process moving toward an end, the systemic theorists of law at the end of the nineteenth century believed that there was indeed a direction to legal change. They believed, in other words, in progress. This belief functioned as belief in God's providence had long functioned: a faith in the idea of an end toward which the community is moving even if that end cannot be grasped—and thus cannot be intended—by any finite actor.

Newton had offered a systemic understanding of natural forces; Darwin of biological forces. Darwin's system was dynamic, while

Newton revealed change to be only an appearance of timeless laws. One cannot predict the future of evolutionary change, but one can know with certainty where the planets will be on any future date. If the common law was to do the work of system in the late nineteenth century, it had to move from a Newtonian model of timelessness to a Darwinian model of ordered change. We can capture a sense of that movement by briefly comparing three figures: Blackstone, who published his *Commentaries* from 1765 to 1769; Langdell, who introduced a new idea of legal science to the American law school in 1872; and finally Holmes, whose volume *The Common Law* appeared in 1881.

Blackstone still understood system as the product of God's design: that hand was not yet wholly invisible. For Langdell, God was gone, but reason stepped into God's place, as if the mind of God remained even after his departure. For Holmes, such claims to reason were to be washed with what he called a "cynical acid." Order was no longer the product of a timeless reason. Rather, order was bound to history and change.[8] We witness in this movement from Blackstone to Holmes the meaning of the death of God as a political and legal phenomenon. Correspondingly, we see the rise of history as a source of order. Not only does the object of inquiry—the law—change as we move from one writer to another, but the form of inquiry—the method of knowing—changes as well. By the end of the century, the clash between Langdell and Holmes offers an early version of the continuing tension in legal study between the doctrinalists, who believe opinions should be studied to discover an immanent conceptual order, and the social scientists, who believe the legal phenomena must be reduced to data in order to discover underlying patterns.[9]

The story to be told, then, is of the convergence of the common law, constitutional law, and the science of the social over the course of the nineteenth century. This calls for a rethinking of the common law, a rejection of a constitutionalism of project, and the development of a social science of law. These are my topics in this part. After discussing Blackstone, Langdell, and Holmes, I move on in the next chapter to the attack on the early nineteenth-century constitutionalism of projects—an attack that began during the Civil War itself.

Arguments are now made that the real constitution is "unwritten."
It is unwritten in the same way that the common law is unwritten—
"in the same way" becomes, by the end of the nineteenth century,
"the same as."

Blackstone: A Science of the Common Law

Blackstone was the first lecturer on English law at Oxford. His
most famous and influential work, *Commentaries on the Laws of
England*, was written as a series of lectures to be delivered each year to
students, who until that time had studied civil law but not common
law.[10] Civil law had the great pedagogic advantage of emerging—
and then reemerging—from the Institutes of Justinian. The Institutes
offered a systematic presentation of a whole legal order in an accessible, textual form. English law was not so organized in practice and
had no comprehensive, accessible text from which it might be taught.
Blackstone set out to create such an organization and such a text—a
project in which he largely succeeded.[11]

Creating such a text made possible an organized scheme of study
that stood apart from an apprenticeship at the Inns of Court, which
had been the traditional place for the study of English law. A university course in law, however, had to construct law as an appropriate
object for an academic discipline. This meant that English law had
to be approached as more than an object of know-how or a habit of
practice.[12] It had to be a science, meaning it had to meet academic
expectations with respect to what it is to be a science.

Eighteenth-century science generally imagined outcomes to follow from a few basic principles that could be identified independently
of any particular set of facts. One studied facts to discover the immanent laws that are themselves the source of the facts. Not surprisingly, Blackstone took as his model Newtonian physics—the
eighteenth-century paradigm of scientific work. Cases became evidence of legal norms—the "real" law—in the same way that Newton's experiments with light provided evidence of physical laws.
Insofar as they were both sciences, there was not any great distinc-

tion to be drawn between the social and the natural sciences. The object of both was to set forth the laws that give order to the phenomena.

The basic form of legal science arises from the need to discover what Blackstone called the "elements and first principles upon which the rule of practice is founded."[13] Those elements form an ordered whole—not merely an eclectic collection of norms as they had been taught at the Inns of Court. Thus, Blackstone described his task as that of providing a "general map of the law."[14] An ordinary map plots each location in relation to all possible locations. A conceptual map of law is to do the same with respect to the field of ideas expressed in legal decisions. If the phenomena cannot be represented by a common set of categories, mapping is not possible. Just as that which cannot be represented spatially cannot appear on an ordinary map, that which cannot be represented in terms of rights and duties cannot appear on a legal map. In addition, if the elements are not well ordered with respect to each other, it will not be possible to map the field. Intersections will, in that case, be haphazard; contradictions will appear.

Blackstone complained that the student taught at the Inns of Court never advanced beyond practice: "If practice be the whole he is taught, practice must also be the whole he will ever know."[15] Blackstone's map of the law was meant to allow the student/scholar to move from a memorized repetition of observed phenomena to deduction from first principles. Absent the map, the student will not know what to make of "the least variation from established precedents" and will "seldom expect to comprehend, any arguments drawn a priori, from the spirit of the laws and the natural foundations of justice."[16] The latter point is important: if law is a science, then argument a priori must be possible, because the basic rules must be independent of their particular appearances. Just as the laws of physics make it possible to predict the motion of the planets or the movement of the tides, the laws of the social order make it possible to predict the distribution of rights and duties in any controversy that might arise. Of course, in any actual case, a judge might err in his ruling, but the point of a science is to enable us to identify those errors. A natural scientist too might err in his measurements of planetary motion.

If laws are independent of their particular appearance in practice, Blackstone believes they must owe their origin to something or someone that precedes their actual deployment in the cases. He can conceive of only one possible source: God. A science of law rests on natural law, the origin of which is in God. Here, too, Blackstone follows Newton, who thought the origin of physical laws had to be in God. Neither could imagine any other ultimate source of order, and thus of truth.

Blackstone understands the most fundamental norms of natural law to make no less a claim on man than the claim that physical laws make on objects in space and time. The difference between a person and a stone in free fall or the moon circling the earth is not in the extent to which each is subject to nature's law. Rather, the difference lies in the fact that man alone has free will. That there is a gap between the natural law and our behavior is accounted for not by a difference in law, but by a failure of the will. The problem, as long taught by Western religion, is in us, not in God's creative act. Man has turned away from the truth of his nature. Kant will capture this idea in its secular form when he writes that a perfectly rational subject would follow the rule of reason with the same necessity as objects in space and time follow Newton's laws of nature.[17] Such a subject would have "no reason" to do otherwise.

Laws, Blackstone believes, are not the sort of thing that can change, for they express the unchangeable nature of God. Law, in all its forms, expresses authority, and authority according to Blackstone is a matter of hierarchy. The fundamental hierarchy is that between the creator and the created. The created are dependent upon their creator, and therefore must follow the rules set forth for them. "[A]s man depends absolutely upon his maker for every thing, it is necessary that he should in all points conform to his maker's will."[18]

This idea of hierarchical authority supports another common assumption of eighteenth-century thought: the ultimate source of lawful order can only be an intelligence. The systemic order of nature must be grounded in God's mind. We are still within the mythical imagination that models explanations of order on our ordinary experience of acting in the world. To experience order and purposiveness is to experience the product of an intentional act. If law displays an order of reason, then it must be the consequence of the intention of some subject. Accordingly, to assert the existence of natural law is to assert the existence of a subject to whom we can trace the nature of law. That subject is, of course, God, which means that the metaphysical claim about the origin of order is equally a theological claim about the nature of authority. On this reasoning, faith is not challenged by science; rather, science is an expression of faith. The system of law may be a science of immanent principles for us, but that science still depends on an idea of God's project. This was just the reasoning of Christian theodicy that I described in Part I.[19]

The Blackstonian worldview, like that of so many early modern thinkers, puts an immense amount of pressure on the idea of reason, which stands simultaneously for man's ability to discover truth, the mind of God, and the order of things. Blackstone writes that God gave man "the faculty of reason to discover the purport of [natural] law."[20] Reason characterizes simultaneously the object of theory, the theorizing subject, and the moral demand upon that subject. Blackstone captures this multiplicity of meanings in his easy resolution of the deep structural conflict between the Scholastics and the Nominalists. The former insisted on God's reason; the latter on his unfettered will. For Blackstone, God wills the product of reason, for he has no reason to create any other sort of law. Not to follow reason would be a failure of God's goodness:

> Considering the creator only as a being of infinite *power*, he was able unquestionably to have prescribed whatever laws he pleased to his creature, man, however unjust or severe. But as he is also a being of infinite *wisdom*, he has laid down only such laws as were founded in those relations of justice, that existed in the nature of things antecedent to any positive precept.[21]

Thus, for Blackstone, reason is both a faculty and a state of the world. Reason (the faculty) is the capacity to discern law (objective reason): the reason of the mind grasps the reason of the world. This symmetry is logically—and theologically—necessary even if it is not evident at the level of ordinary appearances. Nature—as in "natural law"—just is the showing forth of God's power and his wisdom. From his power comes the force of the claim of law upon us; from his wisdom comes the well-being that will accrue to us if we follow that law. Coming from God, natural law supervenes all other authority: "This law of nature, being co-eval with mankind and dictated by God himself, is of course superior in obligation to any other. . . . [N]o human laws are of any validity, if contrary to this. . . ."[22]

There is, then, for Blackstone a single system of law: natural law is not a separate field from what he calls "municipal" law. The laws that operate in a society "derive all their force, and all their authority, mediately or immediately, from this original [natural law]."[23] By "mediately," Blackstone refers to those positive laws that determine an issue with respect to which natural law left discretion. Even there, discretion is always limited by reason. Discretion can be abused, in which case its result is not law at all, but only a false appearance of law.

Blackstone has little faith that man can deploy his reason alone to "discover the purport of [natural] law[]."[24] After Adam's fall, "reason is corrupt, and . . . understanding full of ignorance and error."[25] Here again there is an analogy between the natural and the social sciences. That man has the capacity to discern the truth of the physical laws of nature does not mean that every man is a Newton. We do not trust most people's opinions about nature, but only the beliefs of those who have cultivated reason in order to achieve a scientific outlook. Similarly, we should not trust everyone's opinions about the law, but only those who have cultivated their capacity for reasonable discernment. In the first instance, those are judges. The judges "are the depositary of the laws; the living oracles, who must decide in all cases of doubt, and who are bound by an oath to decide according to the law of the land."[26]

Judges decide controversies only after they arise. We, however, need to know what the law is before we act, that is, before a judge is available. God's sympathetic response to man's failure of reason has traditionally been revelation. Blackstone takes it for granted that the content of revelation is the same as that which reason reveals: "[T]he moral precepts of this [revealed] law are indeed of the same original with those of the law of nature, so their intrinsic obligation is of equal strength and perpetuity."[27] Indeed, because law is the expression of reason, any addition would have to be a negation—that is, it would express an unreasonable element in God's will.

Revelation stands to natural law as Blackstone's *Commentaries* stand to the common law of the courts. Neither is exactly the law itself, but each is a resource for learning the law. A science of law, then, takes the place of revelation, the aim of which had always been to ground an ethical practice. This is an aspect of a larger Enlightenment project of man taking responsibility for himself through the cultivation of reason.[28] Thus, Blackstone begins by explaining to his students, who came from the privileged classes of English society, just why they should study the science of the common law. Without this knowledge, he tells them, they will be unable to perform their public responsibilities well or adequately to defend their private interests. Blackstone's science of the law is always both theory and practice because man must work to achieve his own reasonable nature. Just as science displaces revelation, the scientist-academic displaces the theologian-minister.

Because Blackstone's God wills the order of reason, modern readers tend easily to dismiss the theological claims of the work as unnecessary, looking directly to the claim for reason. They think that reason can do without God, that appeals to reason point to a latent secular attitude. This is a mistaken reading. For Blackstone, science and reason remain the path to, not away from, God. They have the normative valence of recovery from the corruption of the will. The truth of the law, that which makes a proposition law at all, is that it rests ultimately upon the authority of natural law. That body of law, in turn, rests upon the sovereignty of God. Absent that foundation, there is no ground whatsoever for the authority of law, even if it is adopted with the consent of those it governs.

This does not mean that consent has no place in Blackstone's theory. He is well aware of Hobbes's idea of the social contract. Indeed, Blackstone takes up directly Hobbes's theory about the origins of the political union through "the consent of all persons to submit their own private wills to the will of one man, or of one or more assemblies of men, to whom the supreme authority is entrusted."[29] Yet, this theory of the origins of civil authority does not tell us what it is the sovereign should do: what is the content of that will? Consent can create a possible site of authority, but to be authoritative, the sovereign must subordinate itself to reason in the form of law. Failure to do so would be unjust as a matter of politics, law, morality, and religion.[30]

Consent, then, cannot ground the authority of a law. It can, however, be indicative of authority well used. A custom that has long been practiced operates with the consent of the community that it regulates. Blackstone assumes that the unreasonable could not long survive. The irrational is always aberrational. The accumulated consent of generations is, therefore, evidence—not necessarily conclusive—that a custom is not contrary to natural law.

Failing to take seriously the theological assumptions behind Blackstone's understanding of legal science, modern readers emphasize instead his use of history. Blackstone at times encourages this view, because of the link he sees between consent, practice, and reason. He writes, for example, that his exposition of the primary rules and fundamental principles requires, among other things, that "their *history* should be deduced, their changes and revolutions observed."[31] Much history is set forth in the work, but history is hardly the point of the inquiry. History, even a history of consent, is not offered as explanation of the authority of law. History serves rather as empirical evidence from which the truth of the law can be discerned. History stands to law as experiment stands to physics. The experiment is the site of a kind of reasoning that discerns a universal principle. So too, history is the site for the discernment of reason immanent in the law.[32]

Blackstone's appeal to history is actually quite the opposite of our expectations with respect to the uses of history. For him, the history that counts is time immemorial. "[I]n our law the goodness of a custom depends upon its having been used time out of mind; or, in the solemnity of our legal phrase, time whereof the memory of man runneth not to the contrary. This it is that gives it its weight and authority. . . ."[33] Only when a practice emerges from a past beyond contemporary discernment does it gain value as support for legal authority. To know the actual history of a norm—who created it and why—is to render the norm accidental. Of such accidental, political interventions in the immemorial common law, Blackstone writes: "[I]t hath been an antient observation in the laws of England, that whenever a standing rule of law, of which the reason perhaps could not be remembered or discerned, hath been wantonly broke in upon by statutes or new resolutions, the wisdom of the rule hath in the end appeared from the inconveniences that have followed the innovation."[34] An actual intervention—a project—is likely to express the corruption of reason, while time immemorial overcomes the bad effects of any such corruption.

There is a deliberate slippage between time immemorial and time eternal. A custom that appears to us as always having been slips into the normative order of reason itself, for that which is without reason could not survive in a world ordered by God. "[H]ence it is that our lawyers are with justice so copious in their encomiums on the reason of the common law; that they tell us, that the law is the perfection of reason, that it always intends to conform thereto, and that what is not reason is not law."[35] So strong is his belief in the coincidence of reason and time immemorial that he will affirm it even when "the distance of time" has made it impossible to discern the actual reason for a customary norm.[36]

When a rule—or more precisely a judicial ruling—appears to be "flatly contradictory to reason," it cannot be the case that it is correct. The law exists independently of the judicial rulings, which are only evidence of the law. They are the best means for discovery of law, but they are not the thing itself. Thus, a ruling can be wrong: "the judge may *mistake* the law."[37] The law does not change as judicial rulings change. Rulings can make the law more or less clear. When they are wrong, they obscure the law.

Blackstone provides his most elaborate explanation of the coincidence of custom and reason in his discussion of "particular customs." These are recognized exceptions to the more general customs that constitute the common law proper. He sets forth seven "necessary requisites" to determine if such a custom is "good," that is, legally controlling. Since a particular custom and a general custom are similar in their relationship to authority—differing only in jurisdictional range—these seven requisites guide judgment whenever a customary claim is put forth.

The first two requirements go to the temporal character of the custom. The custom cannot have a historically identifiable beginning: "[I]f any one can shew the beginning of it, it is no good custom."[38] The second requirement complements this one: the custom must have operated without any break. "Any interruption would cause a temporary ceasing; the revival gives it a new beginning, which will be within time of memory, and thereupon the custom will be void."[39] The order of rights and responsibilities established by the common law is cast here as an analogue to the laws of nature. Just as the latter have always been and continue without interruption, so must the former. Just as a break in the operation of a law of nature would suggest that it is not law at all, a break in a customary norm suggests that it too is not law.

Not only must a custom emerge unbroken from time immemorial, its operation must have been "peaceable, and acquiesced in; not subject to contention and dispute."[40] Acquiescence is taken by Blackstone to be an expression of consent: "For as customs owe their original to common consent, their being immemorially disputed . . . is proof that such consent was wanting."[41] Blackstone is not suggesting that consent grounds the law. If that were the case, there would be no sense in linking consent to time immemorial. The consent that matters, when making a claim of political legitimation, is contemporary: we bind ourselves, as in a contract. Rather, Blackstone is observing that a practice imposed by force cannot have the normative quality that comes with adhering to a rule for the right reasons. Custom in that case could not be evidence of a rule grounded in reason and ultimately in divine authority.

This chain of argument leading from practice to reason is immediately evident in the next requirement: "Customs must be *reasonable*; or rather taken negatively, they must not be unreasonable."[42] The immediate movement from the positive requirement to the negative constraint is necessary to account for the arbitrary element of many rules: for example, drive on the left. Blackstone has already set forth the proposition that the common law generally is "the perfection of reason . . . and that what is not reason is not law."[43] Much of the law, however, falls into the area of discretion—line drawing—about which we can ask no more than that it not be unreasonable.

The combination of this requirement of reasonableness with the prior one of consent works to limit the domain of those whose consent matters. After all, wherever there is law, there are law violators. If everyone consented to all law all the time, then the common law would work like the laws of nature. Accordingly, the consent that matters is that of those who are reasonable, by which Blackstone means those who possess the "artificial and legal reason, warranted by authority of law."[44] That group consists, for the most part, of the judges and those who expound the meaning of their judgments.

The next two requirements are that customs be "certain" and "compulsory." A rule that does not determine a specific course of action does not have the quality of legality. It may set forth a moral principle or a value that citizens should seek to achieve. Such norms are appealed to all the time in our personal and social lives: be charitable, take care of your health, respect those with whom you deal, spend cautiously. These open-ended norms no doubt inform our general expectations with respect to specific laws. Thus, early on Blackstone writes of "three general precepts" to which Justinian had reduced the whole doctrine of law: "we should live honestly, should hurt nobody, and should render to everyone it's due."[45] These are among "the eternal, immutable laws of good and evil," which all law—natural and municipal—must follow. Yet, these general precepts do not determine any particular act. They must be implemented by laws that are both certain and compulsory.

The final requirement goes directly to the idea of systemic order: "customs must be consistent with each other."[46] Since all relevant customs must have existed from time immemorial, contradiction is unimaginable. We can see this as a practical consequence: inconsistent norms could not control behavior without objection over a substantial period of time. Or we can see it as a demand of reason: a contradiction is a violation of reason. Just as physical laws of nature operate systemically without contradiction, so must customary laws. Again, we see that time immemorial and reason are overlapping ways of describing the same normative claim.

The net effect of the seven requisites is to imagine the common law as an immanent system of artificial reason that establishes the order of a political community maintaining itself as a single whole over time immemorial. It is artificial not in the sense of illusion or appearance, but in the constructive sense of reason informing an artifice. Because we stand within that artifice, which is creation, laws appears immanent to us: they are not the product of our deliberate acts. From the perspective of the creator, the order of law remains his project. Reason is the pivot around which simultaneous claims of project and system can be organized. All subjects, finite or infinite, must follow reason as a rule for action. God does so as part of his project; man does so as the immanent principles of order in the system that is his world.

Blackstone uses the argument from reason not to attack but to support customary practice. That practice, for him, stands in a direct relationship to God—a relationship traditionally mediated by the reason of judges, but now by scholars. The scholar's role is to identify the immanent system of reason within the plethora of precedents. At no point, however, does Blackstone set reason free of custom, as if man's unaided reason could come to the law as a field for new projects.[47] The common law displays not a history of self-ordering, but the nature of God's providence.

Daniel Boorstin, in his book on Blackstone, correctly points out the deeply conservative nature of Blackstone's work.[48] Appeals to natural law, however, just like appeals to reason, are not necessarily conservative. They can serve a reformist or even a revolutionary purpose; they can offer a standard against which to measure existing laws and practices. It is not the appeal to reason, but the turn to an immanent system that accounts for Blackstone's conservatism. Reason set free of system will quickly come to inform the revolutionary project of American law.

Customary practices are, for Blackstone, evidence of the universal system of reason—the immanent principle of order—that extends from God to man, from the physical world to society. Those practices are the object of the judge's expertise, just as his judgments are the form in which the practices are given renewed, explicit expression—thus providing further evidence of the customs themselves. As this system of thought extends across late nineteenth-century America, it sheds its theological context and metaphysical assumptions. The judicial opinion shifts its position from evidence to source. Even Christopher Langdell, whose work has a decidedly Blackstonian cast, will describe himself as a positivist: law's origin is in the actions of the authoritative decision makers of this world.

Langdell: From God to Reason

Langdell, like Blackstone, was simultaneously designing a course of legal pedagogy and offering a theory of the nature of law.[49] Again like Blackstone, he believed these dual aims point to a need to make the study of law a science. In the modern university, a science refers to both a course of study and an object of study—for example, chemistry or biology. And like Blackstone, Langdell believed that the object of scientific interrogation is, in the first instance, the case. For Langdell, cases increase dramatically in importance: they are not only evidence of law; they are the source of the authority of law. The reason of law is no longer made authoritative through the divine will; the system of law is no longer a part of God's creation. God disappears from the account of legal authority. System cuts its tie to a divine project.

This shift toward a deeply historicized understanding of the order of social (and biological) phenomena is characteristic of nineteenth-century thought. Stories of originary acts no longer offer explanations; rather, they serve only as myths. Darwin is paradigmatic of this shift. Langdell shows us that the shift does not necessarily take a Darwinian form. Yet, absent something like a Darwinian account of competition within environmental constraints, Langdell's appeal to history absent God produces more of a conundrum than a coherent account.

Blackstone's interest in history had a kind of antihistorical bias. He was interested in history only at the point at which it escapes the reach of narrative. The history that actually counted in Blackstonian law was that of time immemorial; the history beyond the memory of man. This was the span of history within which natural law and customary law could somehow fuse into a single unit. To trace a point of origin is to identify a decision maker. Since Blackstone believed people operate with only a corrupted capacity for reason, he saw no ground to assume a convergence of the law of nature and the work of particular decision makers. Time immemorial was, accordingly, Blackstone's answer to the corruption of reason.

Langdell reverses this set of assumptions. There is no longer any point at which a legal decision escapes the fallible character of human reason; there is no purity in an imagined point of origin beyond recorded time. Accordingly, the perfection of law as a system of reason depends not upon its origin, but upon its progressive development. The idea of systemic order no longer finds its paradigmatic expression in the static organism—Aristotle's timeless form—but in the dynamic of evolution.

Langdell expresses the idea of an evolving legal system quite concisely in the preface to his first casebook—the first casebook in legal education:

> Law, considered as a science, consists of certain principles or doctrines. . . . Each of these doctrines has arrived at its present state by slow degrees; in other words, it is a growth, extending in many cases through centuries. This growth is to be traced in the main through a series of cases; and much the shortest and best, if not the only way of mastering the doctrine effectually is by studying the cases in which it is embodied.[50]

Growth is imagined as a process of social learning. The cases trace a pattern of learning by judges. The student replicates that learning by following the development of the cases. Progress displaces origins in the account of authority. Progress is generated spontaneously and immanently within the legal order. No one imposes order on the courts.

What exactly are the judges—or anyone else—learning when they study the cases? Langdell and his followers are very weak—indeed, fatally weak—in their answer to this question. There is a suggestion that law's progress is like that of the natural sciences: the sciences get better over time as scientists test the laws they have hypothesized against new observations and experiments. This is true not just of pure sciences like physics, but also of applied sciences like civil engineering. Just as we get better at building bridges, perhaps we get better at doing law.[51]

Yet, as others—beginning with legal realists—have pointed out, the analogy to the natural sciences won't quite work for Langdell. Having stripped law of its theological support, what exactly could be the external object of this science? The natural sciences get better over time as scientists learn more about an objective order that exists independently of the state of science at any given time.[52] But for Langdell, unlike for Blackstone, the principles of law don't precede the decisions of the judges. The law is not being discovered by the judges; rather, it is being created. Decisions are not just evidence of the law; they are its source. There is a collapse of the epistemic and the ontological, of knowing and being. God is no longer available as the point at which to break out of the circle. Theorizing this collapse as the "hermeneutic circle" will be the task of twentieth-century thought, but Langdell has no conceptual tools to confront the conundrum he creates.[53] Thus, he claims that he is both a positivist and a scientist. What he cannot easily do is make both claims simultaneously.

If the model of progress in the law is not that of the natural sciences, perhaps Langdell believes it is more like progress in the practical arts. Do judges get better at ordering complex social arrangements simply because they come to see what works best, all things considered? This too will not quite work, for the Langdellians are deeply invested in the idea that the law, however it is produced, is an autonomous system; it is not simply an application of otherwise available evaluative judgments. Properly read, the cases reveal a rationally ordered conceptual system within which particular rules can be derived deductively from general normative principles.[54] There is no available theory by which we could explain the emergence of an immanent, rational order through a judicial practice driven by judgments of what works best overall.[55]

Langdell explicitly acknowledges that legal rules deductively derived from fundamental principles may not always accomplish ends that accord with our overall sense of justice; those rules may not be best overall for those involved.[56] The Langdellians insist that there is a difference between legal rights and the morally just or the economically efficient. Indeed, part of the burden of a theory of law is to explain why some things that seem unjust are nevertheless right as a matter of law. Systemic theories of law are, in this sense, never far from their theological roots in theodicy. Absent an answer to this question, we don't know why politics should defer to law in cases in which the legal result is unjust. What is it exactly that the lawyers know? Not too much later, the legal realists will respond that what the Langdellians know is nothing but "transcendental nonsense."[57] This is the legal equivalent of pronouncing the death of God and the end of theology as a field of knowledge. It is to abandon systemic theodicy and open a space for new projects of law: the administrative, social-welfare state of the twentieth century.

The work history does for Langdell, accordingly, remains indeterminate. For history really to do the work explicitly assigned to it, Langdell would have either to establish the authority of law as an object to be discovered—the natural-law perspective—or explain why a practice that depends upon experience as a source of progress would choose logic over justice.[58] Langdell chooses neither option, leaving the foundations of his account of law indeterminate and obscure. His assumption about the movement of history toward system puts him somewhere between Hegel's appeal to the cunning of reason and Darwin's appeal to the struggle for survival. Law remains a "mysterious science."[59]

The truth is that the work that Langdell and his followers do in developing legal formalism generally pays little attention to history. The promise of a historically oriented account is never seriously pursued. It is not history that determines the small set of relevant cases judged to be relevant, but the scholar who brings to the cases a systemic ambition. Langdellians are interested primarily in the logic of the law at a very high level of abstraction—too high for history to offer much guidance. History's role is little more than to serve as a pedagogical device: cases are to illustrate rules, which the instructor has well in mind before he turns to case selection.

Langdellians descend from those high-level principles to ground-level rules through a process of reasoning that pays little attention to a history of development, but instead deploys a pseudodeductive form. "Pseudo" because in law the weight of the deduction is always carried by the minor premise, which must be constructed by analogy. The minor premise is not just a self-evident statement of objective fact. For example, that all persons must be treated equally at law (major premise) does not tell us whether women or minorities are persons in the relevant sense (minor premise). It does not even tell us that all men qualify as legal persons. It does not tell us whether or when corporations qualify as persons. We don't learn the elements of the class from deduction, but only by making arguments of likeness and difference starting from some commonly accepted cases.[60] The conclusion of the deduction, however, can be no stronger than the analogy upon which it relies. Similarly, the principle of equality in itself tells us nothing, for example, about the legitimacy of "separate but equal" as an application of the principle.[61] Langdellians have nothing to say about the cultural assumptions—historical, social, ideological, economic, religious—built into the construction of minor premises. They assume that the facts take care of themselves, which is just what the pragmatists, developing at the same time, were going to deny.[62]

Rather than developing a history of the case law, Langdell identifies certain paradigmatic cases. Those cases are used pedagogically to present doctrinal principles. Seeing through the case to the doctrine, the case itself drops out of the account. The presentation is not actually one of doctrinal development, but rather of the logical character of doctrine. That the doctrine gains its authority by virtue of its development in and through judicial decisions is only a framing assumption, not an operative element of legal reasoning. Thus, Langdell saw no problem in looking primarily to British case law—a remnant of Blackstone. Yet what authority does a British judge have in the United States?[63] The force of law, Langdell assumes, is conceptual; reason does the actual work. It is the immanent, if unspoken, source of systemic order. Reason plays the role, then, of Blackstone's God, but now working over time rather than through an original creative act.

When history does appear in the Langdellian account, it is usually in the form of allegations of error. Courts can go wrong in their application of principles; they can, for example, decide for reasons of justice, instead of following the abstract logic of legal rules. As many have noticed, this produces the paradox of Langdell claiming both that the cases are the authoritative source of law and that many of the cases are wrong.[64] We need some criterion other than the fact of decision by which to separate out the good cases from the bad. Blackstone appealed to an "artificial reason" at this point—a reason the authority of which was ultimately grounded in God.[65] Modern lawyers often appeal to the cultivated sensibilities of the professional lawyer.[66] They do so, however, at the risk of losing the democratic legitimacy of law, for what is it that gives authority to a legal elite in a system of popular government?[67]

Holmes: From Reason to Reasonableness

Deflating the self-conception of elite practitioners of law is part of the ambition of Oliver Wendell Holmes's famous lecture of 1897, "The Path of the Law."[68] Holmes begins with what he calls the "bad man's" view of the law. The bad man, whom he describes as the lawyer's client, wants to know only one thing about the law: what would be the consequences to him were a court to find some proposed action a violation of the law. He wants to know, in other words, what he stands to lose from a judicial decision. Presumably, he already knows what he has to gain by the action he proposes. Holmes's bad man is engaging in an informal cost-benefit analysis as he consults his lawyer.

Holmes uses the idea of the bad man to introduce his claim that in the law office, the law is nothing but "prophecy" of what courts will do with respect to any controversy.[69] That is all that counts to the client, so any greater claims as to the nature of law are matters for the speculative imagination. Such speculations make no difference in the actual practice of law—the domain into which law students (his audience for the lecture) are about to enter.

For the bad man and his lawyer, it makes no sense to describe the law as a set of norms that carry independent weight rooted in God or reason. The legal order, for those who must act within it, does not describe a morally best world. Rather, laws are nothing but facts about the world, which a client must take into account as he decides what it is that he will do. The law is like the weather: we ask a meteorologist to predict the weather in order to figure it into our plans; we ask a lawyer to predict how a judge will rule in order to figure that ruling into our plans. Like the weather, law may have its own order, but that is of no relevance to the individual planning some particular course of action.

Holmes's bad man is anyone who has reasons for his actions independent of the law. The client approaches the law as a potential obstacle; he asks whether his plan is worth the cost. From a moral point of view, the bad man may actually be quite good. He may be moved by justice or charity. He may think that justice requires him to steal to feed a starving person. He wants to know from his lawyer what penalty the law sets if he is caught. Accordingly, even the good man becomes a "bad" man when he consults his lawyer.

Holmes's point is that everyone, both the morally good and the morally bad, has the same interest in knowing what the law is. Each wants to maximize his interests, whatever they may be. The bad man, accordingly, can be perfectly law-abiding, while the good man may be driven to disobey the law. Law is about observable actions, not an individual's maxims.[70] Conversely, that someone abides by the law tells us nothing about his moral character.[71]

Holmes's lecture begins with the bad-man view of the law, but the lecture is misread if one takes that starting point as a complete expression of Holmes's understanding of the law. At most, it is his understanding of practice in the law office. The lecture traces the *path* of the law, which begins with the bad man's view but ends with an "echo of the infinite, a glimpse of its unfathomable process, a hint of the universal law."[72] This is not a glimpse available to the bad man, whose concerns with law are distinctly finite. Nor is it ordinarily available to the practitioner, whose tasks are defined in relationship to the needs of his or her client. It is, rather, that glimpse of the infinite available to the scientist in any field. Each looks for the universal in and through particular objects of knowledge. Each finds a path to self-transcendence by achieving knowledge, which is necessarily divorced from a narrow, personal perspective. Reading Holmes, we are reminded of Kant's remark in *The Critique of Practical Reason*, where he speaks of the starry heavens above and the moral law within as inspiring admiration and awe. To Kant's pair, Holmes would suggest adding the law. Thus, he writes, "I venerate the law, and especially our system of law, as one of the vastest products of the human mind."[73]

The path of the lecture parallels the path of the law; it moves along this arc from the narrow self-interest of the bad man to the echo of the infinite. If the bad man's view were all there was, then there would be no path to traverse and nothing to glimpse at the end. The calculation of interest would work no less in the construction of law than in the application of law: judges and legislators would pursue their own interests in the same way as everyone else. To understand the law, we would ask whose interests are being advanced by these rules.

That, of course, is the approach of much of positive political science today.[74] This is distinctly not Holmes's view. Even though he speaks of his work as applying a kind of "cynical acid" to theories of law in order to get to the "operation" of the law itself, he also proclaims that his approach to law is not to be mistaken for cynicism: "The law is the witness and external deposit of our moral life. Its history is the history of the moral development of the race. The practice of it, in spite of popular jests, tends to make good citizens and good men. When I emphasize the difference between law and morals I do so with reference to a single end, that of learning and understanding the law."[75]

If we step away from the bad man—if we begin to ascend the path—and ask about the substance of the law, rather than the consequences of its violation, Holmes tells us that the law generally sets forth the dominant public opinion. The content of the law, accordingly, develops along with the moral views of the community. Law is a kind of depository of norms of sociability, of expectations of behavior, of the general sense of the public good, and of beliefs about what can be demanded of each person for the sake of the community. The law generally reflects the common sense of right and wrong that operates in a prereflective way in the community.

The history of the law, then, is a history of the moral development of the political community. Famously, Holmes will write in his dissent in *Lochner* that a dominant opinion tends to become the law.[76] Holmes has a sense for what Rawls will later theorize as "reflective equilibrium."[77] Public opinion arises in part from law, but law is just as much the product of public opinion. Accordingly, a community will generally get the law it deserves, for the law reflects its own beliefs about the good and the just. As beliefs change, so will the law.[78] For Plato and Thomas More, who each pursued a politics of project, this reciprocity of law and public opinion presented what I termed "the paradox of new foundations."[79] That same reciprocity appears to the systemic understanding as the condition for the development of an immanent order.

Holmes tells us that most of our beliefs and legal practices—good and bad—are simply inheritances from the past. We cannot reinvent everything for ourselves. We can, however, address one "small corner" of the law at a time. There, we can bring reason to bear by identifying the "social advantage" that the law seeks, measuring how well the law succeeds, and improving it where possible. This is intervention as repair. The systemic quality of law depends on judges taking up this responsibility to repair.

The man of the future, Holmes tells the students, will be the one who knows how to use statistics in the examination of the costs and benefits of a law. For Holmes, this is the method of a remedial science: as laws age, they no longer provide all the benefits they once produced. Famously, Holmes wrote, "It is revolting to have no better reason for a rule of law than that it was laid down in the time of Henry IV."[80] The science of law, on this view, is not the Langdellian ideal of identifying the immanent principles of order at a high level of conceptual abstraction; rather, it identifies the ends of social policy toward which particular laws are reaching. The program Holmes foresees is that of the modern regulatory state that systematically applies cost-benefit analysis to improve the efficiency of particular laws. Each area of law becomes the subject of an administrative order led by experts trained in social sciences.

While Holmes approves of the general method of cost-benefit calculation, he certainly does not believe that the range of human behavior can be completely accounted for in terms of calculations of interest. Elsewhere he writes, for example, that a soldier's duty exhibits the sublime precisely when his willing sacrifice exceeds all personal interest and rational calculation. In the lawyer's office, we may all be bad men, but on the battlefield men willingly sacrifice for each other without regard to personal cost. These values too work their way into the law.[81]

The order of law for Holmes, then, is not the immanent order of a timeless reason. This is the critique he levels against Langdell. Universal reason is not working itself out in the law.[82] Instead, the law we have is the consequence of accumulated shared beliefs about what is reasonable and how to behave. Because our beliefs change as a result of our experience, laws come to be out of sync with contemporary public opinion. Legal change imposes its own costs and difficulties, which means that law lags behind our beliefs. The law we have at any time may reflect less of our moral development and more that of our predecessors. This is the reason we have to study history if we are to understand our law. History is the propaedeutic to statistics, and statistics is the method of reform. In a vivid metaphor, Holmes says that while historical inquiry gets the "beast out of the cave," statistics allows us to slay it.[83]

To advance on the path of law is to move from the bad man, to the man of ordinary moral sensibilities, to the modern policy analyst. Holmes's closing invocation of the infinite is not a step within the law, but the point at which the reflection on the law—on this entire progression of study—becomes a matter for self-reflection. In the study of law—no less than in other disciplines—we can affirm our capacities for reason, self-ordering, and understanding; in this, we are near to the very heart of things.

Holmes's major work in jurisprudence, *The Common Law*, was written about twenty years prior to "The Path of the Law." In it, he does not yet catch a glimmer of the infinite, but he does elaborate his understanding of the nature and development of the immanent order of law. *The Common Law* remains within the field of history; Holmes does not yet have a view of the place of statistics in the reform of law. The volume agrees with the lecture, however, in its resolute critique of Langdellian legal science. Thus, Holmes opens the work with one of the most famous lines of American legal scholarship: "The life of the law has not been logic: it has been experience."[84] This does not mean that reasoning is irrelevant. Rather, it means that there is no hidden world of abstract logic behind the cases. The cases are not epiphenomenal, resting upon reason itself. Concepts are not guiding the development of law as if it were an abstract science: "[T]he law embodies the story of a nation's development through many centuries, and it cannot be dealt with as if it contained only the axioms and corollaries of a book of mathematics."[85]

The *Common Law* puts the experience that is the source of law into a dynamic form, effectively offering a theory of history. The common law is a body of doctrines, rules, and precedents that come to us as a sort of inheritance. No doubt, the origins of any particular rule lie in a past judgment that this would be a good way to realize an acknowledged end. All such judgments, however, rest upon the knowledge and practices of the moment. The legal rules change much more slowly than do the surrounding beliefs in which they had been anchored. That they endure independently of the reasons for their creation opens law to a practice of apologetics as new reasons are offered to justify old rules. What had been adopted for one end comes to be seen as a means to satisfy a different end—one that is compelling to contemporary public opinion. Thus, the substance of the law changes even as the form endures. History develops in this gap between genealogy and justification. That gap is filled by the moving, practical force of experience.

Legal reasoning, precisely because it justifies what it does not create, is always playing a catch-up game. As the reasons offered in defense of a rule depart more and more from the original reasons for the creation of the rule, the gap between means and ends grows. Judged by contemporary beliefs and values, law is always inefficient, for we are using tools invented for one purpose to reach new and different ends. Law is, therefore, always in need of reform; it is never quite as dynamic as public opinion. The latter moves continuously, while the law moves in distinct steps.

This entire process is what Holmes means by "experience"—as in "the life of the law. . . ." It is not without reason, but its reason is not abstract, universal, or deductive. Law grows as a sensible and sense-giving practice; it is not a matter of ordering highly abstract concepts. As our justifications for the law shift, they will eventually ground an effort to reform the law. Holmes describes a kind of dialectic of invention, drift, redirection, and reform. This dialectic is the path of the law that Holmes summarizes in his 1897 lecture.

Holmes's account of the dialectic of legal experience is not exactly Darwinian, but it is surely offered in the spirit of Darwin. It describes how order emerges from history, not as the realization of an abstract plan, but as a practical matter of accomplishing a community's actual ends. Like Darwin, Holmes sees life as a kind of striving to succeed. Order, including legal order, is the product of that striving. History brings order because we are purposive and critical in our efforts.

If the growth of the law often comes through new reasons offered for old rules, the study of the law can easily fall victim to anachronism. We project our contemporary reasons back onto the earlier stages of the law, as if our predecessors were already us. For example, Holmes argues that the origin of our liability rules is in a practice of vengeance on the thing or person that accomplished the injury. That end grounded a rule of surrender, that is, the giving over of the offending object or person. Payment in lieu of surrender was an exceptional possibility that protected the interests of some innocent owners—for example, if a slave was the offending party, but acted without the owner's knowledge. At some point, Holmes says, the norm and the exception shifted position. Liability came to be the ground, and surrender came to be seen as a way of limiting liability. We engage in anachronism if we project back onto the origin of the rule our current beliefs about the limits of liability.[86]

We see in this example that identifying the genealogy of the rule puts us in a position to see the gap between the formal rule and the substantive reasons we offer in its justification. Our legal practice of liability continues to include rules grounded in the earlier social practice of vengeance. Understanding the history frees us from any belief in the necessity of the rule or its various elements.[87] History creates the possibility of a critical perspective—and thus of reform—for history is the work of neither God nor reason.

The dialectic of law reform, Holmes claims, has not awaited the arrival of the modern scholar. It has been pursued by "able and experienced men, who know too much to sacrifice good sense to a syllogism. . . ."[88] Their work has, however, been unconscious: they fitted new reasons to old rules, while claiming only to apply the law. "[H]itherto this process has been largely unconscious. It is important, on that account, to bring to mind what the actual course of events has been. If it were only to insist on a more conscious recognition of the legislative function of the courts . . . it would be useful. . . ."[89] Again, we see that systemic consequences were not dependent on systemwide intentions.

Holmes identifies an important characteristic of modern legal theory here. He argues that the reform of law is and has always been a part of law. Judges applying the rules are actually "legislating," for even if they keep the form of law the same, they reform its substance. That which the judges have been doing unconsciously should be brought to deliberate awareness in the modern age. The man of "good sense" will be replaced by the man of statistics. Genealogy is, in this sense, the Enlightenment project of taking responsibility, and cost-benefit analysis is the reform of law internal to the law itself. This modern form of legal reform, however, is strikingly beyond the power of the courts; judges are not economists. Thus Holmes's famous plea in his *Lochner* dissent for judicial deference to legislative experimentation.[90]

In Holmes, we see a figure who has absorbed much of nineteenth-century thought. At its center is a new understanding of history. Even Langdell had formally to acknowledge history, although his real concern was decidedly an ahistorical, conceptual order close to that of Blackstone. Holmes's idea of history relies on reasonableness rather than reason. Reason has been stripped of its theological pretension by which it was imagined as an independent force pushing us from behind, whether as a visible or invisible hand. For Holmes, the future is our calling; it is that toward which we are moving. The law, Holmes writes, "will become entirely consistent only when it ceases to grow."[91] For us mortals, that would be death.

Between Holmes and Langdell we see the possibilities of an immanent system of order in the absence of God. For both, reason remains even as God departs. What used to be imagined as the mind of God remains immanent in the phenomena. Langdell has no account, however, of how reason got there. Holmes offers a theory of the growth of law as the progress of civilization itself. The reason is our own and the burden of enlightenment is to make conscious and therefore deliberate what had been unconscious and intuitive. Reason is not a brooding omnipresence in the sky; it is our collective work understood not as a grand project, but as a system developing in history.

Appealing to cost-benefit analysis, Holmes is theorizing system under the model of Adam Smith. History must be approached as system, but the capacity for critique always allows us to view the system from without, even as we are a part of it. That is precisely the position that Holmes imagines himself to occupy, combining judge, soldier, scientist, and critic. Even as we analyze law's systemic character, we imagine a place for reform as adjustments within the interstices of the system. Thus, the legal scientists of the late nineteenth century will lead to the twentieth-century movements of legal reform.

Project and system were long the attributes of God's reason. Now, they have become our own. This new attitude toward law that develops in the latter part of the nineteenth century characterizes not just the study of private law, but that of American constitutional law as well. Indeed, if law is the systemic expression of the growth of our common beliefs about order, then there is no ground upon which to imagine a strong distinction between public and private law.[92] As I explain in the next chapter, the common law and constitutional law converge in the idea of system.

Approaching the Constitution as a project, we may find ourselves tracing the contribution of identifiable individuals or groups to its drafting, ratification, and maintenance. Some of those individuals will be judges—for example, Chief Justice Marshall—whose decisions have contributed to—or perhaps undermined—the project. The nature of these inquiries follows from the intentional character of a project. These attributes of a *political* project would have made Blackstone skeptical that the Constitution was properly classified as law at all, for law governs from time immemorial. Yet, in the first half of the nineteenth century, constitutionalism was distinctly a project, and that project was one of law.

Because a political project is chosen for reasons that the actor must evaluate for him- or herself, a democratic political project speaks to citizen character as much as to beliefs about political institutions. We can relate the project of constitutional construction, for example, to the project of constructing prisons during the same period.[1] Both projects appealed to norms of citizenship, and both constructed institutions in order to realize those ideals. Both projects linked the formation of individual character to the creation and maintenance of order. A prison, too, has a constitution that establishes rights and institutions of governance over a particular jurisdictional space. A prison, like the polity it imitates, can also succeed or fail in its project.

A political project of reflection and choice imagines citizens to be open to the reasons and reasoning of political science. To follow a practice—including law—merely because it is customary was exactly what Kant—and later Holmes—imagined as unenlightened and irresponsible.[2] A constitution is the Enlightenment's answer to the common law. Strikingly, by the end of the nineteenth century, scholars are writing that law, including constitutional law, is necessarily grounded in custom.[3]

The idea of a constitutional project remained vivid in narratives of the founding and in the reasoning of judicial opinions right through the first half of the nineteenth century. It captured a sense of the United States as new and responsible for itself in ways that distinguished it from the Old World. This is not to say that there was a single view of the nature of the constitutional project. Rather, the model of the Constitution as project enabled and directed interpretive contestation.[4] The idea of project structured the multiple, competing narratives—a contest that came to focus especially on the issue of whose project it was. Project offered a way of imagining constitutional authority, judicial role, and citizen character. It determined the shape of an argument; it did not determine the content of that argument. What, for example, was the project with respect to the distribution of authority between state and national governments? What was the project with respect to the regulation of slavery? Political arguments, then as now, were often structured as constitutional claims, for despite interpretive controversy, the Constitution was authoritative: to win the constitutional claim was to win the political dispute. Or so it was imagined until *Dred Scott*, when Southern interests discovered that winning on the law was hardly the end of the matter.[5]

By the time of the Civil War, this narrative of constitutional project was no longer generally persuasive. There was stress on every element of the model: disagreement on the principles as well as on the question of whose project it was. These points were connected, for assertions of constitutional principles by some made it impossible for others to see that Constitution as a text they had authored. For the radical abolitionist, if the Constitution protected slavery, then he could not imagine himself as its author; it was not his project. The Southern slaveholder took exactly the opposite position.

In response, writers began to think differently about the ground of constitutional order. They argued that the *real* Constitution is not the written text, but unwritten customs of practice and belief. The Constitution is not a project initially put in place through deliberate, intentional action in 1789; it is, rather, an immanent order of reason—a system—that has no definite beginning and operates quite independently of the deliberate efforts of the Founders. This system of law is not the common law of time immemorial, for it is bound to the growth and development of the nation. It did not precede recorded history, but neither is it a product of the deliberate intentions of political actors. History is the field within and through which the internal logic of political institutions has worked itself out. The Constitution is the systemic order constituted by the gradual realization of these immanent principles of order.

The Founders might have thought they were pursuing a scientific project in writing and ratifying a text, but the truth of the matter—a truth revealed to a new science of the social—is that the fundamental legal order of the community is not determined by our deliberate acts, no matter how rational we believe those acts to be. A community's fundamental order is a function of experience and growth. Legal science can no more make political order than biology can make organic order. In both cases, the role of science is only to discern the systemic character realized in and through natural growth. The *reason* of the actual political system is not the *reasons* of those who pursue projects. Accordingly, to look to the deliberate intentions of Founders is to look in the wrong direction for the meaning and nature of our law. Instead, scholars must turn to the social.

The social is not a category of the ordinary understanding; it is, instead, the object of a new science that studies regularities among populations. To see the social requires that we give up the individual perspective that generates accounts of order in the form of narratives organized around reasons for decisions. Those narratives are accounts of individual and collective projects. From the perspective of the social, all such accounts are merely anecdotal. They can no longer explain order. What had been the perspective of Enlightenment responsibility is now seen as continuous with myth—a prescientific understanding. The reasons of law, to use a term that will become popular at the end of the century, are now seen as "unconscious."[6] They are unconscious because they are no one's reasons. Law is the immanent order of a collective as it develops historically.

There is not a single phenomenon of the social. There are as many forms of the social as there are sciences of studying the practices and beliefs of a group or groups. There are as many social sciences as there are ways of organizing data. Today, we too quickly think that organizing data is a matter of quantification, and that its natural form of expression is statistics. The social sciences of the nineteenth century, however, included qualitative approaches to social forces. We still have some of this in cultural anthropology and in some forms of social psychology. One such social science of the late nineteenth century was law. "Qualitative" does not quite capture the character of those social sciences, for they deployed mechanical, and especially hydraulic, ideas of order—a "qualitative mechanics" of fluid, social forces. Today, we read such language as metaphor, but it was thought then to be quite descriptive.

Constitutional law might seem particularly recalcitrant to this way of thinking of the social as a system of forces shaped by immanent principles—the model for which was the economy. The project of constitutional construction, after all, was not so far from living memory. Moreover, that project is continually reflected in the opinions of the Justices; it is also the object of popular histories. The turn to system, then, required a critique of the possibility of a constitutional project: such projects were only a false appearance. Whatever might have been thought by the Framers and their early successors, a constitutional project was not possible. If it was not possible, identification and explanation of the constitutional order that actually operates had to be found elsewhere.

The critique of project was not moral but epistemic.[7] The Founders may have had the best of intentions, but the task they set themselves was literally impossible. The much-repeated point was that no human hand or hands could take the place of the invisible hand. No one could possibly know enough or see far enough to build a political system.[8] Sidney George Fisher puts the point bluntly in his critique of the Founders in his 1862 book *The Trial of the Constitution*:

> A written constitution is one constructed by one man or an assembly convened for the purpose, granting and distributing political power, and providing security for personal rights. It has two inherent defects,—it cannot adequately provide for the future, and its meaning is necessarily uncertain. No man or convention, or single generation, can furnish wisdom and knowledge to foresee all exigencies that may arise, and supply the needed powers to meet them, and it is impossible to use language, so clear and explicit, as to exclude doubt as to the meaning, often, of the most important clauses.[9]

Fisher's first point is that the project won't work because the future differs too much from the present. His second is that any such effort will have to speak at such a level of generality that it will determine nothing of real importance. The first point suggests that we should not try; the second, that we cannot succeed. The critique is not just that a project of constitutionalism will do a poor job; it is that it is impossible. An impossible project cannot create actual law. The real constitutional law of the nation has never been that of the written project; it has always been that of the unwritten system.

Imagining constitutional law as the product of a project is not merely a cognitive error, as if project stands to system as alchemy stands to chemistry. Fisher believes that misidentifying the source and nature of law can undermine political practices, precisely because constitutional claims are such an important part of our politics. We will not manage our political affairs properly if we proceed under the idea of project. Under some circumstances, that misunderstanding can become deadly.

The point, however, is more general and reflects a broader critique pursued in fields as diverse as economics, psychology, biology, and theology. The common theme of the era was the turn to system. This form of explanation linked the work of Sigmund Freud to that of Karl Marx and Alexander von Humboldt.[10] The explanatory form of system carries an idea of self-transcendence through adoption of a scientific perspective that stands against the form of self-privileging in narratives of project. The scientist now displaces the founder as the paradigm of a free subject.

On the systemic view, to remain bound to the idea of project is to be in thrall to an archaic, mythical way of thinking. Myth must be replaced by a new science of system. Kant's idea of enlightenment is seen now as just another form of mythical imagining. It would replace a creator God with a sovereign man, but the narrative of project remains the same. To replace a God-centered perspective with a man-centered perspective is only to replace one myth with another.[11] Similarly, a moralizing psychology must be replaced by an account of the systemic relationship of psychic forces: Freud's account of the unconscious as a field for the dynamic development of erotic forces. The science of sociology will emerge when these same epistemic shifts are applied to group behavior.[12]

If system is to displace project in the public imagination of politics, the identification of the Constitution with the written text must be broken. Accordingly, the new teaching is that the real Constitution is "unwritten." Constitutional law has its own immanent principles of order that develop independently of individual intentions and regardless of whether they have been set forth in the text. The signature move, then, of late nineteenth-century constitutional scholarship is the identification of the real Constitution as unwritten and the written Constitution as only an appearance.

The problem with a written constitution, theorists now argue, is that while society is in motion, a written text is not. Only an unwritten constitution can be as progressive as the society that it purports to order. The unwritten constitution grows in ways not accountable to the deliberate project of the Founders. The unchanging character of a written text guarantees that it will become increasingly anachronistic in a growing, changing polity. This attack upon written texts represents a reversal of the founding idea of a project of writing, which had been the progressive, scientific response to the unchanging character of the common law—the law of time immemorial.

Of course, in themselves neither a written nor an unwritten constitution makes a greater claim to stasis or progress. How these broad paradigms of order figure in the imagination is a matter of the uses to which they are put. That, in turn, is a function of the larger practices, beliefs, and empirical contingencies within which the paradigms are operating—including the practices and beliefs against which they are arguing. To understand that, we have to turn to an analysis of some texts. Fisher's *The Trial of the Constitution*, written while the outcome of the Civil War was in doubt and legal controversy raged about Lincoln's emergency wartime measures, is a good place to start.

Sidney George Fisher, The Trial of the Constitution

In Fisher's view, the war was caused, at least in part, by a misconception that informed the Framers' project of constitutional construction. They tried severely to limit the possibility of constitutional amendment, as if their text were near to perfect. The amendment procedure of Article V imposes requirements that are extraordinarily difficult to meet. Despite the unchanging text, Fisher contends that constitutional reform is going on continuously by other—that is, unwritten—means. Article V, then, contributes to a popular misconception about the nature of the real Constitution. That misconception contributed to the turn to political violence.

Article V creates the false impression that Americans are bound to the text as the sole source of constitutional order. Believing this, political disputes become disputes over interpretation of the text. Every department of government and every political actor makes a claim to have the correct interpretation. Each accuses the others of failing to follow the constitutional text. Irreconcilable conflicts arise, with no process available for resolution. Even the Supreme Court's constitutional constructions are measured against alternative claims to the meaning of the text. A written text always empowers a determined dissent—on or off the bench—simply to stand by its position, declaring a judicial majority wrong. Dissenters will say that the majority is "making" law, rather than applying the legal text.[13] They will pull out their copy of the Constitution and point to the text, while denouncing a judicial opinion as merely the personal opinion of some judges. A text that creates interpretive controversy cannot itself put an end to political controversy.

None of this can happen in England, according to Fisher. Parliament has the authority to settle political disputes by making law. It is not bound to any text, so it cannot commit a legal error. Neither can political actors accuse it of making such an error. Judicial review, instead of being a strength of the American constitutional order, is its weakness. It disempowers Congress while simultaneously opening the Court to the charge that it has misinterpreted the text. To make matters worse, the written Constitution disempowers the collective agency of the people by establishing a wholly impractical amendment process. It lets loose an endless contestation among political actors by locating authority at a point exogenous to all of them.

Fisher offers this analysis of the failure of the Founders' project not as a plea for law reform, but rather as an example of how a misunderstanding of the nature of law can lead to political pathology and violence. He is not arguing for better law, as if we need to perfect the project. Rather, he is arguing that we have failed to understand the law that we already have. A formal text that cannot be put into practice does not, in Fisher's view, qualify as law at all.[14] Conversely, a custom that orders practice and is supported by popular belief is the law.[15] A legal text, accordingly, is best thought of as a "proposal" for law. Until and unless it is taken up and becomes a custom followed by the community, it is little more than a fiction. If it falls into desuetude, it is no longer law.

To understand the actual law, then, one has to examine not the text of the Constitution but the customs and practices of political institutions as they have been accepted by the people. By this measure, Article V is not the law regarding the possibility of actual amendment. Lincoln's wartime measures, even if not ratified in accordance with that article, are the law because they have been accepted as such.[16] An institution has the capacity to make law just to the degree that its proposals advance into practice and popular belief.

In a democracy, Fisher believes, the dominant law-making institution is inevitably the representative body.[17] Its law-making function cannot be restrained by abstract limits, even if those limits are embodied in a constitutional text. The Founders' idea that the courts can exercise a check on congressional power was a fiction grounded on a failure to understand the nature of democratic authority.[18] The same is true of efforts to create checks on the exercise of political authority through separation of powers and the constitutionalization of rights. It is not that such measures are never effective, but that there are circumstances—emergencies—in which they cannot possibly work. The first rule of every political order is that it will take whatever measures are required for its own self-survival.[19] Self-maintenance is a defining attribute of systemic order. The Civil War offers one example after another of the exercise of this emergency authority operating quite regardless of anything the courts might say about it.[20] The unwritten constitution is not and cannot be a "suicide pact."[21]

The war brings out a startling comparison to the British constitutional order, which not so long before was that which the American constitutional project had rejected. Fisher does not just measure the American legal order against the British; he actually collapses the distinction between the two. Whatever the Founders' project, the actual law emerges from customary practices that are themselves determined by the underlying nature of the society. American and British practices converge—if they ever differed—because both express the truth of the Saxon people.[22] There is, at least for this people, only one way to be free under law. The war, then, is the trial of the Constitution because it is a winnowing away of all that the constitutional project got wrong with respect to the necessary system of Saxon self-government. This is the order of a natural, organic growth. This race bears the immanent principles of order of the social.

Fisher's text begins with an acknowledgment of the model of a project. His very first line describes government as a "machine." Citing the unlikely authority of Plato, he elaborates, "[Government's] 'real being' . . . consisting of the idea or truth it is intended to manifest and execute."[23] As in any project, the machine embodies the idea that formed the intent of its maker. Fisher goes on, however, immediately to reject the idea that this machine was made by anyone in particular: "[T]he only safe foundation for government is custom—another name for experience—the best guide in temporal affairs. No man or assembly of men is wise as the generations or as time. . . ."[24] A machine without a maker is the traditional way to describe a natural system. The natural system of political order is produced by history.

Fisher maintains a sort of popular Platonism, arguing that acts and institutions are the outward expression of Ideas. These Ideas, however, are not the subjective intentions of particular individuals. Nor are they timeless, as Plato imagined. Fisher uses various expressions to refer to their status. They are necessary truths of popular government, laws of nature, the work of reason, the endpoint of the development of customary practices, or the objects of a science of law. All of these expressions point to the idea of immanent principles of order. There is a sort of confused metaphysics behind his popular Platonism. What comes through, however, is his faith that for a civilized community, there is a natural truth to their political organization: "[W]e cannot throw aside the natural laws that govern society, which declare that a government is made for a people, not a people for the government, and that an intelligent people will have a government to satisfy their intelligence."[25] These natural laws will govern regardless of what the text of the Constitution might say or fail to say.

From this, it follows that the government must represent the contemporary community, not that of 1787:

> If the Constitution be immutable, what was law in 1787, must be law as long as the Constitution lasts. To maintain it, therefore, the Judiciary must be stronger than the people, stronger than the representatives of the people. In a popular government this is impossible. It contradicts its elementary principles.[26]

Fisher's point is not just that representative government *should* respond to the present, not the past. It is the stronger point that it cannot be otherwise. "We know that [the Constitution] must conform to the truth of nature or perish."[27] Any efforts to impose ideas that are inconsistent with the true ideas of governance will fail as a matter of custom and practice. "We may be sure of one thing, that whatever portion of the Constitution is unnatural, that portion must be got rid of by some process or other. . . ."[28] War is one such process.

The true Constitution, then, is not the text that represented an eighteenth century constitutional project. The true Constitution is that which expresses the natural law of democratic governance.

The task is to describe the actual Constitution, which is bound neither to interpretation of the text nor to implementation of the Founders' project. Both of those approaches fail to understand the systemic character of a Constitution grounded in the organic nature of the society.

Much of Fisher's work is an elaboration of what the constitutional project got wrong when measured against the truth of a legal order that constantly assimilates the advancing intelligence of a community. The central idea of this unwritten constitutionalism is that there must be an unmediated relationship between the people and their government, such that law gives expression to the people's idea of themselves. Any effort to construct a judiciary that can check the legislature in the name of the written Constitution must fail: "The judiciary is armed with no means of resisting the people or their organ, the Legislature, and its alleged power for that purpose does not exist."[29]

Effectively, this means that Congress is sovereign in its law-making power. The Constitution, to the degree it suggests otherwise, is empty—at best "declaratory of the wishes and feelings of the people."[30] The Court's power of judicial review can correct unintentional mistakes by the legislature, but it does not extend to reversal of actions to which the people have given their consent. That which the people take up into their practices is necessarily law, and that law will converge on the truth of reason by virtue of the intelligence of the people.[31]

Fisher is effectively using the conceptual tools of midcentury political theory to describe a new idea of constitutional order. He borrows the language of natural law, but strips it of any connection with a creator God. Natural law now refers to the necessary, immanent order of the social. God has no place in a science of the social. Thus, Fisher reasons about power, personal or political, as follows: "[Power] is an invisible force existing in nature, and revealed by visible effects. It is therefore controlled by natural laws, which cannot be resisted by any human contrivances."[32] In place of the reference to "contrivances," we might put the word "projects." The new science of immanent order labels as fiction the American constitutional project.

If constitutionalism is not a project, Fisher needs some other explanation of its motive force, that is, of the movement from Idea to practice. He appeals to custom, which serves as a sort of black box in which reason and will intersect. If his metaphysics remains vaguely Platonic, custom is doing the traditional work of the gods, mediating between Ideas and becoming. This rather mysterious role of custom is a reminder of Blackstone, for whom time immemorial served to link God's reason and man's will. Over the course of the century, this black box of custom will come to be filled in with an idea of public opinion.

Customs, for Fisher, are like languages in that they embody an intelligible, rule-governed order. Like a language, they are independent of any particular person's contrivances. And like a language, they are as much a form of practice as a set of ideas. Customs, on Fisher's view, grow. Using a term that will soon become dominant, he says customs "evolve." This is to naturalize the work of reason in human affairs. A nation's experience is its schooling; it learns to survive and to flourish. It can only do so insofar as it realizes the natural truth of its own condition. It is an article of faith that the truth of nature is the realization of law and that law is the form of reason.

This array of ideas will dominate constitutional thought well into the twentieth century. We already saw many of these ideas of custom, growth, and reason in the thought of Langdell and Holmes. It may be surprising to see that Fisher's work in constitutional law predates their work in private law. Fisher's insistence on the collapse of any distinction between American and British constitutionalism is an early expression of the assimilation of the Constitution to the common law. How could it be otherwise, if the truth of law is custom? And of custom, Fisher writes as an American Blackstonian: "The mere existence of a customary law . . . is proof that it is founded on truth, for such only does time respect."[33]

Tiedeman's Unwritten Constitution as Social Science

Fisher was writing in the middle of the Civil War. That context determined his focus on the emergency measures pursued by the Lincoln Administration as well as on the procedural inadequacy of Article V to work a normalization of those measures. His work is a meditation on power as it drives the formation of law. This process, he observed, was moving substantially faster than the formal amendment process could bear. The growth of the law, he argued, proceeds according to its own truths, the first of which is the survival of the state whose law it is.

Thirty years later, when Christopher Tiedeman writes *The Unwritten Constitution of the United States*, the emergency has passed. The issues that most concern Tiedeman no longer involve the power of the state to survive. Rather, he focuses on the limits on state power—issues associated with the rise of a newly interventionist state. The state had begun to pursue new forms of social-welfare legislation. In the language of the era, this raised issues of the reach and limits of the "police power."

It is one thing to speak of an unwritten law under exceptional circumstances where the existence of the state is at issue, but quite another to speak of an unwritten law that operates in normal times to limit the social-welfare functions of a democratic state. The exception, after all, is that which cannot be normalized: no text can provide legal means and methods for a civil war. Existential necessity always has an unpredictable, ad hoc character. But social-welfare legislation is the product of the ordinary political processes. It is controversial, but not exceptional. The unwritten law of the exception empowers government to save the state. The unwritten law of ordinary politics limits government in order to vindicate a contested policy choice. The wartime radical has become the peacetime conservative. In itself, the idea of an unwritten constitution has no particular political valence.

The postbellum shift in constitutional law to a focus on the police powers marks a move toward unwritten constitutional norms, for the extent of the police power is nowhere set forth in the constitutional text. Along with this shift in focus comes a shift in scholarly form. Tiedeman had already written a very popular treatise on the extent of—or rather, the limits on—the police powers of the state and federal governments.[34] His work follows that of Thomas Cooley, who had produced the most important constitutional-law treatise of the era.[35] These treatises focus on judicial opinions; they are in the tradition of Blackstone. Both Cooley and Tiedeman write about constitutional law with little regard for distinct state sources of authority. This is law as system unbound to the separate projects of producing texts in different political communities. The idea of unique constitutional projects has simply disappeared.[36] The constitutional order is the system that emerges in and through judicial opinions working as precedents. That the opinions arise in different jurisdictions does not bear on their capacity to set forth an immanent order.[37]

The police power, for the treatise writers, is not simply a residual category of those government powers not prohibited by written constitutional norms. Rather, the police power is a customary practice of authority; it is a system of governance already in place and undisturbed by the Framers' constitutional project. Like every system, it has an immanent order that simultaneously empowers and limits. Policing, we are told by writers of the period, includes action to advance the public safety, health, welfare, and morals. These are not mere labels. Nor do they refer to the subjective intentions of legislators. Each of these categories has its own structure of granting power and limiting authority. The treatise writers' ambition was to set forth the content of each of these categories. The treatises, accordingly, go into substantial detail as to what can and cannot be done under these various categories of public policy.

Of interest here is how these legal scholars imagined law such that a treatise on constitutional limits became a possibility. In the project model, a constitution is produced by the deliberate actions of a particular people who together create and approve a text. While there is reason to believe that the constitutional projects of each of the states (as well as of the nation) would agree upon some general principles, there is no reason to think they would converge on particular rules. Different states would likely create different forms of the police power, assigning different powers and drawing different limits. Each state's Supreme Court would function only to maintain its own constitution. A treatise of national scope would, therefore, have to be a work in comparative law. It could not set forth the substantive law of police power as it operates over discrete subject matters. Thus, the very idea of the treatise announces that constitutional law is not a project, but a system. We learn the content of the system by turning to the expert, who is now a scholar/scientist of law. He is likely to be located in the university.

By the end of the century, the general scholarly view is that while the written Constitution was a project, the true Constitution is an unwritten system. The police powers are the rules of living bodies politic. These various political bodies have evolved in the same direction. What concerns Tiedeman are not "dead letters" but "living rules."[38] The former refers to those aspects of the written project that fail to correspond to the systemic character of the organism that is the state.

Tiedeman shares with the leading scholars of the period a firm belief in laissez-faire economic principles.[39] Herbert Spencer, Tiedeman believes, was right to collapse the distinction between the biological and the social: both are systems evolving toward more complex forms through a process of competition. In politics, the natural development is toward increased protection of private property and individual autonomy.[40] Accordingly, the concern with police powers has nothing to do with policing as we understand the term. Rather, it expresses an interest in limiting the capacity of a democratically elected government to advance a social-welfare agenda responsive to the political interests of the poor and working classes. Tiedeman's essay, for example, turns strikingly personal when he writes:

> Contemplating these extraordinary demands of the great army of discontents, and their apparent power, with the growth and development of universal suffrage, to enforce their views of civil polity upon the civilized world, the conservative classes stand in constant fear of . . . the absolutism of a democratic majority.
>
> In these days of great social unrest, we applaud the disposition of the courts to seize hold of these general declarations of rights [the Fourteenth Amendment] as an authority for them to lay their interdict upon all legislative acts which interfere with the individual's natural rights, even though these acts do not violate any specific or special provision of the Constitution.[41]

In context, what is most striking about this assertion is that Tiedeman had just argued that natural rights are nothing more than a myth.[42] The power of claims of natural rights, he argued, derives from the belief in those rights, not from any sort of objectivity of the rights themselves. The Court in ruling on such rights is not identifying a truth independent of public opinion, but acting to support what he calls "the prevalent sense of right." This would seem thin ground upon which to base judicial opposition to a democratic majority.

Tiedeman characterizes this clash of beliefs about the ends of government power as one between a democratic majority's views of the civil polity and the contrary views of the "civilized world."[43] The idea of the civilized world is a construction that rests upon his view of the end toward which social forces are moving. The civilized world is simultaneously the object of scientific description and the set of beliefs of those who are civilized—in particular, the legal experts.

The burden on Tiedeman is to reconcile his claim that law is based on nothing more than the prevalent sense of right with his belief that the public's actual opinion can be substantively wrong. It is fair to say that Tiedeman is no more successful in achieving this reconciliation than the numerous democratic, constitutional theorists who come after him.[44] All must offer a theory of how the public binds itself. They all face the paradox of invoking democracy against itself or one expression of democratic law making against another. The deep attraction of turning to unwritten law as the constraint that "already exists" lies just here.

Tiedeman's work reflects not only a different context from that of Fisher, but a different understanding of his own expertise. Fisher wrote as a reflective observer of the phenomena going on around him during the Civil War. Tiedeman wrote as a social scientist of the law trained in the new European approach to the social.[45] The social scientist, like the natural scientist, offers explanations that make use of laws that are not a part of our everyday discourse. These laws operate independently of the reasons that individuals, including judges, ordinarily offer to account for their actions or those of others. The social scientist abandons the narrative form and replaces it with a causal account of "forces," which may not be visible to the ordinary observer.[46] Tiedeman, accordingly, repeatedly expresses the idea that "constitutional law is the resultant of *all* the forces at play in society. . . ."[47]

Tiedeman announces his scientific perspective in the opening pages of *The Unwritten Constitution*. Indeed, the first sentences identify the scientific error in Blackstone's definition of law. Blackstone, he tells us, fails to rise above the narrative perspective when he defines law as "a rule of conduct *prescribed by the supreme power of the state. . . .*" That definition imagines law as if it were the project of a person or group of persons. Such an approach misunderstands "the origin and development" of law.[48] The origin of law is not in any person's power. Law, rather, "is the product of social forces, reflecting the prevalent sense of right."[49] That "popular sense of right does not remain stationary. In its growth and evolution it follows an easily recognized law of development."[50] The science of the social identifies the origin and development of law in the "vigorous contest between opposing forces."[51]

Rejecting Austin's command view of the origin of law, Tiedeman writes, "I cannot believe that he [Austin] was unconscious of the natu-

ral sequential development of the law, operated upon by all the social forces, out of which civilization is in general evolved."[52] In the
next sentence he refers to this as "scientific development." Science
here refers simultaneously to the object and the study of that object—
just the move by which nineteenth-century science naturalizes
itself.

The basic elements of Tiedeman's view are all evident in the first
few pages. Law is in movement; it is "living."[53] That movement is a
natural evolution toward greater civilization. The movement is produced by, and to be analyzed in terms of, "the aggregation of all the
social forces, both material and spiritual, which go to make up our
civilization."[54] The bearer of these forces is "the prevalent sense of
right," which operates in and through the opinions of "the mass of
the people."[55] The study of all of these forces is a science. That science is both descriptive and normative, for its end is to identify the
content of "the prevalent sense of right."

That the law is naturally evolving toward higher levels of civilization does not mean there will not be missteps by those with the power
to decide. A social science of law identifies those missteps by showing how the particular decision is inconsistent with the system. Such
errors are imagined as pathologies, for which the scientist can offer
a cure. The scientist of the law will claim to distinguish the passing
whims, the caprice of mass opinion, from the prevalent sense of right,
which alone is the legitimate source of law. Public opinion, accordingly, is not necessarily the actual opinion of the public. The legal scientist knows what we think because he knows what we should think.

The systemic order of the democratic state is the unwritten law
that arises spontaneously as the internal order of a free people as they
become more civilized. From the perspective of system, they could
not be other than they are. "American constitutions are, in the main,
an evolutionary development of the British Constitution; and a closer
study of the two systems reveals the fact that every principle, brought
into play by the American constitutions . . . was either of English
origin, or was the direct product of the social forces then at play in
American life."[56]

Like Fisher, Tiedeman believes that political pathology can arise from a mistaken idea of the nature of law. A common mistake about the nature of law is, for example, to look to the intentions of those who wrote the law in order to understand its meaning. Tiedeman vigorously denies any interpretive authority to those whose acts bring the law into being:

> It is true that a true interpretation of the law must disclose the real and full meaning of the lawgiver; but in countries in which popular governments are established the real lawgiver is not the man or body of men which first enacted the law ages ago; it is the people of the present day who possess the political power, and whose commands give life to what otherwise is a dead letter. No people are ruled by dead men, or by the utterances of dead men.[57]

His point is not that law must be a project of the living, not the dead. It is that law is not a project at all. It is a system that evolves toward civilization as a result of conflicts among social forces.

The Unwritten Constitution was substantially influenced by Tiedeman's time in Germany. He frequently cites his teacher, Rudolf von Jhering. Yet, Tiedeman's book is not simply a translation of German jurisprudence into English. Tiedeman is dealing with uniquely American problems. There is, after all, a written Constitution toward which many people feel a substantial, Lincolnian reverence. Their attachment to that text cannot simply be wrong. What could it mean for the public to have misplaced its affection for law?

Whatever the nature of the unwritten Constitution, it does not govern simply in place of the written text. It does not reduce that text to nothing at all. The written and unwritten laws have to be put into some sort of relationship and explained as aspects of a single whole. Sometimes Tiedeman speaks of interpretation of the written text as the device for opening up a substantial domain for the unwritten law.[58] Sometimes he speaks of a range of practices and beliefs that govern legal activities in ways that are not inconsistent with the text, but operate as supplemental limits on government. These, he thinks, can be just as forceful as those set forth in the text.[59] Sometimes he notes that practices have evolved in ways that are not contemplated by the text and are even in some tension with the intent of the Founders.[60] He has, in short, no single answer to the problem of the relationship of project to system.

Tiedeman proceeds by way of examples, beginning with that of the Electoral College. While the Framers imagined an elite institution insulated from the democratic process, it quickly developed into an institution controlled by the voters in each state. His second example is that of the two-term limit on presidential office—a practice begun by Washington. Both examples demonstrate the way in which the living law of the Constitution may begin but does not end with a textual provision.

Tiedeman's subsequent examples of unwritten constitutional law are more complex, for they point not just to a shift in a single practice, but rather to entire methods and domains of law making. This is how he understands both the ordinary work of judicial interpretation and the exceptional law making carried out by the Lincoln Administration during the national emergency of the Civil War. "The prevalent sense of right furnishes, in war as well as in peace, the norm for the formulation of rules of law."[61] Despite the difference between ordinary conditions and the exceptional, Tiedeman relies in both cases on the same substantive understanding of the nature of law: the actual law is not a written text, but those aspects of the public morality habitually followed by a majority and successfully imposed by elite decision makers upon a recalcitrant minority. Judges follow the prevalent sense of right or they produce nothing but "dead letters."[62] In ordinary times, courts have kept the law attuned with public opinion through the process of interpretation; in exceptional times, public opinion followed and supported the actions of a president who became "virtually . . . a dictator."[63] In both cases, the elite decision makers are simultaneously following and constructing public opinion.

Tiedeman's belief in the foundational character of an evolving public opinion makes him deeply skeptical of social-contract theories. The idea of a social contract is just another mistaken idea of project. This idea is doubly wrong, for law is not a project of the one or the many, and citizens do not stand in an equal relationship to the law.[64] Tiedeman writes that "[a]ll governments are either monarchies or oligarchies."[65] The United States is an oligarchy in which the rulers are those who effectively control the formation of public opinion. "When we lay aside our political dreaming, and come down to a consideration of the plain facts of political science, we are forced to the conclusion that there is no community in the world whose inhabitants stand on an equal absolute equality before the law. . . ."[66] One way to affect public opinion is to write a treatise.

These views lead Tiedeman to inquire into who actually exercises the authority to direct the prevalent sense of right. Of course, courts and presidents do so, but so do the actual voters. Noting that only 11 million people will vote in the coming election of 1890, while the population of the country is 60 million, he observes that the relationship between the few and the many is not one of consent. The 11 million consent to be ruled by elected representatives, but the other 49 million simply acquiesce. The minority govern because of their "possession . . . of the superior strength, both moral and material."[67] Strength includes "moral influence," for in the end the law lacks the power to coerce a mobilized citizen body.

Tiedeman returns repeatedly to the idea that "political constitutions are a growth, evolved from all the forces of society, both material and spiritual."[68] The scientist's expertise brings some order to our understanding of the nature of these forces. For example, Tiedeman argues that these multiple forces can work either toward centralization of power or toward its disbursement. "[T]wo opposing social forces . . . are present everywhere in bodies-politic, and . . . were prominently distinguishable at the time when the present Federal Constitution was adopted, viz.: the force of consolidation or centralization, and the force of disintegration."[69] The relative power of these forces remained unresolved until the Civil War: "Then [at the founding] began a contest for the supremacy between those two forces, the forces of disintegration and the forces of centralization. . . . The civil war demonstrated the superiority of the forces of centralization."[70]

The resolution of conflict depends upon the total constellation of social forces as each side tries to win control of the institutions of governance by appealing to popular opinion. At times, Tiedeman suggests that there is no "correct" resolution apart from the outcome in the court of public opinion. This applies particularly to conflict at the largest scale: "Revolutions are nothing more than successful rebellions, while rebellions differ from revolutions only in the fact that the former are unsuccessful. Both have their beginning in unlawful acts. . . ."[71] By definition, whoever wins the conflict possesses sovereignty: "[T]he sovereignty of a nation resides in those who for the time being possess the political power. . . ."[72] Law cannot resolve the conflict between these forces. Rather, law is both the field in which the conflict plays out and a consequence of the actual outcomes.

Courts too make use of all the resources at hand—written and unwritten—to win control of the formation of the prevalent sense of right. Their successes must always be proven anew, for there is no possibility of stabilizing law against the ultimate will of the people. Thus, Tiedeman ends the book by distinguishing between the will and the "whims and ill-considered wishes" of the people. It is, he says, "an absolute impossibility to suppress the popular will." The role of the courts is to follow not the law as written, but the meaning that "would have been imposed by the people, if their judgment had not been blinded with passion, and which in their cooler moments they would ratify."[73]

The prevalent sense of rights is always in process of formation. That these forces of opinion formation will lead to increasing reasonableness—"civilization"—is the faith that comes from linking science to system. The growth in the sciences, including legal science, is the measure and means of progress toward civilization. Civilization defines who we are and who we must be. It is a product not just of our reason, but of our will.

Woodrow Wilson: Between Reform and Evolution

Woodrow Wilson was born in Virginia in 1856 and grew up in the South during the Civil War and Reconstruction. He studied law, becoming a member of the bar in North Carolina, but quickly shifted to the study of political science at Johns Hopkins. He published his first book, *Congressional Government*, in 1885. Wilson's personal move from law to political science is itself symbolic of a larger shift about which he comments in that book: with the war, the age of great lawyers as public figures came to an end. The problem in the postwar era, Wilson believes, is no longer that of lawyerly interpretation of texts, but that of reformulating the institutional plan of government. After the break of the war, the constitutional project must be renewed. This will require a new science of politics.

As a political scientist, Wilson insists that his book is an analysis of the *facts* of American political order. His theme is to contrast the "literary theory" of the Constitution, which focuses on the formal text, with how the government actually works in its daily operations. While he proposes to put off issues of reform for subsequent work, *Congressional Government* is actually deeply committed to a reformist agenda that would remodel American constitutionalism on the British model of parliamentary democracy. As Wilson puts it in the original preface: "I offer, not a commentary, but an outspoken presentation of such cardinal facts as may be sources of practical suggestion."[74] One does not have to speculate as to what those practical suggestions might be.

By the "literary theory," Wilson means more than the original text itself; he means the popular understanding of that text as it has been passed down from the Framers. This is the theory that informed *The Federalist Papers*, as well as the arguments of figures like John Adams and Thomas Jefferson. Wilson understands this as a theory of separated and balanced powers. On this view, the branches of the federal government, along with the multitude of state and local governments, each function to limit and control the others. The literary theory imagines a Newtonian world of balanced powers held together as if in a robust machine of governance.

Wilson finds that mechanical theory to be out of touch with the facts of late nineteenth-century governance. Instead of balance, he finds a federal government that dominates the states, and a Congress that dominates the federal government. No doubt, he is reflecting a deep dissatisfaction with what had been the Radical Republican project of Reconstruction. He has a theory of the stages by which this unintended congressional dominance came to be, but he is less concerned with its origins than he is with describing its actual working. Behind that description lies his deepest concern: the manner in which congressional government—its organization and procedures—undermines the values of a democratic order. He measures congressional government against the British system of parliamentary government and finds the latter far preferable. Its advantage lies in the manner in which it combines legislative and executive functions, thereby creating forms of public debate, party coherence, public accountability, and leadership that are lacking in American institutions.[75]

While Wilson aspires to an objective perspective, he has no privileged point of access to the facts. He has recourse to no new method, no new set of data about the operations of government, no interviews with or testimony from those who wield power. He writes simply as a more informed observer of that which requires no special training to see. His account reads like good reporting; something written by a reporter who does a bit more investigating than one finds in the ordinary press.

Similarly, Wilson brings to his observations a quite ordinary understanding of human motivation and of institutional dynamics. He imagines, for example, what a newly elected congressman experiences when he discovers that he has no ability to exercise legislative initiative outside of the tight procedural control of the Speaker of the

House. Or again, he complains of the absence of men of great character in the Senate or the presidency, and locates the reason for that decline in the unattractive circumstances of office. These observations are based on no more than his own intuitive sense; ultimately, they depend on his character. Today, we would describe this work as impressionistic. Little of it would pass for social science.

In building a theory from the ordinary materials of popular psychology and institutional observation, Wilson is actually much closer to the Framers' approach to the science of government than he is to that of his contemporaries. While like the latter in investigating an "unwritten constitution," he means by that something entirely different from the political scientists of Darwinian-inflected system theories. For the latter, the system is evolving according to an immanent order that perfects an Anglo-American ideal of democratic governance. System is the answer to an inevitably flawed project; it offers the means of self-correction. Growth for someone like Tiedeman means movement toward maturity; it means realizing an immanent order that is both the only possible order in the long run and the best order. System naturalizes, even as it grounds a claim for civilization against the less than civilized.

Wilson too believes that political order is "living," by which he means that it is growing in response to changing circumstances. For him, however, growth means little more than change. Whether that change is toward a more perfect order is a question for observational inquiry. He has divorced change from an immanent order of perfection. When he looks to the growth of the American constitutional order, he finds that change has brought disorder. There has been a decline from the original vision because institutions and individuals make self-interested choices that tend toward no coherent ideal. To return to a beneficial order requires a re-foundation of the project.

Not only is Wilson's method of observation similar to that of the Framers, but he seems to understand himself as similarly positioned to his predecessors. They had been freed to pursue a new political project by the destructive violence of the Revolution. Destructive violence has again shaped political possibilities in the latter part of

the nineteenth century. Wilson argues that his is the first generation since the Framers able to engage in critique of the existing order and to consider the possibility of a new political project:

> We are the first Americans to hear our own countrymen ask whether
> the Constitution is still adapted to serve the purposes for which it was
> intended; the first to entertain any serious doubts about the superior-
> ity of our own institutions as compared with the systems of Europe;
> the first to think of remodeling the administrative machinery of the
> federal government, and of forcing new forms of responsibility upon
> Congress.[76]

Wilson echoes here the language of the Declaration of Independence
on "altering" poorly performing forms of government. He captures
the normative character of a project—the operations of government
must be measured against the ends of the project—and acknowledges
the possibility of "remodeling" that always comes with a project.
Holding Parliament as his model, Wilson would use the tools of a
constitutional project to approximate the immanent system of the
British politics.

Wilson argues that, prior to the Civil War, serious political argument in the country took the form of contesting constitutional interpretations. This was the age of lawyers. Everyone held the
Constitution in reverence and therefore tried to show that his political position was that which the Constitution required. Wilson is
describing the arguments over slavery, state sovereignty, and secession. The war and Reconstruction—"the rude shock of the war
and . . . subsequent developments of policy"—broke the spell of reverence for the text.[77] Together these shocks exposed the new reality
of the federal government: "this model government is no longer con-
formable with its own original pattern."[78] The original balance has
disappeared; it has been replaced by "a scheme of congressional supremacy."[79] If that is so, the role of the analyst is to observe how it
actually works, determine whether the mechanism is accomplishing
its ends, and consider any necessary remodeling.

Congressional Government is meant to inform ordinary citizens
about the real workings of their government and, thereby, help them

to abandon the literary theory of divided powers. "[W]e are," Wilson says, "farther than most of us realize from the times and the policy of the framers of the Constitution."[80] Citizens need this help not because the facts are complex, but because they are not easily accessible. The most important work of government often goes on behind the closed doors of congressional committees. Moreover, that work is divided up among dozens of congressional committees, each with a distinct jurisdiction. The ordinary citizen does not know where to look or who to hold accountable. What is done in public has little relationship to the actual procedures of legislative decision making.

Wilson often complains that there is no person or persons who have the responsibility to give a public account of, and can be held accountable for, a unified program of governance. Instead of a legislative agenda for which a party might campaign and then be held accountable, legislative initiative is distributed among the fiefdoms of multiple congressional committees. No one knows how these committees set their agendas; there is no pressure for a common or coherent agenda across committees or even within parties. Instead, agendas tend to be set in a way that is satisfactory to both the majority and the minority within the committee. We get government by multiple compromises, which are themselves unseen, unspoken, and uncoordinated. Democratic accountability fails.

With many people exercising small amounts of fractured authority in pursuit of their own interests, government will become increasingly chaotic. There is no invisible hand that brings order to all of these disparate, individual actions. Neither is there any visible hand, for the institutions of governance are not well designed to deal with these centrifugal forces. The presidency has become a weak office, thoroughly incapable of imposing a coherent agenda on all of the executive agencies, let alone on Congress. The agencies have come under the domination of the relevant congressional committees, which legislate for them but fail to take public responsibility for the administration of the programs they create. Without accountability, no one has to give an account; without an account, no one can be held accountable. Rather than moving forward toward more perfect order, there is a sort of spiral of disorder.

Congressional Government is written for the ordinary citizen seeking information about his government; it is not speaking to a specially trained academic elite.

> What makes it the more important to understand the present mechanism of national government . . . is that there is plain evidence that the expansion of federal power is to continue, and that there exists, consequently, an evident necessity that it should be known just what to do and how to do it, when the time comes for public opinion to take control of the forces which are changing the character of our Constitution.[81]

This reporting function, however, is framed within a normative theory of how a democratic government should operate. Here, the work has a more contemporary feel, for at its core is an idea about the essential role of public opinion in democratic governance.[82]

Public opinion, as we have already seen, figures in late nineteenth-century theories as the mechanism by which the public informs government and government informs the public. It is effectively the soul of the polity, the mysterious site at which organic, evolutionary growth can occur. It is not only the site, but the mechanism for this immanent process of growth. Ideally, just as a person becomes more reliable as he becomes better informed, so the public's opinion becomes more reliable as citizens gain knowledge and information. Public opinion combines traditional ideas of reason with nineteenth-century ideas of progress.

Wilson believes, however, that congressional government has slipped outside of the view of public opinion. It neither contributes to the formation of that opinion, nor is it a product of a well-formed public opinion. Contrariwise, Wilson believes that British parliamentarianism perfects and is perfected by public opinion. Because there is no gap between legislative and executive power in Britain, the debates in Parliament are about the reality of policy and its execution. The government is constituted from members of the majority party and must give an account of itself in Parliament. Thus, the government is forced to have a coherent plan upon which it campaigns and against which it can be measured. If it fails to convince a majority of members of Parliament, it will fall.

The British structure makes their parliamentary debates far more interesting than the perfunctory statements that pass for congressional debate. Because the British debates matter, they are followed by citizens. Indeed, they are so interesting and informative that Wilson claims even American newspaper readers follow them. While the British debates can shape public opinion, the American system of congressional government falls far short of creating an informed public opinion. Once public opinion has malfunctioned, there is no mechanism by which change can become growth toward order. Without an invisible hand, there must be the visible effort of a new intervention—a new project that better matches institutions to contemporary circumstances.

Wilson does not offer an explicit account of why the American system has failed to evolve in the direction of a perfected parliamentarianism. One has a sense, however, that he believes this failure to be a function of the path dependency of a government that was cast under a mechanical ideal and stabilized through a written text. The problem arises not just from the politics of secession, war, and Reconstruction, but from a flawed design at the origin. Like the British constitutional system, ours "is a living and fecund system." But, on Wilson's view, it does not "find its rootage so widely in the hidden soil of unwritten law. . . ."[83] The literary theory may not be an accurate account of what we have, but it is accountable for the path by which we came to the present, disordered state. It created institutional possibilities that have been realized by politicians moving to satisfy their own interests over the public interest.

Whatever power public opinion may have, it is not enough to salvage a scheme of democratic governance that has drifted away from those ends that it was intended to realize. What was begun as a project must be reformed as a project. *Congressional Government* is to serve the preliminary role of informing the public, so that the real work of reform can begin. That project, however, fails to occur, and by the time Wilson comes back to the themes of the fundamental nature of the constitutional order—some twenty years later—he no longer sees a need for a new project. There is no need, because the system is realizing its own immanent principles of order. Wilson too has become a believer in system over project.

Constitutional Government arose out of lectures Wilson delivered in 1907. The title itself suggests a substantial shift from his earlier focus on Congress and its need for reform. The new book offers chapters on each of the branches of the federal government, with pride of place now going to the president. It also considers the role of states in the constitutional system, as well as the role of political parties. Finally, the new book is much more concerned than the earlier one with offering a theoretical and historical frame for the inquiry.

Wilson's comments on contemporary theory offer some of the most famous passages in the book:

> The government of the United States was constructed upon the Whig theory of political dynamics, which was a sort of unconscious copy of the Newtonian theory of the universe. In our own day, whenever we discuss the structure or development of anything, whether in nature or in society, we consciously or unconsciously follow Mr. Darwin. . . . [84]

Wilson's claim to be a follower of Darwin is more rhetorical than scholarly. His approach is evolutionary, but in the sense of pre-Darwinian, evolutionary theories of common law.[85] There is very little in his work of the main elements of the specifically Darwinian approach: an environment of scarcity, a source that generates random variation, and a mechanism of inheritance.[86] There are, instead, the characteristic claims of nineteenth-century anthropology and legal-cultural thinking: societies and their governments develop through distinct stages; the telos of that development is representative government acting through law; and the engine of change is not random variation but political leadership informed by public opinion.

Wilson's commitment to evolution, in other words, amounts to little more than a teleological view of history, which is actually not Darwinian at all. It is more a remnant of the Christian theology of providence than it is an expression of a new empirical science that explains change without appealing to final causes. Nevertheless, the theme of *Constitutional Government* is change—not only in institutional structure, but also in the individual. Wilson constructs an ideal of political leadership that is bursting with energy. He imagines a symmetry between a nation vigorously asserting itself in the world and a political leadership vigorously leading the nation. One cannot help but see Teddy Roosevelt's image looming above Wilson's text.[87]

Just as Wilson attacks mechanical models in political theory, he attacks models of constitutional interpretation that are too "legalistic." Legal documents, he notes, are generally designed to secure order against change. That, for example, is the very point of a contract. If the constitutional order is a vital, living process, then it fits poorly with the idea of a legal document. "The Constitution cannot be regarded as a mere legal document, to be read as a will or a contract would be. It must, of the necessity of the case, be a vehicle of life."[88] That does not mean that the text can be ignored, but it does mean that it must be constantly reinterpreted to respond to "new aspects of life itself."[89] Or again, "the Constitution is not a mere lawyers' document: it is . . . the vehicle of a nation's life."[90]

The need to bring life to what appears to be a legal document puts a good deal of pressure on the Supreme Court. It must work the necessary, constant "adjustment" of power, public opinion, and law. Wilson is so taken with the importance of this function that he falls back into the mechanical language of balanced parts: the courts are the "balance wheel of the whole system."[91] On investigation, however, their role is less that of a balancing force than of a mediating instrument by which the individual citizen, insisting on his own rights, can force the system to articulate and defend itself before public opinion. The courts function in a sort of educational role, but since public opinion is the vital force of the whole, education is a master metaphor for the life and growth of the state.

In *Constitutional Government*, Wilson sees less of a contrast between congressional and parliamentary government than in his earlier work. Instead, he sees the American and British systems as two variations on a single theme; they are two species of a single genus. Not only are they moving toward a similar end, but they have over-lapping origins. Wilson now argues that the American Framers adopted Whig theory to create in America a constitutional order that corrected the flaws of the British system. What had been seen as a project of creating an entirely new political order is now reduced to a remedial intervention. The British would, in the early nineteenth century, reform themselves in the direction of more representative government, but by then the Americans had split off. Because both systems are dynamic, living orders, there can be no easy assessment that one is preferable to the other. Each is moving toward the same end from a common origin, even though their paths diverge in par-ticular matters.

Wilson's assessment of the nonlegislative branches of government obviously changed considerably in the twenty years between the books. His views about public opinion, however, did not change so much as deepen. In the new book, public opinion plays the sovereign function: it is the beginning and end of the state, as well as the means of constitutional government.[92] Every institution of government, ac-cordingly, is assessed for its contribution to the formation of public opinion, on the one hand, and its capacity to reflect public opinion, on the other.

Public opinion appears in Wilson's very definition of constitutional government. Such a government is not simply government under law or even under written law. It is not formal, but substantive. Wilson, however, is not interested in offering a list of rights—as in our idea of human rights—that must be satisfied for constitutional govern-ment to exist. His assertion, for example, that Americans cannot sim-ply give constitutional government to its colonial possessions is based on this idea that neither legal formalism nor substantive rights are constitutive of constitutionalism. Prior to either, there is an idea of "adjustment." Constitutional government exists when there is a continual adjustment between the people's opinions of their rights and interests, on the one hand, and government, on the other.[93]

A constitutional government is one that reflects a people's conception of themselves and of what they deserve. It reflects their principles and their interests, even as these change. A constitutional government, accordingly, must have the means continually to work the adjustment. It is, for this reason, alive. Just as an organism adjusts constantly or dies, so a constitutional government must continually adjust in response to changing opinions: "There can be no constitutional government where the organs of government are not constantly under the control of public opinion."[94]

Wilson takes this last point into the very substance of the state. A state is constituted neither by its territory nor by a chronology of events. It is more than an aggregation of individuals and families who live or have lived within a defined territory. A state is defined by its consciousness of itself as a historical phenomenon; a state is a community that knows itself as a unity over time. It maintains a common public opinion with regard to its own identity. That which holds the state together across generations is public opinion. One hundred years earlier, Hegel spoke of the state as objective Spirit. Wilson continues this idea but without the metaphysics. That spirit is now public opinion. Its metaphysical status is only that which arises from beliefs commonly held by a group of individuals. Today, we might make the same point by speaking of an "imagined community" that lives in and through public opinion.[95]

Just as public opinion is not some sort of world spirit, it is not simply an aggregation of individual opinions of the sort revealed by polling data. It is not an aggregation, but rather a systemic, organic whole. Wilson speaks of "life" to convey this idea. The life of the state, while making no metaphysical claim, nonetheless makes a normative claim upon the individual citizen. The citizen stands to the state as an organ stands to the whole of the organism. If, for example, public opinion ranks honor as its highest virtue, the individual receives this as a demand upon his own behavior and beliefs. Responding to the demand, he offers his own opinion as an additional source of strength of the prevailing opinion.

We see something like this process of reciprocal influence in Wilson's reflections on the changing character of what constitutes a scientific outlook: the science of politics used to be Newtonian; now it is Darwinian. The person who wants to make a scientific contribution to the study of politics must frame his own inquiries accordingly. A Newtonian analysis in the age of Darwin is not viewed simply as idiosyncratic, but as wrong.[96] What is true of the theorist replicates itself in all fields of belief and action. Most important, it replicates itself in the meaning of citizenship.

> Every man's thought is part of the vital substance of [the state's] institutions. With the change of his thought, institutions themselves may change. That is what constitutes citizenship so responsible and solemn a thing. Every man in a free country is . . . put upon his honor to be the kind of man such a polity supposes its citizens to be. . . . Every generation in a free state realizes that the perpetuation of its institutions depends upon the thought and disposition of the generations which are to follow. . . . [97]

Just as public opinion shapes and is shaped by citizens, it shapes and is shaped by political leadership. Institutions are, for this reason, somewhat secondary in Wilson's account, for they are themselves only the expression of the opinions of their members. Those members, in turn, must respond to a public that maintains common views. Thus, in a book organized around institutional and legal forms, Wilson writes "[T]here never was such a government [of laws and not of men]. Constitute them how you will, governments are always governments of men, and no part of any government is better than the men to whom that part is intrusted."[98] While the earlier book focused on institutional structures that regulate legislative production, the new book focuses much more on character. It becomes, in substantial part, a book about leadership.

In Wilson's earlier work, the president appeared as a minor figure wholly eclipsed in importance by the Speaker of the House. Even his executive role was dispersed to the heads of agencies. In what many see as an expression of his own political ambitions, Wilson now describes the president as the central figure in the national drama. He is the only person on whom the whole public focuses; the only one who can speak directly to the public. He represents the nation to itself. To be a success, he must simultaneously express the public's deepest beliefs and lead the public into whatever adjustments new circumstances require. When a president fulfills this role, he is unstoppable, for he carries the entirety of the nation with him:

> [The president] is the only national voice in affairs. Let him once win the admiration and confidence of the country, and no other single force can withstand him. . . . His position takes the imagination of the country. . . . If he rightly interpret the national thought and boldly insist upon it, he is irresistible; and the country never feels the zest of action so much as when its President is of such insight and caliber. . . . A president whom it trusts can not only lead it, but form it to his own views.[99]

This presidential role did not come about by design, but rather "by the operation of forces inherent in the very nature of government. . . ."[100] Wilson argues that the Framers cast the president to fulfill their ideal of a king. The president was to be that which they had wanted George III to be. He was to execute laws passed by a representative assembly; he was to appoint officials and negotiate treaties in cooperation with the Senate as his council of advisors. The president was to be a part of a balance of powers, but in no way dominant. The modern president as leader of party, government, and nation is not what the Framers imagined in their Newtonian world. Yet, the structure they created remained open to the "sheer pressure of life. . . ."[101]

> Fortunately, the definitions and prescriptions of our constitutional law, though conceived in the Newtonian spirit and upon the Newtonian principle, are sufficiently broad and elastic to allow for the play of life and circumstance.[102]

While Wilson believes the Whig theory of machinelike balance is now an anachronism, he still views the president as functioning in the traditional role of the king. Not the king as executive and administrator of the law, but the king as the figurative embodiment of the state. Wilson's theory of the president as the singular representative of the state echoes the belief in the king as the mystical corpus of the state. He is selected to be the "representative man," standing before public opinion.[103] In the people's perception, the president is the state. In him, public opinion takes on a corporeal form.

The reappearance of this political-theological remnant should not be surprising. Before the rise of the Whig theory of a constitutional project of balanced powers, the state was imagined as an organic body both extensively and intensively. The metaphysical organism of the body politic was instantiated, not represented, in the body of the king. The Christological influence was explicit: the Church is extensively the body of Christ, but Christ is intensively the body of the Church.[104] The reappearance in Wilson of this earlier form of the political imagination reflects the difficulties of abandoning the Whig theory of balanced institutions. The unity of the state no longer comes from the idea that informs the project through the intentions of an author. But what provides the unity of a political order cut off from the intentionality of a project? The unity of a system must somehow precede its realization. Public opinion is asked to serve this function of unifying without intending. Politics differs from markets in the necessity of self-awareness of this unity. Citizens are not simply consumers of political order. To create citizens, the state needs an object that reflects the public back upon itself. That is the function of the president, as Wilson imagines it.

A system that relies on public opinion is always in danger of slipping into incoherence in the face of the diversity of actual opinions. Wilson, like others, believes that "civilization" can be the lodestone in negotiating the truth of public opinion. But actual political disputes are unlikely to be settled by claims to civilization. They are more likely to be settled by a vigorous political leadership that successfully claims to express the truth of the nation to itself. The claims for public opinion may be linked to science and civilization by academics, but they gain political force insofar as they are linked to nationalism. Not surprisingly, the systemic theorizing of the late nineteenth century is precursor to a bellicose American imperialism of the twentieth century. System may be without need of an author, but in its place it often turns to charismatic leadership.

The nation appears to itself as a new, dynamic force in the world at the beginning of the twentieth century. It appears as scientific in an age that privileges science. But behind all of the appeal to Darwin, evolution, and civilization is little more than a new form of faith: a faith that the nation is an organic whole that has already grown into what all nations are seeking to be. The public is confirmed in this sense of itself when it has a visible symbol of its own faith. As a young man, Wilson had no such symbol; twenty years later, he had seen the possibility of such a symbol in the presidency. With that, he too became a believer in America as the realization of the immanent order of civilization. The new science of politics, in the end, makes contact with some of the oldest forms of political theology.

System and the Supreme Court's Constitution at the Turn of the Twentieth Century

Wilson was no doubt right when he wrote that his was the era of Darwinian thought. As Wilson himself demonstrates, however, there was no single meaning of Darwinism, especially as it passed from the biological to the social sciences. None of the theorists who appealed to public opinion as the mechanism by which a polity realizes its immanent principles of order was actually much of a Darwinist. Public opinion simply does not generate the sort of scarcity that drives Darwinian evolution. The battle for public opinion is not a fight for survival, except metaphorically. Metaphor, however, cannot exactly work the mechanisms of Darwinian evolution.[105]

Efforts to link public opinion to social evolution were actually moves in a two-front battle. On the one hand, they were efforts to overcome the constitutionalism of project that informed the first half of the century. Public opinion, it was argued, created a systemic order like that of a market: neither was the object of a project; each was sustained by endless, particular expressions or transactions.[106] Pointing to the dynamic growth of public opinion was a way of undermining those static models of a well-balanced machine that informed the political project of earlier generations. On the other hand, public opinion as the site and mechanism of growth was an alternative to the views of more radical Social Darwinists who focused on actual markets and real scarcity as the mechanism of social evolution.[107] We still live with a somewhat confused idea of the relationship of a marketplace of ideas to a marketplace of goods—a confusion that comes into focus, for example, in the adjudication of cases involving commercial speech and campaign finance.[108]

The more radical Social Darwinists imagined the market in the same terms in which Darwin imagined natural evolution. There was scarcity, a struggle for survival, and the endless generation of innovations. At stake was not just the competition among goods and services, but a competition in life chances for individual subjects. Those who fared well in the market survived; those who did not could literally find themselves without the means to support themselves and their families.

There were multiple variations on the way in which theorists placed these two ideas of market—in the exchange of goods and in the competition of ideas—in relation to each other. Tiedeman, for example, thought they intersected: public opinion properly understood supported laissez-faire policies toward markets. A Court could appeal to public opinion—in the form of the "prevalent sense of right"—to support its judgments declaring progressive market interventions unconstitutional. Holmes, in contrast, believed in the evolution of public opinion, but he did not privilege markets as the site of evolutionary social growth. A dominant public opinion was constitutionally free, in his view, to regulate markets in order to advance various social policies. In retrospect, we can see that a constitutional faith in public opinion as a system with an immanent principle of order outlasts a faith in markets. The former idea will be central to twentieth-century, liberal political theorists—for example, Habermas and Ackerman.[109] Contrariwise, by the time of the Depression, unregulated markets are viewed by many as operating with an immanent principle of *disorder*.[110] Economic systems are, consequently, denaturalized and made into projects to be informed by a new economic science. Macroeconomics becomes a science of regulation alongside microeconomics.

The most famous site of conflict between these different views of the meaning of constitutional order was *Lochner v. New York*, in which the Court struck down a New York statute that imposed limits on the working hours of bakery employees.[111] Holmes, in dissent, famously denounced the Social Darwinist views of the majority: "The Fourteenth Amendment does not enact Mr. Herbert Spencer's Social Statics."[112] We should not take the reference to Spencer literally, for Spencer's Social Darwinism was actually complex in its relation to markets and utilitarianism. It is highly unlikely the Justices read Spencer.[113] But Holmes is not teaching philosophy, he is observing the Court's tendency to constitutionalize laissez-faire economics. They are constitutionalizing a general view of the nature of economic science from a generation earlier—the state of the discipline that informed their own education.

Lochner suggests that the Court accepted an identity of American constitutional law and the common law. The path from the Founders' project to a laissez-faire constitutionalism was through the common law—a proposition I explored in discussing the work of Tiedeman above.[114] Evolving common-law doctrines protected contract and property against government intervention. This is what the formal science of law, taught in America's new law schools, had been inculcating in a generation of law students. The Constitution, by the end of the century, was imagined as an expression of the immanent, systemic order of the common law.[115] This was the common constitutionalism of the Anglo-American race.

This identification of common law and constitutional law is seen in *Lochner* in the treatment of a constitutional right to contract. "The general right to make a contract in relation to his business is part of the liberty of the individual protected by the Fourteenth Amendment of the Federal Constitution. *Allgeyer v. Louisiana*, 165 U.S. 578."[116]

Of course, contract is nowhere mentioned in the text of the Fourteenth Amendment. If there is a constitutional right to contract, its source is the unwritten Constitution. Thus, the only authority that the Court cites for this proposition is a single precedent of its own, *Allgeyer*. Turning to that case, one finds no additional authority for the proposition. This is common-law constitutionalism in both substance and form. The unwritten Constitution emerges from the Court's precedents; its substance includes the common law's protection of contract.[117]

To the modern reader, *Lochner* appears deeply puzzling when the Court writes: "Contracts in violation of a statute, either of the Federal or state government, or a contract to let one's property for immoral purposes, or to do any other unlawful act, could obtain no protection from the Federal Constitution as coming under the liberty of person or of free contract."[118] But how is this not the case here? The contract at issue required employees to work more than sixty hours per week, in direct "violation of a statute [of the] state government." It required the doing of an "unlawful act," if we follow ordinary usage of the term. Obviously, the Court means something else by "unlawful" than literal violation of a statute. The same reasoning had appeared in *Allgeyer*:

> The "liberty" mentioned in [the Fourteenth] amendment ... is deemed to embrace the right of the citizen to be free in the enjoyment of all his faculties, to be free to use them in all *lawful* ways, . . . to earn his livelihood by any lawful calling, . . . and for that purpose to enter into all contracts which may be proper, necessary, and essential to his carrying out to a successful conclusion the purposes above mentioned.[119]

But in that case, too, the state had passed a statute that made Allgeyer's contract "unlawful" in the ordinary sense. Nor can we interpret these references to "unlawful" statutes as if the Court were merely anticipating its holding that the statutes are unconstitutional. Rather, the Court in *Allgeyer* and *Lochner* holds the statutes unconstitutional because they violate a prior lawfulness—a common-law lawfulness.

The Court is writing in the Blackstonian tradition in which law precedes politics, including the statutes produced by politics.[120] Lawfulness, in these opinions, means the system of the common law. The relevant common-law principle is that of the police powers—again nowhere mentioned in the Constitution. But to the *Lochner* Court, a statute that does not fall within the police power is not law:

> There are, however, certain powers, existing in the sovereignty of each State in the Union, somewhat vaguely termed police powers, the exact description and limitation of which have not been attempted by the courts. . . . Both property and liberty are held on such reasonable conditions as may be imposed by the governing power of the State in the exercise of those powers, and with such conditions the Fourteenth Amendment was not designed to interfere.[121]

What then was it with which the Fourteenth Amendment was designed to interfere? Anything beyond the police powers as defined by the common law, for there is no such definition in the Constitution itself. This is just another way of saying that laissez faire begins where the common-law recognition of police powers ends. *Lochner* shows us that this end is well before the point at which the progressive agenda begins.

State intervention, on this view, is never permissible simply because of a substantive dissatisfaction with market outcomes. Those who lack market power may not deploy political power to compensate for that lack. Such interventions would not have a public purpose. In contemporary terms, these would be interventions for the sake of a faction or an interest group—even if that group constitutes a political majority. Permissible interventions appeal to an idea entirely outside of markets, property, and contract—an idea of domestic dependence. The Court uses the metaphor of "wards of the state," meaning those for whom the state is especially responsible because they lack the competence to take care of themselves:

> There is no reasonable ground for interfering with the liberty of person or the right of free contract by determining the hours of labor in the occupation of a baker. There is no contention that bakers as a class

are not equal in intelligence and capacity to men in other trades or manual occupations, or that they are not able to assert their rights and care for themselves without the protecting arm of the State, interfering with their independence of judgment and of action. They are in no sense wards of the State.[122]

The Court has in mind children, women, and those for whom it elsewhere uses the antiquated label "imbeciles."[123]

The state is not constitutionally required to protect these classes of individuals who cannot survive on their own; the Constitution does not require an exercise of the police powers. These interventions are imagined as acts of charity. Charity is one face of assuming responsibility toward such wards of the state; eugenics is another.[124] The Constitution is indifferent to state decisions in either direction—exercises of the police powers. Whatever the state decides, however, the decision will be cabined in its effect on markets, contracts, and property. Indeed, not too much later women will move from the category of wards to that of ordinary employees who are on their own in the market.[125] The critical jurisprudential move is that of categorization—in which category do women belong? To be recognized as autonomous agents is to be left to the immanent principles of order realized in the market. In the strange logic of systemic constitutionalism, this amounts to a privilege of citizenship. Thus, the change in status of women is linked by the Court to passage of the Nineteenth Amendment, which gave women the right to vote.[126] There is no necessary relationship between actual well-being and constitutional dignity under such a view of system.

For the *Lochner* Court, the only other exception to the rule of laissez faire countenanced by the common law, and now by the Constitution, is contracts that generate severe public-health externalities. But just as bakery employees are too ordinary to regulate, so are the health risks they suffer or that they might impose on others. There is no real danger to be found at the bakery to workers or customers. In a dissent that makes ample use of expert studies of the conditions of labor, Justice Harlan asks how the Court knows any of this. The Court knows it as it knows the common law, by observing the immanent order in the practices and beliefs of society. No one, the majority suggests, really believes that bakeries are public-health hazards. As Tiedeman would say, such a claim is outside of the "prevalent sense of right." Indeed, the Court ridicules the idea that there is a public-health problem here that would allow an exception to the general rule that government must not intervene in contracts.[127]

The fundamental idea of the *Lochner* Court, then, is that there is a law before the law. This is not just a point of chronology, but a point of status. The project of the Constitution is set against the system of the common law; the terms of the former are read in light of the substance of the latter. Liberty becomes contract; state authority becomes the police power. This idea of an unwritten law that informs what it is that the Constitution could mean is evident when the Court writes: "It seems to us that the real object and purpose [of the New York legislation] were simply to regulate the hours of labor between the master and his employees (all being men *sui juris*) in a private business, not dangerous in any degree to morals or in any real and substantial degree to the health of the employees."[128] The statute, in other words, was intended to do just what it does. Today, we are hardly shocked. We might even say that it expresses the opinion of the people of the state of New York as worked out through their representative institutions. Nevertheless, for the *Lochner* Court it fails the test of public opinion as the system of law that has developed through common-law adjudication, which now constitutes an unwritten Constitution. From the perspective of that system, the New York statute is a pathological intervention that the Court must remedy.

Exactly the same story of the collapse of constitutional law into common law through the idea of a legal science of immanent order can be told about one of the era's most famous commerce clause cases. In *Lochner*, the issue had been state, not federal, power. In *Carter Coal*, the issue is the reach of federal power.[129] When acting domestically, the federal government's most extensive power arises under the commerce clause, which gives it the power to regulate commerce among the several states. But exactly how far does this power extend? The issue becomes acute with the New Deal effort to pass federal legislation in response to a severely depressed national economy. The Court's resistance to this effort marks the end of the long nineteenth century.

In *Carter Coal*, the Court holds unconstitutional the Bituminous Coal Act. Among other things, that act sought to establish minimum wages and maximum hours for coal workers. The law was complex, but none of that matters to the Court, which finds any effort to intervene in these matters to be beyond the reach of the commerce power. Wages and hours, the Court holds, concern production of, not commerce in, coal. Commerce refers to trade; it begins only after production has been completed. One might note here the narrow reliance on the constitutional text—on the word "commerce"—while that same Court had no trouble interpreting liberty to mean contract in *Lochner*. The text could easily be interpreted to extend commerce to the regulation of objects soon to enter commerce or to objects the production of which deeply affects commerce. Indeed, this is just what happens a few years later.[130] The point is not that the Court is narrowly textualist in this case, but that it has a substantive view that understands markets as a site of an immanent, constitutional order. Government interventions, whether state or federal, in this systemic order must be narrow exceptions to a general rule of nonintervention.

The strength with which the Court holds to this view is apparent in its response to the argument that absent regulation of the conditions of production of coal, the entire commerce of the nation will be jeopardized. Disturbances in the coalfields will have ripple effects not just on commerce in coal but on all elements of the nation's commercial life. The majority does not deny this possibility, yet it concludes that this harm is constitutionally noncognizable.[131] No doubt it is an economic problem, but that does not make it a constitutional problem. That would not be so even if the federal government were the only political institution with the ability to solve the problem. We might, in other words, be constitutionally disabled from curing our own economic problems. How can the Court justify this position?

The Court's argument does not appeal to the science of economics but to that of the common law as the frame for interpreting the Constitution. Regardless of the magnitude of the effects on commerce, they are of the wrong sort. The commerce clause gives the federal government the authority to regulate only matters that have a "direct effect" on commerce, not those the effects of which are indirect.[132] Direct and indirect are not quantitative relationships, but qualitative. The reasoning here comes from the common law of tort: a person is liable for a tort only if his action is the direct or proximate cause of the injury. It does not matter that he is the actual cause of the injury, if that causal relationship is indirect. In the Court's view, the relationship between production and commerce is indirect. It has that quality because the Court imagines an intervening agent between the two: the person who puts the product into commerce. That third party destroys the proximity required for a direct causal relationship. The Court is literally moved by its imagining that the agent might change his mind before the goods actually enter the stream of interstate commerce. Were that to occur, federal regulation would, in fact, operate on a wholly domestic transaction. On this imagining, the Court would sacrifice the economic well-being of the country.

To further support its argument, the Court reasons that at common law the relationship between an employer and his employees fell into the category of domestic law—alongside familial relationships. This is quite remarkable: the Court is treating one of the largest commercial ventures in the country—the production of coal—as if it might be thought of as an aspect of family law. Regulation of domestic matters traditionally falls to the states, not to the federal government. But of course the states are limited by the due process doctrine of *Lochner*, which was precisely about regulation of the employment relationship.

No doubt, the Court thought it was being scientific, applying the formal categories of an immanent order of the social that was the object of the expertise of a well-trained legal elite. As the Court dramatically puts it, if one person shoveling coal has only an "indirect" effect on interstate commerce, then multiplying the number involved still does not directly affect interstate commerce.[133] One can well understand why legal realists responded that the Court was speaking "transcendental nonsense," for the whole system was a legal fiction.[134] The legal realists will win this battle over the meaning of constitutional law, sending the systemic theorists of law into retreat for much of the rest of the century. That story, however, comes later. The important point now is to see that the Court, like the theorists of the late nineteenth century, was deeply in the grip of a formation of the social imaginary in which law meant the immanent principles of order through which and in accordance with which a society grows into itself. In American law, that meant that the Constitution and the common law had to converge. The vehicle for that convergence was public opinion rightly understood.

Sheehan and Wahrman point out in their book about the eighteenth-century rise of systemic thought—what they call "self-organization"—that such an approach tends to support conservative political positions.[135] Burke's defense of an evolving constitutionalism as against the project of the French Revolution is an obvious example. The *Lochner* Court is another. The Constitution, the text of which says nothing at all about the design of economic order, becomes the unwritten law protecting markets from government regulation. In the 1930s and 1940s, when the jurisprudence of the *Lochner* era was dismantled, it became accepted wisdom that the earlier Court was simply protecting corporate interests from a political and economic contest with labor. Today, it is accepted wisdom that the story is more complex, for there was a dark side to much progressive legislation. It was designed, in part, to protect white men from competition by blacks, immigrants, and women.[136]

Undoubtedly, a mix of motivations powered both sides in these debates. When we connect the unwritten Constitution to the common law, the common law to the systemic science of law emerging in the new American law schools, and all of this to the enthusiasm for Darwinian ideas of growth and Social Darwinist ideas of progress, we get a fuller picture of the imaginative resources that made possible the *Lochner* Court. Standing against the results of popular democracy, it nevertheless claimed to stand with public opinion, which was theorized as the very force of civilization itself. If law was to be approached as a science, its object was the systemic, immanent order that showed itself equally in political and economic life, in markets of ideas as well as of goods. The Court's unique role was to link both of these in the opinion of the Court and, through that, to the Constitution.

This is pretty much what Wilson told us when he urged the Court to stand against politically popular social legislation in order to maintain the proper adjustment between public opinion and political institutions. He too believed the Court must do this in the name of constitutional liberty—a liberty of ideas, contracts, and property all moving toward the realization of an immanent order. This is the imagination of constitutional order and citizen identity that will allow the United States to move into the twentieth century as a tremendous force for both destruction and creation. It allows the nation to believe that in acting in its own interests, it is acting in the interests of a universal civilization.

CONCLUSION: HAS THE NINETEENTH CENTURY ENDED?

America achieved something genuinely new when it showed that politics could be both secular and a source of ultimate meaning for citizens. With its concluding words, the Declaration of Independence announced this change to the world: "[W]e mutually pledge to each other our Lives, our Fortunes, and our sacred Honor." Politics had become a matter for which citizens would sacrifice themselves—not to realize God's will, but to realize the state as the historical presence of a people.[1] Hobbes had argued that the founding social contract ran from citizen to citizen, not from citizen to sovereign. The Declaration agrees that the founding relationship is among citizens. It is, however, not a contract but a pledge, for a contract is limited by the ends the parties seek to achieve in their bargain. The pledge is the initial act of self-transcendence that is constitutive of the popular sovereign.[2]

A secular politics of ultimate meaning—of citizens pledging their lives to each other—came to characterize nineteenth-century politics throughout the West. A turn to the secular no longer meant a turn to the mundane, ordinary, or insignificant. Ultimate meanings no longer came to history from an eternal God or a timeless being. The significance of history was no longer limited to that of the space within which the transcendent appeared. Even the idea of the miracle was secularized.[3] The pledge at the conclusion of the Declaration had nothing to do with realizing God's will in the state, but everything to do with bringing into being something new that was the citizens' own creation. History was now the source of the ultimate claim that politics could make upon citizens. The Declaration, as well as the Constitution that follows, is not a recovery of something lost; both are the realization of a new possibility at this moment.

American politics has been in large part a process of universalizing the idea of the political pledge of a life expressed at the end of the Declaration. That process moves from participation in local militias, to mass conscription and the spectacle of mass sacrifice on the field of battle, to the threat of weapons of mass destruction in the twentieth century. In the twenty-first century, this expansion continues in the random threat of terror that is imagined as a possibility that can appear anywhere, at any time, and against anyone. In the Second World War, every family felt the loss of loved ones, close friends, and relatives. In the new millennium, every family imagines that it could find itself literally on the front lines of the War on Terror. Political identity, we have been reminded, remains a matter of life and death.

This universalization of sacrifice proclaims that the transcendent has entered history not in the form of a new representation of the divine—there was no second coming—but as pure political presence. Politics no longer refers to anything outside of itself; it is not a means to other ends, whether secular or religious. The ultimate claim of politics appears now as an existential condition in which citizens find themselves. A state that can claim a life—indeed, can claim everyone's life—does not rest on a promise of individual welfare. That the poor and suffering will defend the state with their lives was one of the great discoveries of the nineteenth century. That they can, just as easily as the rich, be victims of random acts of terror in the twenty-first century reflects the same independence of political identity from standards of justice. Holmes, who expresses so much of late nineteenth-century thought, captures this aspect of politics when he reflects on his experience of battle in the Civil War:

> I do not know the meaning of the Universe. But in the midst of doubt . . . there is one thing I do not doubt . . . and that is that the faith is true and adorable which leads a soldier to throw away his life in obedience to a blindly accepted duty, in a cause which he little understands, in plan of campaign of which he has little notion, under tactics of which he does not see the use.[4]

Holmes is saying that our experience of meaning extends beyond our knowledge. We experience the claim, and we act. Whatever meaning we find in life is here, in history: it is not in some other world to come.

Reflecting on this growth of the political as a site of ultimate meaning, Carl Schmitt, in the early twentieth century, used quantitative terms to describe its nature: the political is the highest or most intense concern. That quantitative approach does not quite work to convey the status of politics, but it is close. The point is not that politics scores higher on a common quantitative measure, but that politics has no measure outside of itself.[5] A politics of ultimate meaning has no measure because it has no necessary content. There is nothing it is supposed to be or do. Thus, politics can attach to any issue, practice, institution, or belief once it becomes a sign or symbol of a community.[6] As sign and symbol, it will be defended through acts of sacrifice.[7]

Politics, like faith, is an existential fact; it is not the conclusion of an argument. Thus, the relationship of America's wars to justice has always been problematic—indeed, this is a problem that begins with the Revolution itself. Historians continue to explore the relationship of revolution to colonial interests in slavery, debt relief, and dispossession of Native Americans. Injustice, American history teaches us, is not inconsistent with legitimacy. Even well-working, representative governments commit injustices. For precisely this reason, reform is an endless task: a constitution can be amended; laws can be repealed and redrafted.

Scholarly exploration of an exceptional politics of ultimate meaning requires a kind of phenomenology of practices and beliefs. Politics can no longer be understood apart from the experience of political life that it makes possible. Schmitt will go on to attack the constitutions created by the liberal, democratic projects of European nation-states, arguing that the institutions they put in place are incapable of making the decisions necessary for the life and defense of the state.[8] In place of a politics of projects, he sets forth the friend-enemy distinction as the fundamental political category. For Schmitt, this distinction is entirely internal to political experience. There is no nonpolitical justification of this distinction. The enemy is whoever is perceived as an existential threat to a way of life. That perception follows no general rule: it applies no abstract categories.

Schmitt is a sort of political existentialist. He will be succeeded by a range of thinkers who turn toward a new political value: "authenticity." A politics of life and death—the politics of the pledge—moves toward a symbolism of realizing or failing to realize the truth of the self. By the late twentieth century, much of our political experience, as well as our political theory, will be concerned with "identity politics." That idea will give a new meaning to representation. What had been a mechanism for mediating the effects of popular participation in government becomes, instead, a form of political self-expression. A history of twentieth-century political practice and belief will have to trace the changing meaning of authenticity, representation, and identity in American life. Project and system do not disappear from the late twentieth-century imagination of law, but they must be reinterpreted in light of this new set of concerns with identity.

Schmitt was theorizing the appearance of the sacrificial state: the citizen of such a state imagines an enemy. Against the enemy, the citizen imagines the possibility of killing and being killed. That the secular state can make a claim on the life of every citizen had been the fundamental feature of the modern political imaginary. This is the nineteenth century's legacy to the twentieth century—a period that begins with the slaughter of the trenches in the First World War and ends with the threat of nuclear holocaust. Secularized politics had become deadly serious. The Leviathan may have first been theorized as an artificial construction that would protect citizens from the threat of violence and death. What actually emerged was a new site of ultimate meaning that protected citizens from murder while substituting a practice of sacrifice. The state conquered the threat of murder—Hobbes's starting point—by creating a cult of sacrifice. In this, as in so much else, the modern Western state displayed its Christian roots. The Christian martyr has been universalized and secularized in the form of the citizen soldier. In an age of terrorism, the citizen soldier can be anyone at all. The distinction between war and peace is no longer sharp, which means that the distinction between combatant and civilian is no longer maintained.

Nineteenth-century politics, then, had a double aspect. It no longer looked to an extrahistorical source for meaning, but secularization effectively intensified the political experience. It killed the king who claimed authority from God, but it sacralized the people. This political transformation was parallel to the movement of familial love from a sacrament that derived its meaning from its relationship to God to a romantic ideal that was autonomous and self-sustaining. This was not a lessening in the experience of love. Rather, it was a reorientation of the imagination, which then showed itself in multiple narratives. More, not less, was invested in the love of family.[9] The same was true of the new political formations of the nineteenth century.

Political theorists confronting these transformations had to offer an account of the possibility of order that could make sense of the citizen's experience of the political as a matter of ultimate significance. Facing this task, nineteenth-century writers followed in the steps of the theological accounts of their predecessors. This is hardly surprising, for to pose the question of the sources of order is already to feel the weight of the theological tradition. Those earlier accounts offered two grand narratives: project and system. Order derives from an intention, or order is immanent in the phenomena. These competing master ideas were put to new uses to account for a secularized politics of ultimate meaning.

The revolutionary politics of the founding was imagined as a new act of creation. With that, project became an essential element of the American political imaginary. Political order can be evaluated, negated, and reconstructed. This becomes a permanent possibility once there is a separation of the popular sovereign from the institutions of government, including law. This gap is now read as if it were a relationship of an author to a text or of the maker to the made. This newly imagined democratic politics of projects privileged theory, but it did not privilege philosophers. The people themselves were to deliberate and choose; they had to be persuaded to order themselves one way rather than another. The entire community was to imagine politics as a project that they did together. They could, accordingly, evaluate the products of the project; they could remake those products whenever they were judged to be inadequate. Revolution is always imagined as a possibility, but then so too is amendment. A politics of projects embeds an idea of experiment at the center of the imagination of the legal order. Constitutions are experiments, just as statutes—state and federal—are experiments. They are experiments because they are always open to a practical evaluation and reconstruction.

This idea of project remains an essential aspect of the popular political imaginary. In a democratic project, citizens must be persuaded to see themselves as if they are the author of the laws. In the competition to persuade, claims of reason assert a rhetorically privileged place, for only a project based on reason can hold itself forth as universal. The irrational is identified with faction: what can persuade only a part of the citizen body relies on interest not reason. If law can be grounded in a science, then it will claim the same universality as other forms of science. A democratic politics of legal project requires, therefore, a political science that extends from the most general principles of rights and institutional organization to the narrowest issues of policy. As I argued in Part II, many of our ideas of the Court's role, and particularly of judicial review, have their origins in this Enlightenment idea of law as a project grounded in a science of politics.

The idea of the legal project was challenged in the course of nineteenth century by the rise of new social sciences that shared little with the classical ideas of reason that had informed the project of constitutional construction.[10] The idea that the polity should be approached as a single organic whole, as well as the idea that the laws that govern this body constitute a system that evolves, already had long histories in Scottish Enlightenment thought about civil society (particularly in economics), in Burkean conservatism, and in the nationalisms that arose on the continent in response to the political projects spawned by the French Revolution. In the course of the nineteenth century, society became the naturalized object of a number of new empirical sciences that explored the systemic, immanent order of the social.

By the end of the century, law too had been captured by the imagination of system. Experts in the law were now academic scientists. Their expertise was a capacity to identify the immanent order of a regulatory domain, including constitutional law. Having identified the principles, they could then reason deductively to explain how those principles applied to particular circumstances. Political choices to act in ways that deviated from this immanent logic were now understood as pathologies to be remedied. They were pathologies even if embraced by a democratic majority. This systemic order of law had become the measure of politics; it was not itself the outcome of political projects. Law was still linked to reason, science, and truth, but the locus of reason had changed: what had once been abstract theory supporting a project had now become immanent in social practice.

The systemic imagination gave a radically different meaning to the idea and practice of judicial review. The Court was no longer engaged in a continuation of the Founders' project; it was now a site for the identification of law through the study and the application of precedents. By the end of the century, the constitutional measure could be located in a common-law concept like the police power, which the Court acknowledged was not capable of precise definition because its meaning was embedded in the developing case law.[11] No one created the police power as an element of a project of state construction. Rather, the police power is identified as a truth limiting political choice. Notably, the term does not appear in the constitutional text. Its meaning is that which the Court discerns through the case law. It is immanent to the system.

The new experts of legal system attacked their project-minded predecessors as naïve. Even the revered Founders now appeared to have lacked knowledge of the true science of the law. The Founders wrongly confused the analytic categories of the social with the discourse of ordinary experience in the life-world. In that world, we do indeed imagine ourselves pursuing projects, but science must abandon appearances.

Bringing the science of the social to the study of law meant a re-evaluation not just of the nature of law but of the nature of political virtue. As with the new science of economics, that which had been seen as vice could now be imagined to serve a public good. For example, the law of property might seem to produce poverty for many, but that is only an apparent evil, for the system as a whole will realize the best possible outcome. Similarly, low-paying wage contracts should be viewed not from the perspective of the family that suffers, but from the perspective of systemwide productivity that will arise naturally from a social order that respects individual liberty.[12] If these were the truths of the new systemic science of law, then a politics determined by voters, who were often suffering these apparent evils, would be viewed as a potential source of pathology.

Courts, accordingly, confronted what I have elsewhere called "the majoritarian difficulty."[13] Majority opinion could no longer be taken as the truth of the people's opinion. To discern the latter requires a new form of scientific expertise. Politics is reimagined on a medical model. Individuals want health; they may, however, have ill-founded opinions on what will lead to their own health. The doctor's expertise is a knowledge of the "true" will of the patient. The truth of law stands to the political opinions of the many in the same way.

Project and system support different attitudes across a wide range of issues relating to the scope of possible government interventions in the social order, as well as to the nature of interpretation. Project imagines politics as always open to the reform of law. Its essential nature is to be experimental. Reform-minded interventions can be radical, embracing the fundamental principles of the legal order. At that point, the project is to create a constitution. That radical possibility opens up endless smaller possibilities of legal reform—the greater includes the lesser—in a continuous effort to align political practices with abstract ideas of political order. New ideas of equality, for example, will inform new projects of legal reform. There is no natural limit to the reach of this reform. Politics is part of that larger Enlightenment idea of freedom as taking responsibility for one's own beliefs and practices by subjecting them to the critique of reason. Politics is that aspect of this project of free construction that we pursue together; its product is law.

Contrariwise, system sees radical interventions as likely to fail, for we can never know enough to predict and control the consequences of our actions. Any act, no matter how deliberate, will have unimagined and unanticipated consequences, because everything is linked across time and space. Political order is the product not of abstract ideas, but of the actual forces at work in the transactions, exchanges, multiple relationships, and competing beliefs that constitute a community. Successful interventions are those that rightly identify and correct a pathology that blocks the natural path of immanent order. The proper role of courts is limited to protecting the conditions under which the laws by which a society self-organizes can actually do their work. Other than that, a successful, positive legal norm is only declaratory: it identifies an aspect of this order that precedes the legislative project. Law is a function of the social; the social is no one's project.

When these ideas of project and system cross, we can be in dangerous territory. For example, when the social is itself taken as a project, we may find ourselves in the politics of total revolution, as in late nineteenth-century Europe. The disasters of twentieth-century totalitarianism might be thought of as arising at the point where these separate narratives of project and system intersect, producing a politically incoherent, but extremely dangerous, space—one in which basic elements of the social, including family and religion, are to be remade on the basis of theory.

Just as the ethos of project and that of system are different, so are their approaches to interpretation. Questions of interpretation for the imaginary of project can take the form of matching intentions to practices. We ask, what were the norms or principles to which those whose project it is looked? What did they intend? Project theories of interpretation take different positions within this framework. Some argue that these norms must be framed narrowly; others broadly. Some argue that we must ask what the law's authors would have intended had they known what we now know. There are also arguments over the identity of the subject whose project it is—and thus of whose intentions count. Some look to the Framers; others look to those whose votes ratified what the Framers proposed. Still others argue that the identity of the authorial subject shifts over time, and that the relevant subject is the people today. All of these positions begin from the idea that order is the product of intentionality, that is, of subjects who deliberate and choose among ideas in order to carry out a project. The idea of a project won't settle these disputes, but it does explain why interpretive controversies take the shape that they do.[14]

Questions of interpretation for systemic approaches focus not on deliberate intentions, but on practices. Those practices are evidence of law. The idea of law comes after the fact of its operation, not before; it is discovery, not intention. Identifying the immanent laws of the social puts us in a position to correct pathology. Today, we are familiar with this approach when law and economics scholars argue that the common law developed in the direction of increasing efficiency.[15] Most of these scholars are not saying that judges had an idea of efficiency toward which they deliberately directed their decisions. Rather, efficiency grounds the immanent order of legal development. Having identified that general principle, the scholar is likely to be skeptical of laws that cannot be justified on economic grounds. These are seen as political interventions that are best cabined by the courts, for they amount to little more than the pathology of rent seeking. The move from the descriptive to the normative—from what law is to what it should be—is inevitable in systemic jurisprudence. Avoiding it would be like avoiding the idea of health once one has identified the immanent principles of order of an organism. Health just is that condition of realizing the immanent order.

The law and economics movement has no monopoly on contemporary systemic approaches. Ronald Dworkin, the leading jurisprudential thinker of the late twentieth century, offered a theory of legal interpretation grounded in what he called "integrity." By integrity, he meant that the interpreter (judge) had to read the cases as evidence of an immanent normative order that is working itself out over time.[16] Integrity is the virtue that links the descriptive and the normative—in Dworkin's vocabulary, "fit" and "interpretation."[17] Law is evolving into the best order that it can be, and the role of the judge is to act as a part of this larger whole—an idea Dworkin captured in his metaphor of the chain novel.[18] Each judge writes a chapter, no one designs the whole. The meaning of the judge's chapter, even if it appeared to him as a project, only becomes clear over time as it takes its place in the whole of the novel. Integrity in the entirety of the legal order is not anyone's particular project, except Dworkin's imaginary judge, Hercules. Hercules plays the role that God played in eighteenth-century theories of immanent order—the asymptotic point of origin in a hypothesized imaginary consciousness.[19]

Project and system will also divide in their ideas of the ground of citizen identification with the polity. The imagination of project will appeal to an Enlightenment idea of the citizen statesman, emphasizing politics as an exercise of reason before it is an exercise of will. On this view, reflection must precede choice. Statesmen should be those who can lead a national debate. This idea too has a late twentieth-century echo in those theories of judicial review that present the Supreme Court as if it were conducting a vast national seminar on political principles. The Court is to instruct citizens on the nature of their deepest values.[20] Theories of deliberative democracy continue in this line, viewing citizens as giving and responding to reasons. We deliberate together in order to form our common project.[21]

The systemic imagination offers a narrative within which the citizen finds himself as a part of an organic whole that is always more than reason alone can grasp and more than anyone's project. Political identity is not chosen, and it is certainly not grounded in abstract theory. The citizen must, on this view, take up his political task with the confidence that he is, like the Holmesian ideal soldier, moving to orders that he may not fully know or understand. Edmund Burke used the metaphor of "the little platoon."[22] The citizen experiences this literally on the battlefield and metaphorically in the Pledge of Allegiance. The same experience of reverence is at stake in law: the citizen considers law to make a total claim upon the self, independent of the content of that law. Thus, the citizen believes in the law and the claims of law, even as she waits for the decision in a contested case.[23] Regardless of which way a court decides, we claim there has been an affirmation of the rule of law.[24] In the project view, citizenship is grounded in respect; in the systemic view, it is grounded in reverence. Respect sounds in justice; reverence in faith. Justice tends toward the universal; faith toward the particular.

These two different approaches to law always exist in an uneasy tension. We often imagine laws that are the object of scientific inquiry to be immanent in the natural order, while the laws of the state are the result of projects. But this distinction falls apart when we turn to the social. We wonder, for example, how far legal projects can actually change embedded social practices. This idea is famously expressed in one of the most notorious Supreme Court cases of the late nineteenth century: *Plessy v. Ferguson*.[25] There, the Court upholds a Louisiana law that required segregated cars for railroad travelers: "separate but equal" was the legal doctrine. In reaching this conclusion, the Court argued that efforts to change embedded patterns of racial segregation through legislative projects would only exacerbate racial conflict, defeating the very purpose of such legislation:

> The argument also assumes that social prejudices may be overcome by legislation, and that equal rights cannot be secured to the negro except by an enforced commingling of the two races. We cannot accept this proposition. If the two races are to meet upon terms of social equality, it must be the result of natural affinities, a mutual appreciation of each other's merits, and a voluntary consent of individuals.[26]

According to the Court, race relations are not subject to a politics of projects, despite the Fourteenth Amendment and the Civil War itself. They are, rather, evidence of an immanent order of the social that must develop according to its own laws. The opinion thus rejects the possibility of what had been the broader political project of Radical Reconstruction.

The priority of the social expressed in *Plessy* was not simply an excuse used by the Court to further an underlying racism, although that was certainly an element of the decision. As I explained in Chapter 6, post–Civil War constitutional law generally took such a systemic approach, even in areas that did not involve race. Even as we condemn *Plessy* today, we cannot help but be reminded of the recalcitrance of the social when we look at America's public schools. Sixty years after *Brown v. Board of Education*, many student populations are as racially segregated as they were then.[27] The *Brown* Court may have thought it was beginning a constitutionally mandated project of integration—the Second Reconstruction—but it failed. The social may move according to its own laws.[28]

Conversely, we worry that a failure to take up the project of law will leave us bound to a social and economic order that does not meet our standard of a just political order. Thus, in another famous Supreme Court case, *Nebbia v. New York*, the Court wrote that so far as the Constitution is concerned, the economic order is to be determined through the ordinary politics of reflection and choice.[29] There is no privileged social order—economic or otherwise—beyond the reach of a possible political project. Generalizing this point of view is one way to characterize the legal realists. For them, the system imagined as the ground of legal science was nothing more than a fiction protecting certain well-off interest groups. Out of that critique of legal system emerged the endless projects of the modern welfare state. Law must be refashioned in a way that acknowledges the role of the new policy sciences in grounding a modern reformist agenda of political projects.

Once we start thinking about project and system as competing formations of the social imaginary, we find evidence of them in multiple directions. The appeal of project, for example, helps to explain the persistence of originalism as a form of constitutional interpretation. The appeal of system explains the persistence of common-law doctrinalism in constitutional law. Consider the recent division within the Supreme Court over the question of a constitutional right to same-sex marriage.[30] The majority argued that the idea of constitutional freedom is not properly interpreted by looking to the intentions of the drafters or ratifiers of the Fourteenth Amendment because they could not know the meaning of liberty as it would evolve over time. Constitutional liberty, on this view, is no one's project. Rather, it is a function of all social forces as they shape the nation's history. The role of the Court is neither to identify an original project nor to impose its own project, but rather to discern the principles of liberty that are already at work behind a wide range of developing social phenomena, including law. Those states that fail to recognize same-sex marriages are now seen to be blocking the development of an immanent principle of order.

The dissenters insist on a constitutionalism of project. The written Constitution is the product of an identifiable project, and there is nothing in that text that speaks of gay marriage. There is no argument to be made that the project imagined by those who drafted or ratified the Fourteenth Amendment included constitutional protection for homosexuals seeking to marry. If the asserted right is not part of that constitutional project, then its only source can be in a willful act of a majority of the Justices: they have attached this intention to the text. According to the dissent, the majority is shaping the law as if it were their project, but a judge has no authority to make, but only to apply, law. We are still arguing over whether the real Constitution is written or unwritten, project or system. Thus, each side in this dispute can accuse the other of failing to decide the case according to law.

The opposition of project and system is again at work in the tension that structures many of our political debates over how law should respond to various social problems. The imagination of project explains order by asserting that someone—some conscious actor—put it there. That same form of explanation can be used to explain a failure of order. Accordingly, our first and most easily available explanation of problematic behavior is as a choice by a responsible agent:

the bad actor adopts a project for which he or she should be held accountable. The criminal becomes a malevolent actor; the tortfeasor should have chosen differently. This narrative approaches its mythical foundation when it becomes the political rhetoric of a paranoid style: if the economy is in disorder, if the environment is degraded, then someone adopted a project for which they should be held politically and legally accountable.[31]

The counternarrative traces forms of problematic behavior to systemic failures. Crime becomes a consequence of a poorly functioning economy. If its source is not in a failure of the economy, then it must be in the systemic failure of schools or families. Accounts that focus on an individual's intention are substituting anecdote for social science. The political problem is to bring to bear the work of the social sciences on the formation of law, which means to resist the rhetorical power of the narrative of ill intentions. Law must recognize and facilitate the immanent forces that order the social.

Understanding project and system as contrasting forms of imaging law clarifies an important point about the appearance of interpretive inconsistency among judicial opinions. The Justices have available to them both imaginative formations. There is no requirement that they deploy them in a consistent fashion. The very nature of shifting majorities on the Court, which tend to form differently in response to different problems, makes consistency across opinions unlikely. Project and system are resources for persuasion, but persuasion is a matter of political belief under particular circumstances. The art of persuasion is to grasp which of the available resources are likely to be most effective in a given case.[32] No one holds the Court to a standard of consistency.[33]

One response to this constantly reappearing tension of project and system is to seek synthesis. Indeed, American constitutional law has been strewn with efforts at synthesis: for example, arguments that the original intent of the Framers was that law should be interpreted as an evolving system.[34] Americans often think of their constitutional project as creating "a machine that would go of itself" through such devices as separation of powers and federalism.[35] Project and system, on this view, are not in opposition in political life any more than they are in opposition in technical fields of construction. We rely on physics to build a bridge; we should rely on political science to construct a legal order. Roscoe Pound, who drew on contemporary social science in order to develop his "sociological jurisprudence," went so far as to define jurisprudence as a "science of social engineering."[36]

The tension of project and system arises not when projects draw on bodies of systemic knowledge, but when the idea of system is offered as an explanation of the legal order despite the appearance of projects. Judges and legislators may think they are pursuing legal projects—as might citizens—but the theorist of system identifies that self-conception as mere appearance. The real work of the law is invisible to these actors, even as it may be realized in and through their actions. That work, on the system view, lies in the movement of history itself. It lies in what the theologians called "providence" and early moderns called the "the invisible hand."

Project and system offer conceptual resources that will be deployed against each other whenever controversy arises, and controversy always arises. Constitutional interpretation is a field of political contestation. Conflict does not represent failure; it is not a problem to be solved. We translate our political disputes into constitutional disputes in order to give them a cognizable shape and to open up possibilities of peaceful resolution. The problem—if it is a problem—is that there is more than one "cognizable shape" to draw upon. Forms of legal argument will always be opportunistically recruited for competing ends. We will not agree on forms of rhetorical address independently of our substantive ambitions. Nor should we, for there is no truth of the matter that can resolve these disputes.

If project and system are conceptual resources employed in a contingent fashion, then my account of the long nineteenth century should not be read as ordinary intellectual history. System may follow project in this account of the social imaginary, but not because this is a development along a causal path or the consequence of greater insight—although this is the discourse of legitimation that late nineteenth-century systemic theorists attempted to offer.[37] The movement from project to system does not express a discovery of a truth; it is not a narrative of progress. The movement does reflect a general enthusiasm for Darwin in the latter part of the century, but the legal movement was by no means a product of the spread of Darwinian science. Ideas of evolution were operating well before Darwin, and legal theorists were actually not very Darwinian.[38] The more compelling explanation of this pattern of development arises from the fact of the Revolution itself, which emphasized a discourse of project. Project is the language of the first-person plural: We the People declare and we act. That constitutional project disrupted the systemic, common-law constitutionalism of the existing British order. If that is the starting point, then recourse to system will reappear as a form of contestation.

This contingent order of project and system becomes quite clear if we shift the focus of the inquiry from domestic law to the law of nations, or what will come to be known as international law. Over the course of the nineteenth century, we see an inverse pattern in the way in which this body of law was imagined: the movement was from system to project. The classic textbooks of the law of nations at the start of the century presented accounts of systemic order. They began from the premise that the law of nature applies to the state because states are collections of men who are themselves subject to that law.[39] The distinctive character of the law of nations is a function of the differences that result when the law of nature is applied to collectivities rather than individuals. These differences can be systematically accounted for, which means that the basic rules of the law of nations can be derived through deductions from first principles of natural law.

To this set of natural-law principles, treatise writers added an account of the "voluntary law of nations."[40] This is not the conventional law of treaties, but rather the law that arises spontaneously among nations acting toward each other as sovereign entities. Here, the treatise writer's work was to interpret the behavior of states in order to identify the principles of order, beyond natural law, that are immanent in the system of relations among nations. The expert, on this view, has the ability to look through the particular events, transactions, and practices among states to see the underlying, immanent principles. Such principles might never have been formulated as an object of sovereign intention. This way of imagining order obviously put a strain on the idea of consent as the ground of all those elements of the law of nations that were not a function of natural law—a strain that continues today in the jurisprudence of customary international law.[41]

In British legal practice, the law of nations was understood as a part of the common law: there could be only one immanent system of legal order.[42] Early American practice tended in the same direction of taking the law of nations as a settled, immanent system. Unlike the common law, however, which was generally brought into the newly independent states by legislative acts of incorporation, the new nation entered the system of the law of nations simply by virtue of obtaining sovereignty.[43] Thus, the Constitution directly grants Congress the power "to define and punish . . . offenses against the law of nations."[44] This set up the problem of the relationship of the system of international law to the American project of law.[45]

When Chief Justice Marshall confronts the question of the relationship of the law of nations to American law, this is precisely how he understands the problem. How does a system of international law that arises spontaneously through the often violent interactions among nations relate to the constitutional project of democratic law making? The former establishes claims of property through enslavement, conquest, and prize. From the perspective of the constitutional project founded on ideas of liberty, equality, and due process, none of these international-law claims are justified. Nevertheless, Marshall gives effect to the law of nations. For example, in *The Antelope*, Marshall relies on the law of nations to order slaves returned to their Spanish owners.[46] In *Johnson v. M'Intosh*, he relies on the right of conquest under the law of nations to uphold the limits on the legal rights of Native Americans.[47] The systemic quality of the law of nations serves the theodical role of justifying that which cannot be legitimated in terms of the constitutional project.[48] Slaves and Native

Americans are no part of the sovereign author of the laws that subordinate them. The legitimating discourse cannot be self-authorship. It turns instead to system to explain what otherwise appears as immoral and inconsistent with the project.

Marshall's movement between system and project serves a rhetorical role of context-specific persuasion. Deploying the law of nations to this purpose, Marshall expresses the two faces of sovereignty. On the one hand, the sovereign nation takes itself as a project of law creation. On the other hand, the sovereign nation is a participant in a system of equal, sovereign states. Claims of sovereignty, in other words, do not help to resolve the tension of system and project; rather, they offer only another site for their appearance.

At the end of the nineteenth century, the places of project and system in explanations of international law reverse.[49] This shift in the social imaginary accompanies the development of institutions within which it is possible to think of a project of authoring international law. International conferences are organized to produce international conventions—for example, the Hague or Geneva Conventions. Before there could be an imagination of project, there had to be something that looked like a multinational facility through which nations could act together to make law: the international equivalent of the Constitutional Convention. By the beginning of the twentieth century, the choice-of-law problem becomes the reverse of that which Marshall confronted: courts will have to reconcile the projectlike character of international conventions with the systemic quality of American constitutional law. That problem persists today in the resistance Americans often have to treating international human rights law as a source of law in domestic controversies. Human rights law is a project of recent origins that cannot easily find a place within our 200-year-old system of constitutional rights. If, instead, we think of American constitutional law as a project, we face yet another form of American exceptionalism, for the international and the constitutional law projects do not share a common author. American law is the project of the popular sovereign; human rights law is not.

One of the advantages of studying the nineteenth century is that the differences in the master narratives appear quite clearly. That these ways of imagining politics should themselves become prominent subjects of reflection—from *The Federalist Papers* to Woodrow Wilson's two books—should be no surprise, for it was a century in which traditional forms of authority were rejected and in which politics competed with theology as the frame and source of a meaningful life. Parishioners became citizens; statesmen displaced ministers. Individual identity came to be formed through the idea of the nation, rather than through that of sectarian religions. Law was central to this transformation. Thinking about law became an aspect of national identity—a trait noted already by Tocqueville.[50]

The distinction of project and system was, for example, reflected in the self-understanding of the dominant nineteenth-century schools of jurisprudence: the utilitarians, following Bentham, approached law as project. The historical school, following Savigny, approached law as system. Both schools had their American representatives. By the twentieth century, while the contrast of project and system continued, it was no longer quite so sharp. Systemic thought as the ground of a legal science never fully recovered from the assault on legal formalism mounted by the legal realists. Claims that law can itself be a social science are fatally discredited in the United States. When social science reemerges in the law, it is through the subordination of law to economics; that is, law is not its own science but becomes the object of a different social science. Similarly, by the twentieth century, there is a new skepticism about political projects, which are often seen as the work of interest groups advancing their own private interests.[51] Law cannot be a democratic project of self-rule if representatives pursue private, rather than public, interests. What space remains for projects of legal-institutional construction tends now to be within discrete regulatory agencies. However, they too are subject to regulatory capture.

By the late twentieth century, there is no single, dominant social imaginary of American law. We don't believe in legal science, and we distrust political projects of law construction. The very distinction of law from politics is challenged as membership on the Supreme Court becomes a defining issue of partisan politics. Under these conditions, we are no longer sure what our law is about or what we owe it. Doctrinally, there is a tendency to imagine statutes as the domain of projects and constitutional law as that of system. Even this assertion, however, is no more than a generalization with many exceptions—for example, super-statutes have a systemic quality, and constitutional originalism is grounded in ideas of project.[52]

Nevertheless, it is striking that by the end of a century characterized by the wide acceptance of the legal-realist critique of Langdellian formalism, the constitutional law casebook remains the strongest redoubt of Langdell's idea of a systemic legal science. This is particularly striking since constitutional law was of little interest to Langdell and his followers. For them, it was too political—and too recent—to qualify as real law. Unlike other legal fields that are now taught with frequent reference to policy debates and social science literatures, law professors still teach constitutional law almost exclusively through the cases, which provide evidence of underlying, immanent principles.

A question of constitutional law remains primarily a question of judge-made law, that is, of precedents. We read the cases as standing for principles, which we describe at a high level of conceptual generality. We try to arrange the principles in a hierarchical order such that we can deduce particular rules from higher-order principles. Precedents are never just points of decision; rather, they are points of rule identification. We must see through the cases to the principle. Then, we can reason down from the general principle to the rule in a particular case. To be an expert is to be able to identify paradigmatic cases that stand for general principles that can give order to ever-emerging controversies.

That the body of constitutional law is both conceptually well ordered and complete is simply a premise of the discipline. A common-law system of order could not operate without this premise, which is as central to Langdell on the common law as it is to our modern constitutional theorists.[53] This model of systemic order links scholarship, pedagogy, and judicial opinions. We teach constitutional law by teaching the cases, just as the Court explains its decisions by reasoning from the cases.

For example, thirty years ago, the Court looked at its precedents and concluded that there was no constitutional principle that protected the relationship of a gay couple.[54] Its opinion in *Bowers* explained the relevant principle of immanent order to be one that protected families, not sexual intimacy.[55] Today, the Court looks at those same cases and concludes that the immanent principle concerns dignity and extends to gay couples: they too have a right to marry and form families.[56] There has been no new project; there has been a reinterpretation of the immanent principles seen through the cases.

Often these immanent principles are not actually mentioned in the text of the Constitution: there is no dormant commerce clause; no clause on dignity; no clause on judicial review. The principles that are mentioned are not set in a hierarchical order; their relative place in the constitutional order shifts over time. Not so long ago, the Tenth Amendment principle of federalism—a high principle today—was dismissed as a "truism" that added nothing to the more specific clauses distributing powers.[57] Similarly, dignity did not exist as a constitutional principle until the end of the twentieth century. Nevertheless, contemporary opinions regard dignity as a foundational principle.

Time enters the social imagination of constitutional law not as a source of change but rather as a source of learning. We are learning the meaning of our constitutional principles, as if they had some existence independent of the decisions. As the Court put it in *Obergefell*, "The generations that wrote and ratified the Bill of Rights and the Fourteenth Amendment did not presume to know the extent of freedom . . . so they entrusted to future generations a charter protecting the right of all persons to enjoy liberty as we learn its meaning."[58] Thus, the history of doctrine is an account of pedagogy—first of the Court, and then of the nation seeing itself in and through the Court's opinions. Together, we are learning the full meaning of principles that are themselves timeless. We imagine the law to be working itself pure through the decisions of the Court. We are not far in this belief from Hegel's "cunning of reason."

Because experts in constitutional law "know" the immanent system of which the cases are evidence, they can also tell us which cases are "wrong." This idea of error is no less puzzling for the modern scholar of constitutional law than it was in the work of Langdell.[59] This claim of error stands on nothing but a presumption that immanent order has some authoritative force independent of the judicial decision. What that might be remains a puzzle of theory. The genealogy of the claim, however, is clear. Reason continues to play the dual role that it has always played in our tradition: it is both the capacity to interpret and the object interpreted. An authoritative opinion identifies the reason of the law. Subject and object converge. A wrong decision is identified as "unreasonable." Not surprisingly, the most powerful critique of modern law has been an exploration of the way in which reason has served as a mask for ideology: behind claims of reason lies the exercise of power.[60] This is the same critique mounted by the legal realists against Langdellian legal science 100 years ago.

Just as Langdell's formalism had to recognize the authority of persistent "error," so does the contemporary constitutional law scholar. He or she might pronounce a new decision of the Court to be wrong, that is, to be inconsistent with the principles that are evidenced by the precedents. But if the Court persists, the expert must reimagine those immanent principles such that the new case is now included in the overall explanation of what the law is. This is not a matter of the Court overruling its prior case law. Rather, the burden is on the expert to offer a new, inclusive interpretation of the systemic order of the whole. The content of reason is never fixed. This too is a theological remnant: a reasonable God acts reasonably, even when that reason is not immediately apparent to us. This is the fundamental idea of a system: we must pierce the appearance of disorder to discover the underlying system. System never sheds its character as theodicy. But does any of this still persuade?

The Court has no less of an obligation to maintain the popular belief in self-authorship than it has to maintain the systemic order of the whole. The more erudite the system becomes, the greater the potential strain on the idea of self-authorship. We find ourselves still puzzling over the legitimacy of our constitutional law as we move between system and project. Theories of the public order of law sometimes respond to these new puzzles by becoming less ambitious. There is a new focus on democracy as process: the process of representation and the processes of procedure. In the phrase of a leading proponent, the role of constitutional law is "to police" the democratic process.[61] Constitutional law is only to provide the form and process for pluralist politics.

Despite this modesty, the Court has remained deeply involved in our largest political controversies. It continues to bear the burden not just of explaining itself, but of explaining who we are. Taking up that burden, it falls back on the language of project and system. Doing so, it steps into a very long tradition of legal argument and, before that, of theological argument. Project and system have been ready to hand for as long as we Westerners have been arguing. It is our fate to live within this tension. Without project, we could not imagine ourselves as free; without system, we could not imagine ourselves to live in a rational world. Our burden has always been to be both rational and free.

NOTES

Preface

1. See Michael Donnelly, "From Political Arithmetic to Social Statistics: How Some Nineteenth-Century Roots of the Social Sciences Were Implanted," in *The Rise of the Social Sciences and the Formation of Modernity: Conceptual Change in Context, 1750–1850*, ed. Johan Heilbron, Lars Magnusson, and Björn Wittrock (Boston: Kluwer Academic Publishers, 1998), 225, 233 ("The great pride of [nineteenth-century] social statisticians was to have discovered hitherto unsuspected laws of social life; and to discern through the regularities of those laws a spontaneously generated order which was in many ways more remarkable than the artificial realms of the legislator and the sovereign.").

2. Ludwig Wittgenstein, *Philosophical Investigations*, trans. G. E. M. Anscombe (Oxford: Blackwell, 1997), 48.

3. Alexander Hamilton, *Federalist No. 1*, ed. C. Rossiter (New York: Signet, 1961), 27.

4. Oliver Wendell Holmes, Jr. offered a paradigmatic expression of the modern attitude toward history as both a source for self-discovery and an object for reconstruction. Of inherited legal doctrine, Holmes wrote that we must "get the dragon out of his cave . . . and in the daylight. . . ." Then we can choose "either to kill him, or to tame him and make him a useful animal." Oliver Wendell Holmes, Jr., "The Path of the Law," 10 *Harvard Law Review* 457, 469 (1897).

5. See Jed Rubenfeld, *Freedom and Time: A Theory of Constitutional Self-Government* (New Haven: Yale University Press, 2001).

6. Grant Gilmore famously wrote, "In Hell there will be nothing but law, and due process will be meticulously observed." Grant Gilmore, *The Ages of American Law* (New Haven: Yale University Press, 1977), 111.

7. See Alexander M. Bickel, *The Least Dangerous Branch: The Supreme Court at the Bar of Politics* (New Haven: Yale University Press, 1962), 16.

8. See Paul W. Kahn, *Legitimacy and History: Self-Government in American Constitutional Theory* (New Haven: Yale University Press, 1992), 135–36.

9. My distinction between project and system is related to, but not the same as, that between positivist and natural law theories. Project

fits the positivist idea of the origin of law, but natural law was at times rooted in God's project. Natural law theories tended as well to be explicitly normative, relying directly on morality, while the social-system idea of the nineteenth century tended to locate itself in the emerging sciences. That did not necessarily make these theorists of system less normative, but it did make them less explicitly so. The contrast of project and system, I hope to show, offers a broader and more useful dichotomy that can include within itself the more traditional contest between the positivists and natural law theorists.

10. Robert Cover captured this aspect of law as project when he wrote, "Law may be viewed as a system of tension or a bridge linking a concept of a reality to an imagined alternative—that is, as a connective between two states of affairs, both of which can be represented in their normative significance only through the devices of narrative." Robert M. Cover, "The Supreme Court, 1982 Term—Foreword: Nomos and Narrative," 97 *Harvard Law Review* 4, 9 (1983).

11. Among modern political theorists, Seyla Benhabib has focused on this idea of constitution as "democratic iterations of universals." See, e.g., Seyla Benhabib, "Defending a Cosmopolitanism Without Illusions: Reply to My Critics," 17 *Critical Review of International Social and Political Philosophy* 697 (2014).

Introduction

1. Famously, Socrates pursues the Delphic admonition to "know thyself." See Plato, *Phaedrus*, 229e.

2. See Jedediah Purdy, *After Nature: A Politics for the Anthropocene* (Cambridge, Mass.: Harvard University Press, 2015).

3. On the relationship of faith to representation, see Paul W. Kahn, *Finding Ourselves at the Movies: Philosophy for a New Generation* (New York: Columbia University Press, 2013), 68–70.

4. Some political and moral philosophers believe that their task is to achieve a universal point of view, but that too is a possibility that characterizes a certain community of belief and action. What does it mean to think one's practices should be evaluated from such a perspective? How did we come to that belief? Reflection on this question accounts for the genealogical turn in contemporary philosophy. See Charles Taylor, *The Sources of the Self* (Cambridge: Cambridge University Press, 1989).

5. On the concept of the social imaginary, see Charles Taylor, *Modern Social Imaginaries* (Durham: Duke University Press, 2004).

6. This idea derives from Kant's "Copernican Revolution" in philosophy. For an important expansion of Kant's approach to cover diverse forms of experience, see Ernst Cassirer, *Philosophy of Symbolic Forms*, vols. 1–3, trans. Ralph Manheim (New Haven: Yale University Press, 1953–57). For an explanation of modern phenomenology's relation to Kant's revolution, see Hubert Dreyfus and Charles Taylor, *Retrieving Realism* (Cambridge, Mass.: Harvard University Press, 2015).

7. The concept of the historical *a priori* was introduced by Foucault. Michel Foucault, *The Order of Things: An Archaeology of the Human Sciences* (New York: Vintage, 1970), xx–xxiii; Michel Foucault, *The Archeology of Knowledge*, trans. A. M. Sheridan Smith (London: Tavistock Publications, 1972), 127.

8. See Paul W. Kahn, *The Cultural Study of Law: Reconstructing Legal Scholarship* (Chicago: University of Chicago Press, 1999), 36; Paul W. Kahn, *Putting Liberalism in Its Place* (Princeton: Princeton University Press, 2005), 23.

9. William H. Sewell, Jr. argues for an approach that combines the sociologist's focus on structure with the historian's focus on events. The event is the mechanism and locus of a change in structure. Precisely because the event is a point of incommensurability, it cannot be predicted as the effect of determinate causes. See William H. Sewell, Jr., *Logics of History: Social Theory and Social Transformation* (Chicago: University of Chicago Press, 2005), 100–03.

10. See, e.g., Thomas Wright, *Circulation: William Harvey, a Man in Motion* (London: Chatto & Windus, 2012), which deploys biography in order to study a changing scientific imagination.

11. See Ronald Dworkin, *Law's Empire* (Cambridge, Mass.: Harvard University Press, 1986), 3–11.

Part 1. Project and System Before the Constitution

1. For a contemporary endorsement of the systemic approach to philosophical inquiry, see Roger Scruton, *The Soul of the World* (Princeton: Princeton University Press, 2014).

2. That matter might be self-organizing without the intervention of an idea was the position advocated in classical thought by Lucretius. See Titus Lucretius Carus, *On the Nature of Things*, trans. Cyril Bailey (Oxford: Clarendon Press, 1910), Book II.

3. Frederick Pollock famously wrote in 1883 of Savigny, Burke, Montesquieu, and Maine as "Darwinians before Darwin." He explained, "The doctrine of evolution is nothing else than the historical method [of jurisprudence] applied to the facts of nature; the historical method is nothing else than the doctrine of evolution applied to human societies and institutions." Frederick Pollock, "English Opportunities in Historical and Comparative Jurisprudence," in *Oxford Lectures and Other Discourses* (London: Macmillan & Co., 1890), 41–42.

4. On the history of the term "society," see Keith Michael Baker, "Enlightenment and the Institution of Society: Notes for a Conceptual History," in *Main Trends in Cultural History*, ed. Willem Melching and Wyger Velema (Amsterdam: Rodopi, 1994), 95.

5. See Jonathan Sheehan and Dror Wahrman, *Invisible Hands: Self-Organization and the Eighteenth Century* (Chicago: University of Chicago Press, 2015).

6. See Michael Donnelly, "From Political Arithmetic to Social Statistics: How Some Nineteenth-Century Roots of the Social Sciences Were Implanted," in *The Rise of the Social Sciences and the Formation of Modernity: Conceptual Change in Context, 1750–1850*, ed. Johan Heilbron, Lars Magnusson, and Björn Wittrock (Boston: Kluwer Academic Publishers, 1998), 225–26.

7. Adrian Vermeule's *The System of the Constitution* (Oxford: Oxford University Press, 2011) describes in contemporary terms both of these directions of movement. On the one hand, he offers systemic analysis as a resource for constitutional designers. On the other, he analyzes the systemic effects of the projects pursued by individual and institutional actors. Outside of constitutional law, aspiration for this form of synthesis in law goes back to the legal reformers of the early nineteenth century, who sought the principles of a rational legal order in the system of the common law. See also Perry Miller, *The Life of the Mind in America* (New York: Harcourt, Brace, & World, 1965), 156–64.

8. See Michael G. Kammen, *A Machine That Would Go of Itself: The Constitution in American Culture* (New York: Knopf, 1986).

9. Immanuel Kant, "On Perpetual Peace," in *Perpetual Peace and Other Essays on Politics, History, and Morals*, trans. Ted Humphrey (Indianapolis: Hackett Publishing Company, 1983), 124.

10. Compare Woodrow Wilson, who at the start of the twentieth century insisted that the Founders had erred in imagining government as a

machine: "Politics in their thought was a variety of mechanics. . . . [G]overnment is not a machine, but a living thing." Woodrow Wilson, "What Is Progress?," in *The New Freedom: A Call for the Emancipation of the Generous Energies of a People* (Garden City: Doubleday, Page & Company, 1913), 46–48.

11. On some readings, the Supreme Court was to play this role of repair by recurring again to the ideas that informed the project. This understanding was, for example, central to the explanation of judicial review in *Marbury v. Madison*, 5 U.S. (1 Cranch) 137 (1803). For those who take this view, the Court must be thought simultaneously as within and without the project, leading to the perpetual ambiguity of whether the Court is making or applying law.

12. For a rigorous examination of the ungrounded assumptions behind many of the claims for the Constitution as a self-sustaining systemic order, see Vermeule, supra note 7.

13. This distinction between project and organism is expressed in the Nicene Creed, which describes Jesus as "born, not made." An important American site of conflation of these two theological traditions is Lincoln's Gettysburg Address, with its language of conception linked to the forefathers' project. Lincoln stands at the intersection of project and system, just as the Civil War marks the transition from one form of thought to the other. See below, introduction to Part III.

14. See, e.g., Francis Wharton, *Commentaries on Law* (Philadelphia: Kay & Brother, 1884), §28, 59 ("It is as impossible . . . to create a system of law in a day by a decree as it would be to create an oak forest in a day by machinery.").

15. Leninist theory has to deal with the projectlike role of the Communist Party within a legitimating theory that appeals to an immanent law of historical development. The resolution is a theory of the party as "vanguard."

Chapter 1. Origins of Order

1. This does not preclude arguments that one lacks self-awareness with respect to the projects one is in fact pursuing: the unconscious may have its own projects. I may, for example, be "deceiving" myself. If I am unable to recognize my own projects, then I am in a pathological condition. An immoral person may refuse to take responsibility for his projects; a psychologically ill or incompetent person cannot take responsibility for his projects.

2. Does a slave freely adopt his master's project? No. The project remains the master's. The slave's own project is properly identified as that of realizing his well-being within the limit of his circumstances. That project may include compliance with the master's demands or revolt.

3. For a long time, for example, Machu Picchu was thought to be a temple complex. Recently, it has come to be seen as a sort of summer palace. See John Noble Wilford, "'Lost City' Yielding Its Secrets," *New York Times* (March 18, 2003).

4. Something similar happens when we try to understand the projects—including political projects—of our own, long-dead ancestors. Originalist theories of constitutional interpretation have this same problem of confronting a largely inaccessible past social imagination. See Paul Brest, "The Misconceived Quest for the Original Understanding," 60 *Boston University Law Review* 204 (1980).

5. When Europeans complain of the democracy deficit of the European Union, they are challenging the legitimacy of a project that they see as imposed upon them from Brussels. Their criticism may not be that the laws are unjust or ineffective, but that they are not their own. See, e.g., Dieter Grimm, "The Democratic Costs of Constitutionalisation: The European Case," 21 *European Law Journal* 460 (2015). Of course, in political practice, these two forms of critique may be difficult to keep separate. In part, this is because the perspective of justice from within a state is never as universal as it is from without the state. The state claims that privileging its own citizens is not unjust, despite the unequal treatment of others. This privileging of the citizen is why Carl Schmitt asserts that universal equality is "a liberal, not a democratic, idea," and as such points to a politically unrealizable cosmopolitanism. Carl Schmitt, *The Crisis of Parliamentary Democracy*, trans. Ellen Kennedy (Cambridge, Mass.: MIT Press, 1988 [1926]), 11.

6. See Quentin Skinner, *Liberty Before Liberalism* (Cambridge: Cambridge University Press, 1998) (on liberty as a lack of dependence); Anthony T. Kronman, *Confessions of a Born-Again Pagan* (New Haven: Yale University Press, 2016), 130–41 (on "the good of self-sufficiency").

7. See Hannah Arendt, *On Revolution* (New York: Viking Press, 1963); Hannah Arendt, *The Human Condition* (Chicago: University of Chicago Press, 1958).

8. This is why accounts of evolution inevitably fall into the language of purpose, even though the theory substitutes random mutation and environmental change for final causes.

9. Immanuel Kant, *Critique of Judgment*, trans. Werner S. Pluhar (Indianapolis: Hackett Publishing, 1987), 65.

10. The insistence on thinking of the constitution as a system of systems is a central point of Adrian Vermeule, *The System of the Constitution* (Oxford: Oxford University Press, 2011).

11. Giorgio Agamben's recent work explores the way in which early Christian thought approached the Trinity as a mysterious economy: an organization that expressed God's providence in history. See Giorgio Agamben, *The Kingdom and the Glory: For a Theological Genealogy of Economy and Government*, trans. Lorenzo Chiesa (Stanford: Stanford University Press, 2011).

12. See Amos Funkenstein, *Theology and the Scientific Imagination* (Princeton: Princeton University Press, 1986).

13. See Jacob Viner, *The Role of Providence in the Social Order: An Essay in Intellectual History* (Princeton: Princeton University Press, 1972) (on the seventeenth- and eighteenth-century practice of appealing to providence to explain the social order, including economic inequality and commerce). See also Jonathan Sheehan and Dror Wahrman, *Invisible Hands: Self-Organization and the Eighteenth Century* (Chicago: University of Chicago Press, 2015), chap. 1 ("Providence and the Orders of the World.").

14. The theological origin of this idea goes back to the working out of God's providence through man's free choices. See Agamben, supra note 11, at 45–46.

15. See Vermeule, supra note 10, at 27–37 (on two-level systems and the second best).

16. The possibility of systemic failure raises the reciprocal question of the origins of a social system. Early moderns split on the issue of whether sociability is a natural quality of man, as it is for other animals. Hobbes famously rejected any idea of man's natural sociability. Smith, too, did not think of man's sociability as natural; rather, social order arose out of a propensity to trade. Those who rejected a natural sociability turned to stylized or theoretical histories to show the origins of the social. History steps into the place of God's project in a myth of origins. See Istvan Hont, *Politics in Commercial Society*, ed. Béla Kapossy and Michael Sonenscher (Cambridge, Mass.: Harvard University Press, 2015), 25, 51–54.

17. Luhmann's theory of autopoiesis makes this point: a system's operative closure does not mean that it is a closed system with respect to the

environment. Closed operations are a way of incorporating what had been outside into the system. Such systems simultaneously have a self-referential, operative closure and are open to the environment. Niklas Luhmann, "The Autopoiesis of Social Systems," in *Essays on Self-Reference* (New York: Columbia University Press, 1990), 1–20.

18. In classical linguistics, we move from langue to parole. See Ferdinand de Saussure, *Course in General Linguistics*, trans. Wade Baskin (New York: Columbia University Press, 2011 [1916]).

19. On the creation myth from the perspective of aesthetics, see Paul W. Kahn, *Political Theology: Four New Chapters on the Concept of Sovereignty* (New York: Columbia University Press, 2011), 50–51.

20. See Job 38:4, where God puts this plainly to man: "Where were you when . . . ?"

21. Note that God's omnipotence cannot figure in a story of disobedience.

22. See Robert A. Burt, *In the Whirlwind: God and Humanity in Conflict* (Cambridge, Mass.: Harvard University Press, 2012).

23. See Hobbes on covenant after defeat. Thomas Hobbes, *Leviathan*, ed. Edwin Curley (Indianapolis: Hackett Publishing, 1994 [1668]), 130–31.

24. See Michael Walzer, *In God's Shadow: Politics in the Hebrew Bible* (New Haven: Yale University Press, 2012).

25. On contract and sociability, see Daniel Markovits, "Contract and Collaboration," 113 *Yale Law Journal* 1417 (2004).

26. Paul W. Kahn, *Out of Eden: Adam and Eve and the Problem of Evil* (Princeton: Princeton University Press, 2007), 1.

27. This is the theme of Moshe Halbertal and Stephen Holmes, *The Beginning of Politics: Power in the Biblical Book of Samuel* (Princeton: Princeton University Press, 2017).

28. We struggle with this conflict of ordering today in the jurisprudence of the religion clauses. See, for example, Stephen L. Carter, *The Dissent of the Governed* (Cambridge, Mass.: Harvard University Press, 1998).

29. See Sheehan and Wahrman, supra note 13, at 15–18.

30. See Susan Neiman, *Evil in Modern Thought: An Alternative History of Philosophy* (Princeton: Princeton University Press, 2002) (arguing that responding to evil is the organizing theme of modern philosophy).

31. One particularly difficult variant on the theological problem of project versus system was Calvinist thought on predestination. If God no longer intervenes in response to free choice, then system implies predestination.

32. See Sheehan and Wahrman, supra note 13, at 6–9. See also below at note 34.

33. See Anthony T. Kronman, supra note 6, at chap. 14.

34. Alexander Pope, *An Essay on Man* (London: Cassell & Company, Ltd., 1891 [1734]).

35. See Paul W. Kahn, *Sacred Violence: Torture, Terror, and Sovereignty* (Ann Arbor: University of Michigan Press, 2008).

36. See Hobbes, supra note 23, Part III.

37. See Bernard Mandeville, *The Fable of the Bees*, ed. E. J. Hundert (Indianapolis: Hackett Publishing, 1997).

38. See Hont, supra note 16, at 91 (on extensive use of the metaphor in the eighteenth century). But compare Emma Rothschild, "Adam Smith and the Invisible Hand," 84 *American Economic Review* 319 (1994) (arguing that Smith's few uses of the term were all ironic).

39. See Émile Durkheim, *The Elementary Forms of the Religious Life*, trans. Karen E. Fields (New York: Free Press, 1995), 208 ("[T]he god and the society are one and the same.").

40. By the end of the century, Holmes will argue for a jurisprudence based on history and economics. See Oliver Wendell Holmes, Jr., "The Path of the Law," 10 *Harvard Law Review* 457 (1897); see also below, Chap. 5.

41. See Aristotle, *Oikonomikos*, discussed in David Singh Grewal, *The Invention of the Economy* (Cambridge, Mass.: Harvard University Press, forthcoming).

42. That it is both at once reflects the Aristotelian idea of the good as both transcendent and immanent, which became the Christian idea of God as both sovereign over and immanent in the order of the world. See Agamben, supra note 11, at 87 (referring to "the ontological fracture between transcendence and immanence, which Christian theology inherits and develops from Aristotelianism").

43. See, e.g., John Rawls, *A Theory of Justice* (Cambridge, Mass.: The Belknap Press of Harvard University Press, 1971). See also Bryan Garsten, "The Elusiveness of Arendtian Judgment," 74 *Social Research* 1071 (2007).

44. See, for example, David Gauthier, *Morals by Agreement* (Oxford: Clarendon Press, 1986).

45. There were four signers of the Declaration of Independence trained as ministers, compared to more than half who were lawyers. Of those four, it seems only one, John Witherspoon, who was the president of Princeton, was active as a clergyman.

46. See Istvan Hont, "The Language of Sociability and Commerce: Samuel Pufendorf and the Theoretical Foundations of the 'Four States' Theory," in *Jealousy of Trade: International Competition and the Nation-State in Historical Perspective* (Cambridge, Mass.: The Belknap Press of Harvard University Press, 2005), 159. See also Hont, supra note 16, at 55 (noting Hume's influence on Smith regarding this point).

47. Even Marx's radical alternative theory of systemic order sees ownership of the means of production as the mechanism of change.

48. See 2 William Blackstone, *Commentaries* *2: "There is nothing which so generally strikes the imagination, and engages the affections of mankind, as the right of property. . . ." See also Catharine P. Wells, "Langdell and the Invention of Legal Doctrine," 58 *Buffalo Law Review* 551, 556 (2010) (on priority of property over contrast in Blackstone); see also Vermeule, supra note 10, at 70–71 (on the necessity of a mechanism in systemic accounts).

49. Consider Hart on secondary rules. H. L. A. Hart, *The Concept of Law* (Oxford: Oxford University Press, 2012), 97–98. See also Bryan Garsten, "Deliberating and Acting Together," in *Cambridge Companion to Aristotle's Politics*, ed. Marguerite Deslauriers and Pierre Destrée (Cambridge: Cambridge University Press, 2013), 324–49.

50. Many twentieth-century postcolonial regimes followed this pattern: they were legitimate, but unjust.

51. These paragraphs were written before the electoral victory of Donald Trump.

Chapter 2. An Age of Suspicion

1. In the European tradition, this became the problem of understanding the relationship of the state to society. In nineteenth-century America, the opposition of project and system operates within contending models of the nature of political order. It is an argument about the nature of law, rather than one about the relationship of law to society.

2. Thus, the Declaration of Independence makes a claim of universal right to revolution: "When in the course of human events, it becomes necessary for one people. . . ." The Declaration of Independence (U.S. 1776), para. 1.

3. This idea of a revolutionary project of new beginnings is precisely what Burke finds so objectionable in the French Revolution. See Edmund Burke, *Reflections on the Revolution in France*, ed. Frank M. Turner (New Haven: Yale University Press, 2003 [1790]).

4. This is related to but not quite the same as Habermas's distinction between life-world and system. Habermas sees these as distinct forms of experience, although system is colonizing the life-world, bringing with it a technical or instrumental relationship to institutions and others. I use system in contrast with project, which has its own instrumental rationality. See Jürgen Habermas, *The Theory of Communicative Action*, vol. 2: *Lifeworld and System: A Critique of Functionalist Reasoning*, trans. Thomas McCarthy (Boston: Beacon Press, 1985).

5. Even before revolution takes hold in France, the figure of the finance minister directing state policy emerges, for example, in the person of Jacques Necker.

6. See Paul W. Kahn, *Cultural Study of Law: Reconstructing Legal Scholarship* (Chicago: University of Chicago Press, 1999) 7–18.

7. Interestingly, Oliver Wendell Holmes already uses this example in his 1897 lecture "The Path of the Law." See Oliver Wendell Holmes, Jr., "The Path of the Law," 10 *Harvard Law Review* 457, 470–71 (1897).

8. See Paul Krugman, "How Did Economists Get It So Wrong?," *New York Times Magazine* (September 2, 2009) (on the failures of systemic analysis to respond to the 2008 recession because of the extension of ordinary thought about debt from the micro to the macro level). We might think of this as Habermas's life-world colonizing the domain of system. See supra note 4.

9. See Charles Taylor, *A Secular Age* (Cambridge, Mass.: The Belknap Press of Harvard University Press, 2007); Immanuel Kant, "An Answer to the Question: What Is Enlightenment?," in *Practical Philosophy* (The Cambridge Edition of the Works of Immanuel Kant), ed. and trans. Mary J. Gregor (Cambridge: Cambridge University Press, 1999).

10. Pope had already captured this basic idea in *An Essay on Man*: "For forms of government let fools contest; Whate'er is best administer'd is best." Alexander Pope, "An Essay on Man: Epistle III," in *An Essay on Man* (London: Cassell & Company, Ltd., 1891), lines 303–04.

11. An exception may have been Hamilton's interest in economics. See, e.g., Ron Chernow, *Alexander Hamilton* (New York: Penguin Press, 2004), 170.

12. Most famously, Publius, of *The Federalist Papers*. Similarly, antifederalist writers called themselves Brutus and Cato. There is a longstanding dispute about which political-theory tradition dominated the views of the Founders. Compare J. G. A. Pocock, *The Machiavellian Moment: Florentine Political Thought and the Atlantic Republican Tradition*

(Princeton: Princeton University Press, 1975) and Louis Hartz, *The Liberal Tradition in America: An Interpretation of American Political Thought since the Revolution* (New York: Harcourt, Brace & World, 1955).

13. Tocqueville's *Democracy in America*, discussed below, is deeply concerned with this question. It remains a central question for Carl Schmitt in his work on the problems of Weimar governance. See Carl Schmitt, *The Crisis of Parliamentary Democracy*, trans. Ellen Kennedy (Cambridge, Mass.: MIT Press, 1988 [1926]), 9–13.

14. See Plato, *Republic* II, at 369c (on creating city in speech—that is, "logos").

15. Sir Thomas More, *Utopia*, ed. Ronald Herder (Mineola: Dover Publications, 1997 [1516]), 81.

16. Ibid., at 82–83.

17. See Plato, *Republic* VI, at 499b–d (appealing to "infinite time" to sustain the possibility of a ruler being also a philosopher). This paradox attaches to all systems, material or social: they maintain themselves, but cannot account for their own origin. Thus the appeal to an "invisible hand" in early economics, and to providence more generally.

18. This is the political-theory equivalent of those theories of the origin of life that rely on an "accidental" conjunction of circumstances.

19. See Plato's *Republic* VI, at 496d.

20. More, supra note 15, at 42.

21. Ibid., at 61.

22. Ibid., at 47.

23. Ibid., at 53.

24. Ibid., at 48.

25. Ibid., at 47.

26. Is this not what we have seen in modern China?

27. Immanuel Kant, *Perpetual Peace and Other Essays*, trans. Ted Humphrey (Indianapolis: Hackett Publishing, 1983), 126.

28. Alexander Hamilton, *Federalist No. 1*, ed. C. Rossiter (New York: Signet, 1961), 27.

29. That it is a structure already apparent in Plato's work suggests the classical influence on much Christian political theology.

30. For discussion of uses of duration to represent possibility, see Jonathan Sheehan and Dror Wahrman, *Invisible Hands: Self-Organization and the Eighteenth Century* (Chicago: University of Chicago Press, 2015), 251, 261.

31. For further discussion of Socratic sacrifice, see Paul W. Kahn, *Sacred Violence: Torture, Terror, and Sovereignty* (Ann Arbor: University of Michigan Press, 2008), 101–07.

32. Compare Chap. 1 above on the problem of Old Testament political ethos and God's project.

33. See Plato, *Euthyphro*, trans. R. E. Allen (London: Routledge, 1970).

34. Blackstone writing just a few years earlier had set forth this same position. See Chap. 5 below.

35. Compare Bruce Ackerman, "Revolution on a Human Scale," 108 *Yale L.J.* 2279 (1999).

36. See Chapter 1 above.

37. This idea was reflected in the long history of the doctrine of "accommodation," under which God was thought to accommodate the manner in which he expressed truth to the capacities of particular communities that are themselves a function of their historical situation. See Amos Funkenstein, *Theology and the Scientific Imagination* (Princeton: Princeton University Press, 1986), chap. 4; Nomi Maya Stolzenberg, "Political Theology with a Difference," 4 *University of California Irvine Law Review* 407 (2014).

38. See Bruce Ackerman, *The Failure of the Founding Fathers: Jefferson, Marshall, and the Rise of Presidential Democracy* (Cambridge, Mass.: The Belknap Press of Harvard University Press, 2005).

39. Arendt, for example, emphasizes the continuity of state and local government throughout the American revolutionary era. Hannah Arendt, *On Revolution* (New York: Viking Press, 1963).

40. Thus did Popper criticize Plato. See Karl Popper, *The Open Society and Its Enemies* (London: Routledge, 1945).

41. On the nature of a performative utterance, see J. L. Austin, *How to Do Things with Words* (Cambridge, Mass.: Harvard University Press, 1962).

42. It is too much to speak of a "single" nation at this point. The actual words of the Declaration are: "[T]hese united colonies are . . . free and independent states. . . ." The Declaration of Independence (U.S. 1776), para. 5.

43. Or to at least take a position of neutrality with respect to the war. The Declaration does, somewhat ominously, refer to "mankind" generally as "Enemies in War, in Peace Friends." The Declaration of Independence (U.S. 1776), para. 4.

44. See Conclusion below.

45. Ferdinand Mount, "That Disturbing Devil," *London Review of Books* (May 8, 2014), 13.

46. Compare Lucretius, who thought order arose spontaneously from aggregates of atoms, but had no way to explain a capacity for self-maintenance. See Stephen Greenblatt, *The Swerve: How the World Became Modern* (New York: W. W. Norton & Company, 2011).

47. See Istvan Hont, *Politics in Commercial Society*, ed. Béla Kapossy and Michael Sonenscher (Cambridge, Mass.: Harvard University Press, 2015) (discussing the two Smiths problem and demonstrating the continuity of Smith's two major works).

48. Compare Bentham, who offered an alternative science of social calculation to support a more activist state: one that would take on projects. *The Collected Works of Jeremy Bentham: An Introduction to the Principles of Morals and Legislation*, ed. J. H. Burns and H. L. A. Hart (Oxford: Clarendon Press, 1996).

49. Adam Smith, *The Wealth of Nations* (New York: Bantam Classic, 2003 [1776]), 22.

50. See Bruce Ackerman, *We the People*, vol. 1: *Foundations* (Cambridge, Mass.: The Belknap Press of Harvard University Press, 1991), 22 (on constitutional moments and deliberation).

51. Like blood in the organic system. See Sheehan and Wahrman, *supra* note 30, at 149–51.

52. Freud too believed that there is a natural flow of energy—now libidinal—that will create a social order of exchange—now sexual. Repression of libido is necessary to productive life, but it also generates pathologies, creating both civilization and its discontents. The problem for Freud is to manage these energy flows by identifying and removing the pathological blockages. This is the same problem that Smith identified with respect to labor and economic functions.

53. On the immanent order of fields, see David Singh Grewal, *Network Power: The Social Dynamics of Globalization* (New Haven: Yale University Press, 2008).

54. Dominant forms of political theory similarly move with the master paradigms of an era. Consider the moves from aggregation (liberalism), to flow (Marxism), to field (networks). On eras of imaginative ordering, see Carl Schmitt, *Political Theology: Four Chapters on the Concept of Sovereignty*, trans. George Schwab (Chicago: University of Chicago Press, 2006), 45–47.

55. See, for example, the Coase Theorem. R. H. Coase, "The Problem of Social Cost," 3 *Journal of Law and Economics* 1 (1960).

56. Smith, supra note 49, at 22.

57. See Mount, supra note 45.

58. See Jon Elster, *Alexis de Tocqueville, the First Social Scientist* (Cambridge: Cambridge University Press, 2009).

59. See Robert Wokler, "The Enlightenment and the French Revolutionary Birth Pangs of Modernity," in *The Rise of the Social Sciences and the Formation of Modernity: Conceptual Change in Context, 1750–1850*, ed. Johan Heilbron, Lars Magnusson, and Björn Wittrock (Boston: Kluwer Academic Publishers, 1998), 35, 41 ("[A] recognizably modern conception of the nature of the social sciences was developed in the course of the French Revolution, at first to conceptualize the ideological programme which it was the Revolution's purported aim to achieve but, subsequently, even more to account for its failures.").

60. Alexis de Tocqueville, *Democracy in America*, trans. and ed. Harvey C. Mansfield and Delba Winthrop (Chicago: University of Chicago Press, 2000), 8.

61. Ibid., at 14.

62. Ibid., at 15.

63. See Chap. 1 above.

64. Tocqueville, supra note 60, at 14.

65. Ibid., at 7.

66. Ibid., at 14.

67. Ibid., at 6.

68. Ibid., at 7.

69. See ibid., at 14. "I am ignorant of [God's] designs, but I shall not cease to believe in them because I cannot fathom them, and I had rather mistrust my own capacity than His justice."

70. Ibid., at 315.

71. Ibid., at 310.

72. See Weber on the ethos of Calvinism under a belief in predestination. Max Weber, *The Protestant Work Ethic and the Spirit of Capitalism*, trans. Talcott Parsons (Mineola: Dover, 2003 [1905]).

73. Tocqueville, supra note 60, at 14.

74. Thomas Hobbes, *Leviathan*, ed. Edwin Curley (Indianapolis: Hackett Publishing, 1994 [1668]), 101–03. As these views on the systemic character of the social enter American thought, they confront not Hobbes's

legitimation of a single sovereign, but the American belief in revolution and constitution as the project of the popular sovereign. The American popular sovereign did not require the alienation of citizen subjectivity, but rather affirmed the political identity of citizens. Sovereignty in the American experience was never represented; it was realized and remembered as popular presence. That presence was realized first in the Revolution and the constitutional project it initiated. It was realized again on the sacrificial battlefields of the Civil War. Absent the Hobbesian sovereign, the claim of social system confronts the identity of the popular sovereign whose project is the law. In America, accordingly, the tension between project and system is a competition between different ideas of democracy. Rather than choose between them, we should pursue the possibility that the modern idea of democracy is dependent on both project and system, despite the tension between them.

Part 2. The Constitutionalism of Project

1. *Bush v. Gore*, 531 U.S. 98 (2000), was subject to universal criticism for its suggestion that the law it set forth applied only to the unique circumstances of the case. That has not kept the opinion from being cited as a precedent in cases such as, for example, *League of Women Voters of Ohio v. Blackwell*, 432 F. Supp. 2d 723 (N.D. Ohio 2005), and *Lemons v. Bradbury*, 2008 WL 336823 (D. Or. 2008).

2. For my own view that this idea of project is inadequate as an account of "what judges do," see Paul W. Kahn, *Political Theology: Four New Chapters on the Concept of Sovereignty* (New York: Columbia University Press, 2011), 62–90. The narrative of project has no place for the moment of decision, that is, the moment when a judge must decide between two outcomes for each of which a project account of the law could be given.

3. See Joseph C. Hutcheson, Jr., "Judgment Intuitive: The Function of the Hunch in Judicial Decision," 14 *Cornell Law Review* 274 (1929).

4. But contrast Richard A. Posner, *How Judges Think* (Cambridge: Harvard University Press, 2008), who defends judicial pragmatism. The general resistance to pragmatism as a form of judicial reasoning is apparent in the frequent reluctance of American judges and scholars to take a proportionality approach to judicial decision making. See Francisco J. Urbina, "Is It Really That Easy? A Critique of Proportionality and Balancing as Reasoning," 27 *Canadian Journal of Law & Jurisprudence*

167 (2014). Compare Robert Alexy, "Constitutional Rights, Balancing, and Rationality," 16 *Ratio Juris* 131 (2003).

5. This principle of the necessity of an antecedent rule is embedded in the constitutional prohibitions on *ex post* laws and bills of attainder. U.S. Const. art. I, § 10.

6. This independence is a matter of form, not substance. Substantively, law and facts are always set in a reciprocal relationship. See Paul W. Kahn, *Making the Case: The Art of the Judicial Opinion* (New Haven: Yale University Press, 2016). This, however, cannot be acknowledged in the opinion without moving beyond the project model.

7. See, e.g., Karl N. Llewellyn, *The Bramble Bush: On Our Law and Its Study* (1930); Stanley Fish, "Working on the Chain Gang: Interpretation in Law and Literature," in *The Politics of Interpretation*, ed. William John Thomas Mitchell (Chicago: University of Chicago Press, 1983), 271. This critique of law application on the ground that facts and norms are not easily separated parallels a broader philosophical critique of knowledge claims that purport to do nothing more than represent objective facts. The critique argues that before we can know anything in particular, we must already have available an entire world. For a succinct defense of this critique, see Herbert Dreyfus and Charles Taylor, *Retrieving Realism* (Cambridge, Mass.: Harvard University Press, 2015). My own position aligns with this critique in general and with respect to law, in particular. See Paul W. Kahn, *Finding Ourselves at the Movies: Philosophy for a New Generation* (New York: Columbia University Press, 2013).

8. I wrote about this chasm more than twenty-five years ago in Paul W. Kahn, *Legitimacy and History: Self-Government in American Constitutional Theory* (New Haven: Yale University Press, 1992), chap. 6. See also Richard A. Posner, *Divergent Paths: The Academy and the Judiciary* (Cambridge, Mass.: Harvard University Press, 2016).

9. See Martha Minow, *Between Vengeance and Forgiveness: Facing History after Genocide and Mass Violence* (Boston: Beacon Press, 1998).

10. See Kahn, supra note 2, at 35–38.

11. But see below on the peace treaty.

12. The "lawless" character of the pardon power was recently vividly demonstrated in President Trump's pardon of Joseph Arpaio after he was convicted of criminal contempt.

13. Whether an opinion actually accomplishes a change that brings facts into line with the judicial statement of law cannot be determined apart

from deploying investigative tools other than law: for example, history, biography, or sociology. We cannot read the opinion to learn the character of its own reception. The classic investigation of the effect of constitutional opinions is Gerald N. Rosenberg, *The Hollow Hope: Can Courts Bring About Social Change?* (Chicago: University of Chicago Press, 1991).

14. Compare Morton J. Horwitz, *The Transformation of American Law, 1780–1860* (Cambridge, Mass.: Harvard University Press, 1977), 1–30, describing emergence of an "instrumental conception of law" even among common-law judges in the early nineteenth century.

15. *Marbury v. Madison,* 5 U.S. (1 Cranch) 137, 177 (1803). Marshall himself was a leader of the Virginia Convention that ratified the Constitution.

16. To this list we should add politics and theory. Again, we see the sovereign as philosopher, founder, and citizen. This convergence goes back at least to Hobbes's theory of the social contract.

17. See Immanuel Kant, "An Answer to the Question: What Is Enlightenment?," in *Practical Philosophy* (The Cambridge Edition of the Works of Immanuel Kant), ed. and trans. Mary J. Gregor (Cambridge: Cambridge University Press, 1999), and his own effort at constitutional construction in "Perpetual Peace: A Philosophical Sketch," in *Perpetual Peace and Other Essays on Politics, History, and Morals,* trans. Ted Humphrey (Indianapolis: Hackett Publishing Company, 1983).

18. See, for example, its prominent place in Joseph Story's *Commentaries on the Constitution* of the United States (Boston: Little, Brown, and Co., 1891) and in Alexis de Tocqueville, *Democracy in America,* trans. and ed. Harvey C. Mansfield and Delba Winthrop (Chicago: University of Chicago Press, 2000).

19. See Daniel J. Boorstin, *The Lost World of Thomas Jefferson* (New York: Holt, 1948).

Chapter 3. An American Legal Project

1. Most famously, Madison kept careful notes of the Constitutional Convention.

2. On May 15, 1776, the Continental Congress asked all the colonies to form new government charters for themselves.

3. By 1786, eleven of the colonies had drafted new state constitutions.

4. Also unsurprising is that the same resolution proposed drafting a model treaty to establish amity and commerce with other states.

Resolution of June 7, 1776. All of these texts speak to the "opinions of mankind."

5. Paradigmatic in this regard was the role of Alexander Hamilton, who started life as an illegitimate, poor child on Nevis, an island in the Caribbean. See Ron Chernow, *Alexander Hamilton* (New York: Penguin Press, 2004).

6. For example, the failure of the recent Arab Spring to produce new constitutional texts makes problematic any claim that those states, with the possible exception of Tunisia, experienced revolutions.

7. Compare Ackerman, who works the question the other way around: whenever there appears new constitutional text (formal or informal), the change must have been preceded by revolutionary action. In his analysis, just as the concept of text is broadened, so are the forms of revolution. What matters is the process by which the people can act directly. Bruce Ackerman, *We the People*, vol. 1: *Foundations* (Cambridge, Mass.: The Belknap Press of Harvard University Press, 1991).

8. Story, following Blackstone, distinguishes three forms of colonial "constitution," depending upon its ground of origin and its relationship to the Crown: provincial, proprietary, and charter governments. Joseph Story, *Commentaries on the Constitution of the United States* (Boston: Little, Brown and Company, 1858), vol. 1, chap. 17.

9. In the early twentieth century, the relationship of map (territory) to law (constitution) was thrown into question in the *Insular Cases*, in which the Court held that the constitution does not always follow the flag. See, in particular, *Downes v. Bidwell*, 182 U.S. 244 (1901). The cases are discussed in Owen M. Fiss, *Troubled Beginnings of the Modern State, 1888–1910* (New York: Macmillan, 1993), chap. 8. That the cases appear after system has displaced project as the paradigm of order helps to explain the result.

10. See Edmund S. Morgan, *Inventing the People: The Rise of Popular Sovereignty in England and America* (New York: W. W. Norton & Company, 1988).

11. Indeed, their site of landing was not actually within the boundaries of their royal charter.

12. See, for example, Baldwin's long account of colonial and common-law practices in setting forth American constitutional origins. Henry Baldwin, *A General View of the Origin and Nature of the Constitution and Government of the United States* (Philadelphia: John C. Clark, 1837), discussed below.

13. See also Ian Watt, *The Rise of the Novel* (London: Chatto and Windus, 1957) (on new forms of fiction in the eighteenth century).

14. See Charles Taylor, *Sources of the Self: The Making of the Modern Identity* (Cambridge, Mass.: Harvard University Press, 1989).

15. Benedict Anderson, *Imagined Communities: Reflections on the Origin and Spread of Nationalism* (London: Verso, 1991).

16. See the discussion of Blackstone below; see also David Lieberman, "Blackstone's Science of Legislation," 27 *Journal of British Studies* 117 (1988).

17. Consider that Locke wrote a constitution for North Carolina; Rousseau wrote one for Poland.

18. Several state constitutions of the period employ similar language to set forth a "right to revolution." See, e.g., New Hampshire Bill of Rights, art. 10; North Carolina Constitution of November 21, 1789, art. 1, § 1.

19. On the revolutionary discourse of rejecting slavery under George III, see Quentin Skinner, *Liberty Before Liberalism* (Cambridge: Cambridge University Press, 1998).

20. The traditional maxim that "inter arma enim silent leges" is another expression of this idea of a return to a state of nature.

21. Arendt will famously make this point about human rights: absent a claim in a specific political project, these rights have no legal consequence. See Hannah Arendt, *The Origins of Totalitarianism* (New York: Shocken, 1951), 291–92, 300.

22. Today, we would speak here of human rights. Can we imagine revolution today apart from claims for human rights?

23. William Rawle, *A View of the Constitution of the United States of America*, 2nd ed. (Philadelphia: P. H. Nicklin, 1829), 2.

24. Known as the "incorruptible." See, e.g., Friedrich Sieburg, *Robespierre the Incorruptible*, trans. John Dilke (New York: R. M. McBride and Company, 1938).

25. See Thomas Paine, *The Age of Reason* (London: Pioneer Press, 1937 [1794]).

26. See James Madison, *Federalist No. 47*, ed. C. Rossiter (New York: Signet, 1961), 301 ("The accumulation of all powers, legislative, executive, and judiciary, in the same hands . . . may justly be pronounced the very definition of tyranny.").

27. See Amnon Lev, "Philosophy, Public Law, and the Scope of Justice" (unpublished paper).

28. On More, see Chapter 2 above. On this same skepticism in Shakespeare, see Paul W. Kahn, *Law and Love: The Trials of King Lear* (New Haven: Yale University Press, 2000).

29. Rawle captures the optimism: "America has distinctly presented to view the deliberate formation of an independent government as a means of resisting external force, and with a full and accurate knowledge of her own rights, provides for, and securing her own safety." Rawle, supra note 23, at 17–18.

30. See Joseph de Maistre, *Considerations on France*, trans. Richard A. Lebrun (Cambridge: Cambridge University Press, 1974 [1797]).

31. Edmund Burke, *Reflections on the Revolution in France*, ed. Frank M. Turner (New Haven: Yale University Press, 2003 [1790]).

32. Ibid., at 82. The contrast of the Burkean idea of retail reform versus the revolutionary idea of reason as wholesale constitutional construction continues as a perennial dispute of modernity. At its heart is the question of whether politics as such can be a project, or whether politics is only the enabling condition of a range of particular, local projects. See Ackerman's comparative work, contrasting a revolutionary model of constitutional origins to a commonwealth model of elite compromises with particular social movements—a model of "muddling through." Ackerman, supra note 7.

33. This, for example, is the strategy of John Rawls: there is a timelessness behind the veil of ignorance. John Rawls, *A Theory of Justice* (Cambridge, Mass.: The Belknap Press of Harvard University Press, 1971).

34. Burke, supra note 31, at 27.

35. By the end of the nineteenth century, revisionist constitutional thinkers will reinterpret the American constitutional project in a Burkean mode, claiming that Americans simply adopted and reformed the British constitution to better fit circumstances on this side of the Atlantic. See Chapter 6 below.

36. See Sidney George Fisher, *The Trial of the Constitution* (Philadelphia: J. B. Lippincott & Co., 1862), discussed below.

37. See *Gibbons v. Ogden*, 22 U.S. (9 Wheat.) 1, 196 (1824) ("This power [commerce] like all others vested in Congress, is complete in itself, may be exercised to its utmost extent, and acknowledges no limitations other than those presented in the Constitution.").

38. This phenomenon fascinated Tocqueville, who saw it in the connection of religious morality to the politics of self-government in American

towns. See Alexis de Tocqueville, *Democracy in America*, trans. and ed. Harvey C. Mansfield and Delba Winthrop (Chicago: University of Chicago Press, 2000), 316–17.

39. One consequence of this set of beliefs is a case like *Burwell v. Hobby Lobby Stores, Inc.*, 134 S. Ct. 2751 (2014), in which the Supreme Court held that a major corporation with thousands of employees has the same rights of religious liberty as an individual. Like the individual, the corporation is private.

40. On the entry of these new sciences into American legal thought, see Part III below.

41. See Chapter 3 below.

42. Uncertain about the source of this "discovered" law, the British developed a myth of the "lost statute," as if law must make contact—even if only mythical—with a sovereign source. One suspects that the lost statute myth reflects the idea that order—even systemic order—must have its ultimate source in an intentional act. See Matthew Hale, *The History and Analysis of the Common Law of England* (Stafford: J. Nutt, 1713), 3–4.

43. *Southern Pac. Co. v. Jensen*, 244 U.S. 205, 222 (1917) (Holmes, J., dissenting).

44. William E. Gladstone, "Kin Beyond Sea," 127 *North American Review* 179, 185 (1878).

45. In 1896, Henry Wade Rogers directly challenges Gladstone's remark, arguing that the United States Constitution, no less than the British, is a "product of the historical forces and influences." He speaks the language of organism and system in order to refute any idea that the American Constitution was an invention, that is, "a work struck off at a given time by the brain and purpose of man." Henry Wade Rogers, "The Originality of the United States Constitution," 5 *Yale Law Journal* 239, 246 (1896).

46. *Gompers v. United States*, 233 U.S. 604, 610 (1914).

47. Holmes also reflected the movement from project to system: "When we are dealing with words that also are a constituent act, like the Constitution of the United States, we must realize that they have called into life a being the development of which could not have been foreseen completely by the most gifted of its begetters. It was enough for them to realize or to hope that they had created an organism; it has taken a century and has cost their successors much sweat and blood to prove that they created a nation. The case before us must be considered in

the light of our whole experience and not merely in that of what was said a hundred years ago." *Missouri v. Holland*, 252 U.S. 416, 433 (1920).

48. Alexander Hamilton, *Federalist No. 1*, ed. C. Rossiter (New York: Signet, 1961), 27.

49. This link of reason to persuasion, or of logic to rhetoric, remains a theme within the legal profession in the first decades of the nineteenth century. Perry Miller describes Joseph Story on this point as follows: "The great lawyer *must* be a great orator, Story insisted, because while aiming to convince the understanding he will have to mingle with the close logic of the law those bewitching graces which soothe prejudice, disarm resentment, or fix attention." Perry Miller, *The Life of the Mind in America: From the Revolution to the Civil War* (San Diego: Harcourt, Brace & World, 1965), 147.

50. The rhetorical nature of *The Federalist*'s argument here is clear from the target of comparison that is chosen—not the multiple state governments, but the Articles of Confederation. One might legitimately have wondered why the constitutional order of the states, including New York (to whose citizens *The Federalist* is addressed), has not already answered the fundamental question of whether politics can be a project.

51. Baldwin, supra note 12, at 1.

52. Baldwin spends considerable time arguing that the Framers looked to the British unwritten constitution and the common law as their source. For Baldwin, these are the sources of the principles the Framers adopted and applied. Fifty years later, systemic theorists will drop this moment of independent agency, seeing the American political order as continuous with the British—a sort of natural growth. See, for example, Rogers supra note 45, and Chapter 6 below.

53. Story, supra note 8, at vol. 1, 237.

54. Ibid., at 295.

55. See the discussion of *Marbury v. Madison* below.

56. Story, supra note 8, at vol. 1, 252–53. See also ibid., at 264 (on reasoning down the "terms of the constitution" from "mere theory").

57. Ibid., at 286.

58. Story, ibid., at 302; Baldwin, supra note 12, at 44–45.

59. Something similar was true of a presidential exercise of the pardon power when it was used to negate a conviction under a law thought to have been unconstitutional. Jefferson, for example, pardoned those

convicted during the Adams Administration of violating the Alien and Sedition Acts, which Jefferson thought to be unconstitutional.

60. See Jackson's veto message of July 10, 1832 (arguing that the president's judgments as to constitutionality are independent of those of the Supreme Court).

61. On Jefferson's assertion of a need for a constitutional amendment to legitimate the Purchase, see letter of Jefferson to John Breckinridge (August 12, 1803).

62. As Alison LaCroix puts it, "Triggering a constitutional amendment appeared entirely feasible to interbellum commentators, in contrast to the modern view of the Article V process as effectively impossible except in rare circumstances." Alison L. LaCroix, "The Interbellum Constitution: Federalism in the Long Founding Moment," 67 *Stanford Law Review* 397, 417 (2015).

63. This was essentially Justice Story's view. He recognized that the executive and legislative branches must decide upon the constitutionality of proposed actions, and often those decisions will be beyond review by the courts. "The remedy in such cases [of abuse of a power] is solely by an appeal to the people at the elections; or by the salutary power of amendment. . . ." Story, supra note 8, at §374. On departmentalism as an expression of this view, see Keith E. Whittington, *Political Foundations of Judicial Supremacy: The Presidency, the Supreme Court, and Constitutional Leadership in U.S. History* (Princeton: Princeton University Press, 2009).

64. *Marbury v. Madison*, 5 U.S. (1 Cranch) 137, 176–77 (1803).

65. Ibid., at 177.

66. See below on why "construction" instead of "interpretation" is appropriate here.

67. On the coincidence of the "is" and the "ought" through the concept of reform, see Paul W. Kahn, *The Cultural Study of Law: Reconstructing Legal Scholarship* (Chicago: University of Chicago Press, 1999) 15 ("What the law is is inseparable from what the law should be.").

Chapter 4. Elements of the Legal Project

1. On the connection of exception, freedom, and decision to the miraculous, see Paul W. Kahn, *Political Theology: Four New Chapters on the Concept of Sovereignty* (New York: Columbia University Press, 2011), chap. 1.

2. The Continental Congress twice decided to petition the king, first in October 1774, and second in July 1775.

3. This continuity of power tends to bring with it some skepticism with respect to the ends of the revolutionaries: how much were they seeking relief from private debt to British lenders or protection of their interests in western lands? See Aziz Rana, *The Two Faces of American Freedom* (Cambridge, Mass.: Harvard University Press, 2010).

4. Among the early leaders of the new nation, Hamilton is the great exception in terms of wealth and class. See Ron Chernow, *Alexander Hamilton* (New York: Penguin Press, 2004).

5. John Adams's *Life and Works*, 283, quoted in Francis Wharton, *Commentaries on Law* (Philadelphia: Kay & Brother, 1884), 30, note 1 ("The revolution was effected before the war commenced. *The revolution was in the minds and hearts of the people*; a change in their religious sentiments, of their duties and obligations.").

6. See Jon Butler, *Becoming America: The Revolution Before 1776* (Cambridge, Mass.: Harvard University Press, 2000), 227 ("Yet even after a dozen years of bitter, hostile protest, American independence was not a reasonable wager until April 1775, after fighting erupted between British troops and the Massachusetts militia. . . .").

7. Ibid., at 90–92.

8. Tocqueville will give the clearest pronouncement of this thesis, tying revolutionary claims of self-government to the long tradition of township self-government. See Alexis de Tocqueville, *Democracy in America*, trans. and ed. Harvey C. Mansfield and Delba Winthrop (Chicago: University of Chicago Press, 2000), 316–17.

9. See Joseph J. Ellis, *His Excellency: George Washington* (New York: Knopf, 2004).

10. On the general problem of political character after the passing of the Founders, see Bruce Ackerman, *Revolutionary Constitutions: Charismatic Leadership and the Rule of Law* (Cambridge, Mass.: Harvard University Press, 2019).

11. George Washington, *Washington's Farewell Address*, ed. Victor Hugo Paltsits (New York: New York Public Library, 1935). Note the Hobbesian point made in the first sentence: "unity of government . . . constitutes" the unity of the popular sovereign. The people are brought into being politically by their representation.

12. See Montesquieu, *The Spirit of the Laws*, trans. and ed. Anne M. Cohler, Basia Carolyn Miller, and Harold Samuel Stone (Cambridge: Cambridge University Press, 1989), Book 4, chap. 5; Marisa Linton, *The Politics of Virtue in Enlightenment France* (New York: Palgrave, 2001).

On constitutionalism, virtue, and happiness, see Peter Stephen Du Ponceau, *A Brief View of the Constitution of the United States* (Philadelphia: E. G. Dorsey, 1834), xxiii, who ends his preface with a plea for virtue: "Let us . . . continue to be virtuous, and we may hope to be long united, happy and free."

13. Abraham Lincoln, "Address to the Young Men's Lyceum of Springfield, Illinois: The Perpetuation of Our Political Institutions," in *Abraham Lincoln: Speeches and Writings: 1832–1858*, ed. Don E. Fehrenbacher (New York: Library of America, 1989), 36. Montesquieu had spoken of democratic, political virtue as "the love of the laws and of our country." Montesquieu, supra note 12, at 4.5.

14. Washington, supra note 11.

15. Immanuel Kant, *Critique of Judgment*, trans. Werner S. Pluhar (Indianapolis: Hackett Publishing, 1987), § 91.

16. Washington, supra note 11. Running through Washington's remarks there is a concern with the source of energy that powers the political project once it is constructed. Even a proper order will not move of itself. Theologically, this was the problem of God's continual, providential force even after his creation of right order. One way to trace the distinction of project from system is in the different concepts of the source and character of this energy. It moves from outside—"choice"—to inside—evolving public opinion.

17. *Marbury v. Madison*, 5 U.S. (1 Cranch) 137, 176 (1803). See also Story's *Commentaries* discussed above at Chapter 3.

18. See Sven Beckert, *Empire of Cotton: A Global History* (New York: Knopf, 2014) on the convergence of ideas of citizen and worker in nineteenth century.

19. Skepticism about the possibility of that alignment leads to a counter-politics of the yeoman farmer as the site of moral, and therefore, political virtue. This will ground an anti-industrialization and anti-urban theme in early nineteenth-century politics.

20. Abolitionists will come to make a double charge with respect to virtue and slavery: first, slavery prevented the slaves from realizing a virtuous moral character; second, slavery corrupted the virtue of the slave owner. See, e.g., Jeremy D. Popkin, *You Are All Free: The Haitian Revolution and the Abolition of Slavery* (Cambridge: Cambridge University Press, 2010).

21. See the discussion of Blackstone below.

22. Compare Hobbes on state control over religion in part III of *Leviathan*.

23. See Chapter 2 above.

24. Thomas Paine, "Common Sense," in *Political Writings*, ed. Bruce Kuklick (Cambridge: Cambridge University Press, 1989), 28.

25. The French Revolution faced the same problem of linking reason and reverence. Some revolutionary leaders responded by calling for a public cult of Reason—a less than successful endeavor. The French too needed a source of character formation apart from politics—a role the Catholic Church was disqualified from playing because of its association with the ancien régime. See Mona Ozouf, *Festivals and the French Revolution*, trans. Alan Sheridan (Cambridge, Mass.: Harvard University Press, 1988), 97–102.

26. Washington, supra note 11.

27. Ibid. See above on the presence-to-hand of the possibility of amendment in the early nineteenth century.

28. Kant, supra note 15, at 74–75. Of course, some artists challenge this generalization—e.g., conceptual artists.

29. See Arthur C. Danto, *What Art Is* (New Haven: Yale University Press, 2013).

30. See Clifford Geertz, *The Interpretation of Cultures* (New York: Basic Books, 1973). See also Paul W. Kahn, "Freedom and Method," in *Rethinking Legal Scholarship*, ed. Rob van Gestel, Hans W. Micklitz, and Edward L. Rubin (Cambridge: Cambridge University Press, 2017); and Paul W. Kahn, *Finding Ourselves at the Movies: Philosophy for a New Generation* (New York: Columbia University Press, 2013), Chapter 3.

31. H. L. A. Hart's distinction between first- and second-order rules in a legal system is useful here. H. L. A. Hart, *The Concept of Law* (Oxford: Oxford University Press, 1961). Describing law as a project refers primarily to the imagination of those responsible for the second-order rules: rules that specify creation, amendment, and judgment. Beyond the first- and second-order perspectives, there is that of the legal theorist, who tries to understand the entire legal order, particularly as it changes over time. I would call this third-order perspective that of "critique."

32. See *McCulloch v. Maryland*, 17 U.S. 316 (1819), discussed below. Marshall was hardly alone. See, for example, Thomas Cooper, "Two Essays:

(1) On the Foundation of Civil Government; (2) On the Constitution of the United States," in *Philosophical Writings of Thomas Cooper*, ed. Udo Thiel (Sterling: Thoemmes Press, 2001).

33. Ibid., at 16.

34. Ibid., at 52–56.

35. *McCulloch v. Maryland*, 17 U.S. 316, 406 (1819).

36. Ibid., at 405.

37. Ibid., at 409.

38. Ibid., at 426.

39. Ibid., at 427.

40. See also *Gibbons v. Ogden*, 22 U.S. 1 (1824), for another example of this form of reasoning from first principles, and, of course, *Marbury v. Madison*, 5 U.S. (1 Cranch) 137 (1803), which I discuss as a paradigm of judicial, projectlike reasoning in Paul W. Kahn, *Legitimacy and History: Self-Government in American Constitutional Theory* (New Haven: Yale University Press, 1992).

41. *McCulloch v. Maryland*, 17 U.S. 316, 401 (1819).

42. It is useful here to distinguish drafting the text from authoring the project. The draft of the Constitution composed at Philadelphia did not create anything in itself. Had it not been ratified, it would have been a sort of fiction—particularly in its declaration of "We the People." The "experts'" draft becomes, or begins to become, the sovereign people's project on ratification; then, as it continues, it shapes the social imaginary as our constitutive project. We the people become authors of the project at that point. On the distinction between drafting and authoring projects, see Paul W. Kahn and Kiel R. Brennan-Marquez, "Statutes and Democratic Self-Authorship," 56 *William and Mary Law Review* 115 (2014).

43. Deductive reasoning from first principles will play a substantial role in Langdell's formalism some fifty years later. Langdell, however, will claim to derive the principles from the cases—the law is an immanent order—while Marshall believes the principles precede the execution of the project. On Langdell, see Chapter 5 below.

44. Marshall famously expressed this in *McCulloch v. Maryland*, 17 U.S. 316, 407 (1819), where he distinguishes a constitution from the "prolixity of a legal code," saying, "We must never forget that it is a *constitution* we are expounding."

45. *Trustees of Dartmouth College v. Woodward*, 17 U.S. 518, 644 (1819).

46. Ibid.

47. See Chapter 1 above (on judicial point of view).

48. *Marbury v. Madison*, 5 U.S. (1 Cranch) 137, 165 (1803).

49. *Fletcher v. Peck*, 10 U.S. (6 Cranch) 87, 139 (1810) (emphasis added).

50. Schmitt captures this point when he describes "constitution in the absolute sense" as some principle of unity and order, some decision-making authority that is definitive in critical cases of conflicts of interest and power." Carl Schmitt, *Constitutional Theory*, trans. and ed. Jeffrey Seitzer (Durham: Duke University Press, 2008), 59.

51. See Chapter 3 above.

52. Approved by the National Assembly, August 26, 1789.

53. See Kahn, supra note 1, at chap. 3 (on freedom as discourse, not project).

54. Hannah Arendt, *The Human Condition* (Chicago: University of Chicago Press, 1958).

55. See Ernst H. Kantorowicz, *The King's Two Bodies: A Study in Medieval Political Theology* (Princeton: Princeton University Press, 1957).

56. On how an inductive science can have self-evident axioms, see I. Bernard Cohen, *Science and the Founding Fathers: Science in the Political Thought of Thomas Jefferson, Benjamin Franklin, John Adams, and James Madison* (New York: W. W. Norton & Company, 1995), 121–32.

57. The classic formulation of this problem was by Hart, with his example of "no vehicles in the park." H. L. A. Hart, "Positivism and the Separation of Law and Morals," 71 *Harvard Law Review* 593 (1958).

58. Roberto Mangabeira Unger, *What Should Legal Analysis Become?* (London: Verso, 1996), 76–77.

59. Compare law and economics scholars, who argue for constraint in statutory interpretation precisely because statutes are bargains. See Daniel A. Farber, "Legislative Deals and Statutory Bequests," 75 *Minnesota Law Review* 667 (1991).

60. Unger goes on to mock judges who become "right wing Hegelians" at this moment of stating what the law is, as if the law were the working out of reason behind the backs of the actual actors. Unger, supra note 58, at 76. In this passage, Unger is making the move from project to system.

61. See *United States Railroad Retirement Board v. Fritz*, 449 U.S. 166 (1980); Cass R. Sunstein, "Naked Preferences and the Constitution," 84 *Columbia Law Review* 1689 (1984).

62. Of course, even in contract there are limits on judicial enforcement of the actual bargains among the parties. See, for example, Ayres and Klass on the unconscionability doctrine in contract law. Ian Ayres and Gregory Klass, *Studies in Contract Law*, 9th ed. (St. Paul: Foundation Press, 2017), 562–601.

63. This is the essential idea behind social contract theories. It is also why human rights advocates can think of their work as democratic even when they intervene in a country from without.

64. Ronald Dworkin's idea of interpretation, which includes an element of "fit" alongside an element of principle, reflects this intersection of history and reason. See Ronald Dworkin, *Law's Empire* (Cambridge, Mass.: The Belknap Press of Harvard University Press, 1986).

65. See Seyla Benhabib, "Claiming Rights Across Borders: International Human Rights and Democratic Sovereignty," 103 *American Political Science Review* 691 (2009).

66. See Owen M. Fiss, "Against Settlement," 93 *Yale Law Journal* 1073 (1984).

67. See, e.g., Robert C. Post, *Democracy, Expertise, and Academic Freedom: A First Amendment Jurisprudence for the Modern State* (New Haven: Yale University Press, 2012).

68. See Jed Rubenfeld, *Revolution by Judiciary: The Structure of American Constitutional Law* (Cambridge, Mass.: Harvard University Press, 2005), distinguishing commitments from intentions.

69. The classic expression of this view was put forth as the "bad man" theory of law by Oliver Wendell Holmes in "The Path of the Law." See Oliver Wendell Holmes, Jr., "The Path of the Law," 10 *Harvard Law Review* 457 (1897).

70. See Scott J. Shapiro, *Legality* (Cambridge, Mass.: The Belknap Press of Harvard University Press, 2011) (arguing that the rule of law is the rule of social planning).

71. See Thomas Hobbes, *Leviathan*, ed. Richard Tuck (Cambridge: Cambridge University Press, 1996 [1651]), 79.

72. Jean-Jacques Rousseau, *Social Contract*, trans. and ed. Charles M. Sherover (New York: Meridian, New American Library, 1974 [1762]), 39 ("[T]he Sovereign, which is only a collective being, can be represented by itself alone. . . .").

73. Rousseau did imagine a role for government, which would administer or apply the general laws that were the work of the popular sov-

ereign. Garsten argues that this distinction brings Rousseau much closer to supporting what we mean by representative government than is generally thought. See Bryan Garsten, "Representative Government and Popular Sovereignty," in *Political Representation*, ed. Ian Shapiro, Susan C. Stokes, Elisabeth Jean Wood, and Alexander S. Kirshner (Cambridge: Cambridge University Press, 2009), 93–95.

74. Rousseau, supra note 72, at 45 ("[T]he general will is always right.").

75. William Rawle, *A View of the Constitution of the United States of America*, 2nd ed. (Philadelphia: P. H. Nicklin, 1829), 8.

76. See Giorgio Agamben, *The Kingdom and the Glory: For a Theological Genealogy of Economy and Government*, trans. Lorenzo Chiesa (Stanford: Stanford University Press, 2011), 68–108; Peter Goodrich, *Legal Emblems and the Art of Law* (New York: Cambridge University Press, 2014).

77. This is why revolution can only be seen through constitution, and constitution only through revolution. Each is the truth of the other.

78. *McCulloch v. Maryland*, 17 U.S. 316, 435–36 (1819).

79. See Chapter 1 above.

80. In the later books of the *Republic*, Plato traces the process of the interaction of individual psychology and political hierarchy in his account of the decline of political order.

81. Rousseau, supra note 72 at 5.

82. Arguments for virtual representation in Parliament failed to convince most colonialists, once Parliament began to raise their taxes.

83. Premodern political institutions attempted to achieve this stability through the metaphysical claim that the king's body was the unity of the state. The king did not represent citizens; rather, the body of the king included citizens in the same way that the Church is the body of Christ. In this sense, the representative character of the nation-state is a product of the Reformation's general move from instantiation to representation. On the importance of the distinction of being from representing for Hobbes, see Bryan Garsten, "Religion and Representation in Hobbes's Leviathan," in *Leviathan*, ed. Ian Shapiro (New Haven: Yale University Press, 2010).

84. Ackerman's work tries to identify moments of American history in which a successful claim to "revolutionary reform" has been made. His "higher lawmaking" identifies the formal elements of a project that

characterizes the American constitutional order. Bruce Ackerman, *We the People*, vol. 1: *Foundations* (Cambridge, Mass.: The Belknap Press of Harvard University Press, 1991).

85. See Paul W. Kahn, *The Cultural Study of Law: Reconstructing Legal Scholarship* (Chicago: University of Chicago Press, 1999), 43–55 (on law's time as situated between these moments).

86. Because different polities make different choices, a constitutionalism of project grounds the academic field of comparative constitutional law, as well as the comparative sociological project of normative institutional design. See, e.g., Juan J. Linz, "The Perils of Presidentialism," 1 *Journal of Democracy* 51 (1990).

87. See Kahn, supra note 40, at 35–36 (discussing *The Federalist* on slavery and Southern interests).

88. See Kahn and Brennan-Marquez, supra note 42.

89. See William J. Brennan, Jr., "Why Have a Bill of Rights?," 26 *Valparaiso Law Review* 1 (1991).

90. See Ackerman, supra note 84, at 14–16.

91. See Samuel Moyn, *The Last Utopia* (Cambridge, Mass.: The Belknap Press of Harvard University Press, 2010) (on human rights and social movements).

92. According to the 2016 American Values Survey cited by *The Guardian*, "Sixty-one percent of survey respondents" indicated that "neither political party reflects their opinions today." David Smith, "Most Americans Do Not Feel Represented by Democrats or Republicans—Survey," *The Guardian* (October 25, 2016).

93. See *Marbury v. Madison*, 5 U.S. (1 Cranch) 137, 176 (1803) (the people's exercise of their right to establish a constitution "is a very great exertion").

94. Ibid., at 167 (the president exercises "political powers" for which he is "accountable only to his country").

95. Alexander Bickel gave modern expression to this idea of a Court representing the people's principles. See Alexander M. Bickel, *The Least Dangerous Branch: The Supreme Court at the Bar of Politics*, 2nd ed. (New Haven: Yale University Press, 1986); see also Paul W. Kahn, *The Reign of Law:* Marbury v. Madison *and the Construction of America* (New Haven: Yale University Press, 1997).

96. See James Q. Whitman, *The Verdict of Battle: The Law of Victory and the Making of Modern War* (Cambridge, Mass.: Harvard University Press, 2012) (on providence and the wager of battle).

97. See Oona A. Hathaway and Scott J. Shapiro, *The Internationalists: How a Radical Plan to Outlaw War Remade the World* (New York: Simon & Schuster, 2017).

98. Hobbes, supra note 71, at 88–89 (on continuation of a state of war). See also Radhabinod Pal, "Dissentient Judgment of Justice Pal," *International Military Tribunal for the Far East* (Tokyo: Kokusho-Kankokai, Inc., 1999).

99. *Marbury v. Madison*, 5 U.S. (1 Cranch) 137, 156 (1803).

100. Ibid., at 177.

101. Ibid.

102. Ibid., at 178.

103. This is no less evident in *McCulloch v. Maryland*, 17 U.S. 316 (1819), decided some sixteen years later. See discussion above.

104. See Kahn, supra note 40.

105. The receding place of science in understanding the project of legal construction is related to the general yielding of the Whig-Federalist lawyers to the Jeffersonian-Jacksonian reformers. See Robert W. Gordon, "Legal Thought and Legal Practice in the Age of American Enterprise, 1870–1920," in *Professions and Professional Ideologies in America*, ed. Gerald L. Geison (Chapel Hill: University of North Carolina Press, 1983), 83–87.

106. *Dred Scott v. Sandford*, 60 U.S. 393, 405 (1857) (emphasis added).

107. *The Antelope*, 23 U.S. 66, 120–21 (1825). See discussion in Conclusion below.

108. To be sure, there is a real question of whether Taney answered even his own question correctly.

109. On the political psychology of this difference in historical position, see Lincoln's Lyceum speech, supra note 13.

110. See Kahn and Brennan-Marquez, supra note 42 (on statutes and regulations); Kevin M. Stack, "Overcoming Dicey in Administrative Law," 68 *University of Toronto Law Journal* 293 (2018). See Conclusion below (on international law and the idea of a project).

111. See *Federalist No. 1*, discussed above at Chapter 3.

112. See Peter Gay, *The Enlightenment: The Rise of Modern Paganism* (New York: W. W. Norton, 1966), 99: [Hobbes's work] "was too great to be ignored," but his "name was too disreputable to be praised."

113. This eclectic combination of sources of theory is why it is difficult to describe the tradition in which they acted as either that of liberalism

or republicanism. They did not think they had to choose. See Ackerman, supra note 84, at 24–32.

114. More precisely, a system is not the consequence of the project of anyone within the system. Creation may be God's project, even as it appears as system to us.

Part 3. System as the Order of Law

1. Abraham Lincoln, "Address to the Young Men's Lyceum of Springfield, Illinois: The Perpetuation of Our Political Institutions," in *Abraham Lincoln: Speeches and Writings: 1832–1858*, ed. Don E. Fehrenbacher (New York: Library of America, 1989), 28–36.

2. See Paul W. Kahn, *Sacred Violence: Torture, Terror, and Sovereignty* (Ann Arbor: University of Michigan Press, 2008), 158–62.

3. Compare Pierre Clastres, "Of Torture in Primitive Societies," in *Society Against the State: Essays in Political Anthropology*, trans. Robert Hurley (New York: Zone Books, 1987).

4. See Moshe Halbertal, *People of the Book: Canon, Meaning, and Authority* (Cambridge, Mass.: Harvard University Press, 1997).

5. In this, the scar is a kind of icon. This relationship of making present what is absent is paradigmatically fulfilled in the relic.

6. *Marbury v. Madison*, 5 U.S. (1 Cranch) 137, 176 (1803).

7. Lincoln will famously describe the Declaration as an "apple of gold" and the Constitution as the "picture of silver . . . framed around it." See Abraham Lincoln, "Fragment on the Constitution and the Union" in *The Collected Works of Abraham Lincoln*, vol. 4, ed. Roy P. Basler (New Brunswick: Rutgers University Press, 1953–55), 169.

8. Thus, in the conclusion of his Lyceum speech, Lincoln writes: "Reason, cold, calculating, unimpassioned reason, must furnish all the materials for our future support and defence. Let those materials be molded into *general intelligence, sound morality*, and in particular, *a reverence for the constitution and laws. . . .*" See Lincoln, supra note 1.

9. Immanuel Kant, *Critique of Judgment*, trans. Werner S. Pluhar (Indianapolis: Hackett Publishing, 1987), § 27 (referring to the sublime).

10. On this view, life is not limited to individual organisms. We might want, for example, to speak of environmental systems as alive. Some think of the earth itself as alive, but why stop there? Life may be the order of the universe. See Lawrence Joseph, *Gaia: The Growth of an Idea* (New York: St. Martin's Press, 1990).

11. See Jonathan Sheehan and Dror Wahrman, *Invisible Hands: Self-Organization and the Eighteenth Century* (Chicago: University of Chicago Press, 2015).

12. On the connection of theorists of European nationalisms to the rise of a historical school of jurisprudence in the United States in the nineteenth century, see David M. Rabban, *Law's History: American Legal Thought and the Transatlantic Turn to History* (New York: Cambridge University Press, 2013), 67–80.

13. On progressive attitudes toward the written constitution, see Aziz Rana, "Progressivism and the Disenchanted Constitution," in *The Progressives' Century: Democratic Reform and Constitutional Government in the United States*, ed. Stephen Skowronek, Stephen Engel, and Bruce Ackerman (New Haven: Yale University Press, 2016).

14. On disillusionment with the formal order created by the constitutional text, see Aziz Rana, "Constitutionalism and the Foundations of the National Security State," 103 *California Law Review* 335 (2015).

15. On Jeffersonian objections to the common law, see letter to Edmund Randolph (August 18, 1799) ("Of all the doctrines which have ever been broached by the general government, the novel one of the common law being in force and cognisable as an existing law in their courts, is to me the most formidable."). On the Jeffersonian and Jacksonian attack on the common law, see Perry Miller, *The Life of the Mind in America from the Revolution to the Civil War* (San Diego: Harcourt, Brace & World, 1965), 105–09.

16. See Roscoe Pound, "Common Law and Legislation," 21 *Harvard Law Review* 383, 383 (1908) ("Not the least notable characteristics of American law today are the excessive output of legislation . . . and the indifference, if not contempt, with which that output is regarded by courts and lawyers."). See also Francis Wharton, *Commentaries on Law* (Philadelphia: Kay & Brother, 1884), §2, 4 ("All laws must be more or less declaratory."). Morton Horwitz sees this attitude as already dominant in the nineteenth century. Morton J. Horwitz, *The Transformation of American Law, 1780–1860* (Cambridge, Mass.: Harvard University Press, 1977), 255–56 (speaking of an "underlying convention held by all orthodox nineteenth-century legal thinkers that the course of American legal change should, if possible, be developed by courts and not by legislatures").

17. See Thomas C. Grey, "Langdell's Orthodoxy," 45 *University of Pittsburgh Law Review* 1, 34 (1983) ("Langdell's Harvard colleagues . . . threatened

to withdraw their offer to help the new University of Chicago Law School get started, because its organizers proposed to teach a substantial number of public law courses, thus violating the Harvard curricular dogma that students must be exposed only to scientific 'pure law' courses. Constitutional law was unscientific, because hopelessly vague . . . political, not legal. . . .").

18. The exception is a brief criticism of the Court's developing doctrine of substantive due process. Oliver Wendell Holmes, Jr., "The Path of the Law," 10 *Harvard Law Review* 457, 468 (1897).

19. Holmes famously put forward a "bad man" theory of law. Ibid.

20. See Rana, supra note 14.

Chapter 5. System and the Theory of the Common Law

1. Francis Wharton, *Commentaries on Law* (Philadelphia: Kay & Brother, 1884), §2, 5. For a similar view emphasizing law as custom working in an evolving system, see James C. Carter, *Law: Its Origin, Growth and Function* (New York: G. P. Putnam's Sons, 1907), 331 ("The body of custom . . . tends from the beginning to become a harmonious system.").

2. An example of this problem of the locus of the sovereign in a systemic approach to law is found in Hans Kelsen's accusation that Carl Schmitt's concept of the sovereign was a reification of what is only a transcendental condition of legal judgment. See Paul W. Kahn, *Political Theology: Four New Chapters on the Concept of Sovereignty* (New York: Columbia University Press, 2011), 73. The locus of the debate today over the nature of a law without popular sovereignty is the regulatory production of the EU.

3. There is a parallel question of the site of popular sovereignty, if not located in law. The answer of the twentieth century will be war: the will of the popular sovereign is expressed in the violent exception to law. This position was famously articulated by Carl Schmitt in *Political Theology: Four Chapters on the Concept of Sovereignty*, trans. George Schwab (Chicago: University of Chicago Press, 2005). See also Clinton L. Rossiter, *Constitutional Dictatorship: Crisis Government in the Modern Democracies* (Princeton: Princeton University Press, 1948).

4. On the countermajoritarian difficulty, see Alexander M. Bickel, *The Least Dangerous Branch: The Supreme Court at the Bar of Politics*, 2nd ed. (New Haven: Yale University Press, 1986); on the connection of that

problem to American exceptionalism, see Paul W. Kahn, "The International Criminal Court: Why the United States Is So Opposed," *Crimes of War Project Magazine* (December 2003).

5. See Jedidiah J. Kroncke, *The Futility of Law and Development: China and the Dangers of Exporting American Law* (New York: Oxford University Press, 2016) (describing the close relationship between law, Christian missionary work, and American efforts in China).

6. See Carter, supra note 1, at 129–36.

7. For this reason, Thayer writes of American efforts in the Philippines not as bringing law and democracy, but as creating the conditions in which a democratic legal order can arise. James Bradley Thayer, "Our New Possessions," 12 *Harvard Law Review* 464 (1898).

8. Holmes does not actually read Darwin until the early twentieth century. See Sheldon M. Novick, "Justice Holmes's Philosophy," 70 *Washington University Law Quarterly* 703, 722 (1992) ("Holmes, who called himself an evolutionist, believed that his ideas were derived from Darwin, but Holmes had not read Darwin's books and his ideas actually reflected an older version of evolution, most strongly influenced by Hegel" (citations omitted).).

9. See, e.g., Jody S. Kraus, "Philosophy of Contract Law," in *The Oxford Handbook of Jurisprudence and Philosophy of Law*, ed. Jules L. Coleman, Kenneith Einar Himma, and Scott J. Shapiro (Oxford: Oxford University Press, 2002).

10. Canon law was also taught until King Henry VIII split with the Church.

11. See Daniel J. Boorstin, *The Mysterious Science of Law: An Essay on Blackstone's Commentaries* (Boston: Beacon Press, 1958), 3 ("In the fourteen centuries since Justinian's Institutes, Blackstone's *Commentaries* are the most important attempt in western civilization to reduce to short and rational form the complex legal institutions of an entire society."). On the enormous importance of Blackstone to early American legal education and legal practice, see Perry Miller, *The Life of the Mind in America from the Revolution to the Civil War* (San Diego: Harcourt, Brace & World, 1965). Miller notes that by 1775, "more copies of Blackstone's *Commentaries* had been sold in America than in all England." Ibid., at 115. Miller traces the unresolved debate about the law's scientific status—its expression of an order of reason—in the first half of the eighteenth century, but also notes that "before the Civil War there is nothing in the American literature of an out-and-out evolutionary

philosophy. Reiterated statements that the common law was 'malleable' seldom came to explicit historicism." Ibid., at 259.

12. Langdell will face exactly the same issue in bringing the study of law into the American university. He writes: "If law be not a science, a university will consult its own dignity in declining to teach it. If law be not a science, it is a species of handicraft, and may best be learned by serving an apprenticeship to one who practices it." Christopher Columbus Langdell, Speech, 3 *Law Quarterly Review* 123, 124 (1887).

13. 1 William Blackstone, *Commentaries* *32.

14. Ibid., at *35.

15. Ibid., at *32.

16. Ibid.

17. For a perfectly rational subject, the categorical imperative would always already form his will. The concept of duty would make no sense to such a subject. His will, Kant says, would be "holy." See Anne Margaret Baxley, *Kant's Theory of Virtue: The Value of Autocracy* (Cambridge: Cambridge University Press, 2010), 55–56.

18. Blackstone, supra note 13, at *39.

19. On Blackstone's work as itself a kind of theodicy, see Boorstin, supra note 11, at 51–53.

20. Blackstone, supra note 13, at *40.

21. Ibid. The proposition is vaguely incoherent, since God's atemporality seems incompatible with an idea of the "antecedent."

22. Ibid., at *41.

23. Ibid.

24. Ibid., at *40.

25. Ibid., at *41.

26. Ibid., at *69.

27. Ibid., at *42.

28. See Immanuel Kant, "An Answer to the Question: What Is Enlightenment?," in *Practical Philosophy* (The Cambridge Edition of the Works of Immanuel Kant), ed. and trans. Mary J. Gregor (Cambridge: Cambridge University Press, 1999 [1784]).

29. Blackstone, supra note 13, at *52. Correspondingly, Blackstone recognized the sovereign law-making power of the king-in-Parliament. The *Commentaries* were meant to instruct legislators in the science of the law such that they would understand that legislation's role is to facilitate, not to negate, the common law. See David Lieberman, "Blackstone's Science of Legislation," 27 *Journal of British Studies* 117 (1988).

30. Blackstone is, in this sense, part of the Christian, stoical response to Hobbes. See Istvan Hont, *Politics in Commercial Society*, ed. Béla Kapossy and Michael Sonenscher (Cambridge, Mass.: Harvard University Press, 2015), 16–17.

31. Blackstone, supra note 13, at *36 (emphasis added).

32. Boorstin expresses this idea well: "[English laws] were institutions which man seemed to have created, and yet which had immanent in them the never-changing quality of God." Boorstin, supra note 11, at 59.

33. Blackstone, supra note 13, at *67.

34. Ibid., at *70.

35. Ibid.

36. Ibid.

37. Ibid., at *71.

38. Ibid., at *76.

39. Ibid., at *77.

40. Ibid.

41. Ibid.

42. Ibid.

43. Ibid., at *70.

44. Ibid., at *77.

45. Ibid., at *40.

46. Ibid., at *78.

47. "[W]hen laws are to be framed by popular assemblies, even of the representative kind, it is too Herculean a task to begin the work of legislation afresh, and extract a new system from the discordant opinions of more than five hundred counsellors." 3 William Blackstone, *Commentaries* *267.

48. Boorstin, supra note 11, at 48–53.

49. See Paul W. Kahn, *Making the Case: The Art of the Judicial Opinion* (New Haven: Yale University Press, 2016) for a contemporary example of this dual approach; for another, see Karl N. Llewellyn, *The Bramble Bush: On Our Law and Its Study* (New York: Oxford University Press, 2008 [1930]).

50. Christopher Columbus Langdell, *A Selection of Cases on the Law of Contracts*, 2nd ed. (Boston: Little, Brown, 1879), viii.

51. Pound, several decades later, will make exactly this claim, describing his sociological jurisprudence as a form of "civil engineering." Roscoe Pound, *Interpretations of Legal History* (Cambridge, Mass.: Harvard University Press, 1946), 15–21.

52. Even with respect to the natural sciences, this idea of objectivity is complicated given the changing character of epistemic paradigms. See Thomas Kuhn, *The Structure of Scientific Revolutions* (Chicago: University of Chicago Press, 1962).

53. On the hermeneutic circle, see Hans-Georg Gadamer, "Hermeneutics and Social Science," 2 *Cultural Hermeneutics* 307 (1975).

54. See Thomas C. Grey, "Langdell's Orthodoxy," 45 *University of Pittsburgh Law Review* 1 (1983).

55. Contemporary evolutionary biologists have the same problem in attempting to explain the evolution of man's scientific abilities. Theory would hypothesize that those abilities evolve toward belief in what works best for survival in different contexts, which may not correspond to an objective truth. See Thomas Nagel, *Mind and Cosmos: Why the Materialist Neo-Darwinian Conception of Nature Is Almost Certainly False* (New York: Oxford University Press, 2012).

56. Famously, his example of the mailbox rule. See Grey, supra note 54, at 3-4.

57. Felix S. Cohen, "Transcendental Nonsense and the Functional Approach," 35 *Columbia Law Review* 809 (1935).

58. The early claims of law and economics—that tort and criminal law are aiming for economically efficient rules—responded to this epistemic need. See Richard A. Posner, *Economic Analysis of Law*, 2nd ed. (New York: Walters Kluwer Law & Business, 1977), chap. 7. See also Richard A. Posner "An Economic Theory of the Criminal Law," 85 *Columbia Law Review* 1193 (1985).

59. See Boorstin, supra note 11.

60. See Kahn, supra note 49, at chap. 5.

61. See Owen Fiss on the necessity of mediating rules: Owen M. Fiss, "Groups and the Equal Protection Clause," 5 *Philosophy & Public Affairs* 107 (1976).

62. On John Dewey's relationship to Oliver Wendell Holmes, Jr., and their common pragmatism, see Thomas C. Grey, "Plotting the Path of the Law," 63 *Brooklyn Law Review* 19, 52-53 (1997).

63. On state incorporation of British common law, see Richard C. Dale, "The Adoption of the Common Law by the American Colonies," 30 *American Law Register* 553 (1882). For an example of state incorporation of the common law of England after the American Revolution, see W. Va. Code § 2-1-1 (LexisNexis 2018) ("The common law of England, so far as it is not repugnant to the principles of the constitution of this

state, shall continue in force within the same, except in those respects wherein it was altered by the General Assembly of Virginia before the twentieth day of June, eighteen hundred and sixty-three, or has been, or shall be, altered by the Legislature of this state.").

64. See, e.g., Grey, supra note 54, at 20–27.

65. See discussion of Blackstone above.

66. See, e.g., Owen M. Fiss, "Objectivity and Interpretation," 34 *Stanford Law Review* 739 (1983) and Owen M. Fiss, "Conventionalism," 58 *Southern California Law Review* 177 (1985).

67. See my critique of Fiss in Paul W. Kahn, *Legitimacy and History: Self-Government in American Constitutional Theory* (New Haven: Yale University Press, 1992), 194–96.

68. Oliver Wendell Holmes, Jr., "The Path of the Law," 10 *Harvard Law Review* 457 (1897).

69. Ibid., at 461.

70. See ibid., at 462–64; see also Oliver Wendell Holmes, Jr., *The Common Law*, ed. Mark Antony De Wolfe Howe (Boston: Little, Brown, 1963), 253: "[A]lthough the law starts from the distinctions and uses the language of morality, it necessarily ends in external standards not dependent on the actual consciousness of the individual."

71. Eric Posner and Jack Goldsmith recently made just these sorts of claims about states in their relationship to international law: they are all Holmesian bad men making calculations of the cost of law. See Jack L. Goldsmith and Eric A. Posner, *The Limits of International Law* (Oxford: Oxford University Press, 2005).

72. Holmes, supra note 68, at 478.

73. Ibid., at 473.

74. See, e.g., James M. Buchanan, *Politics as Public Choice* (Indianapolis: Liberty Fund, Inc., 2000); James M. Buchanan and Gordon Tullock, *The Calculus of Consent: Logical Foundations of Constitutional Democracy* (Indianapolis: Liberty Fund, Inc., 1999).

75. Holmes, supra note 68, at 459.

76. *Lochner v. New York*, 198 U.S. 45, 76 (1905).

77. John Rawls, *A Theory of Justice* (Cambridge, Mass.: The Belknap Press of Harvard University Press, 1971), 20–21.

78. This reciprocity constitutes the mechanism of legal development identified by evolutionary theories of jurisprudence well before the arrival of Darwin. See Herbert J. Hovenkamp, "Evolutionary Models in Jurisprudence," 64 *Texas Law Review* 645 (1985).

79. See Chapter 2 above.
80. Holmes, supra note 68, at 469.
81. See Oliver Wendell Holmes, Jr., "The Soldier's Faith," Memorial Address at Harvard University, May 30, 1895, in *The Occasional Speeches of Oliver Wendell Holmes*, ed. Mark Antony De Wolfe Howe (Cambridge, Mass.: The Belknap Press of Harvard University Press, 1962).
82. See Oliver Wendell Holmes, Jr., "Book Review," 14 *American Law Review* 233 (1880).
83. Holmes, supra note 68, at 469.
84. Holmes, supra note 70, at 1. A sentence that appeared earlier in his review of Langdell. See supra note 82, at 234.
85. On geometry as Langdell's paradigm of a science, see Grey, supra note 54, at 16–20.
86. Holmes, supra note 70, at 10–15.
87. Holmes pursues a Nietzschean theme here—one picked up later by Foucault. See Michel Foucault, "Nietzsche, Genealogy, History," in *The Foucault Reader*, ed. Paul Rabinow (New York: New Press, 1984).
88. Holmes, supra note 70, at 36.
89. Ibid.
90. *Lochner v. New York*, 198 U.S. 45, 76 (1905).
91. Holmes, supra note 70, at 32.
92. James Coolidge Carter, writing in 1907, imagines public law as essentially creating the institutions and mechanisms for applying private law or the customary norms that ground private law. See James C. Carter, *Law: Its Origin, Growth, and Function*, supra note 1.

Chapter 6. The Rise of an Unwritten Constitution

1. See Michel Foucault, *Discipline and Punish: The Birth of the Prison*, trans. Alan Sheridan (New York: Pantheon Books, 1978).
2. See Immanuel Kant, "An Answer to the Question: What Is Enlightenment?," in *Practical Philosophy* (The Cambridge Edition of the Works of Immanuel Kant), ed. and trans. Mary J. Gregor (Cambridge: Cambridge University Press, 1999 [1784]); Oliver Wendell Holmes, Jr., "The Path of the Law," 10 *Harvard Law Review* 457 (1897).
3. See, e.g., James C. Carter, *Law: Its Origin, Growth and Function* (New York: G. P. Putnam's Sons, 1907).
4. In Rawls's terms, project provided the "concept"; interpretive disagreement was over different "conceptions." See John Rawls, *A Theory of*

Justice (Cambridge, Mass.: The Belknap Press of Harvard University Press, 1971), 9; see also Ronald Dworkin, *Law's Empire* (Cambridge, Mass.: The Belknap Press of Harvard University Press, 1986), 70–71.

5. Something similar was discovered after *Roe*. See Douglas NeJaime, "Winning through Losing," 96 *Iowa Law Review* 941 (2010).

6. Holmes had offered a particularly vivid account of what it means to bring to consciousness the unconscious causes of law: "get the dragon out of its cave on to the plain and into the daylight." Discussed in Chapter 5 above.

7. A moral critique of the Framers' actual intentions will appear a little later. See Charles A. Beard, *An Economic Interpretation of the Constitution of the United States* (New York: Macmillan Co., 1913).

8. This will become a standard conservative critique of efforts to construct nonmarket-based economies in the twentieth century. See Friedrich A. Hayek, *The Road to Serfdom* (Chicago: University of Chicago Press, 1944).

9. Sidney George Fisher, *The Trial of the Constitution* (Philadelphia: J. B. Lippincott & Co., 1862), 20.

10. See Alexander von Humboldt, *Cosmos: A Sketch of a Physical Description of the Universe*, published in five volumes from 1845 to 1862; Sigmund Freud, *The Interpretation of Dreams* (1899); Karl Marx, *Capital*, vol. 1: *The Process of the Production of Capital* (1867).

11. Compare Ted A. Smith, *Weird John Brown: Divine Violence and the Limits of Ethics* (Stanford: Stanford University Press, 2015), 91–99 (on multiple sources—human and divine—for mythical violence in support of law).

12. Freud tried to apply his systemic account of psychic forces to explain social/political phenomena as well. See, e.g., Sigmund Freud, *Civilization and Its Discontents*, trans. Joan Riviere (London: Hogarth Press, 1953); Sigmund Freud, *Group Psychology and the Analysis of the Ego*, trans. James Strachey (New York: Liveright, 1951); Sigmund Freud, *Moses and Monotheism*, trans. Katherine Jones (New York: Knopf, 1939).

13. For a recent example, see Chief Justice Roberts's dissent in *Obergefell v. Hodges*, in which the majority declared a constitutional right to same-sex marriage, 135 S.C. 2584, 2626 (2015) ("The majority's decision is an act of will, not legal judgment. The right it announces has no basis in the Constitution.").

14. Fisher, supra note 9, at 41.

15. Ibid., at 91.
16. Ibid., at 60–64.
17. Ibid., at 41.
18. Fisher is less than certain that the Founders actually intended judicial review, but he accepts that reading. Ibid., at 66.
19. Ibid., at 63–64; see also Thomas Jefferson: "A strict observance of the written law is doubtless one of the high duties of a good citizen, but it is not the highest. The laws of necessity, of self-preservation, of saving our country when in danger, are of higher obligation." Letter from Thomas Jefferson to John B. Colvin, September 20, 1810, in *The Works of Thomas Jefferson*, vol. 11 (New York: G. P. Putnam's Sons, 1904–05), 146. These views on the relationship of law to emergency will reappear in the early twentieth century in the work of Carl Schmitt.
20. Fisher, supra note 9, at 73.
21. This language is used by Justice Jackson, dissenting in *Terminiello v. Chicago*, 337 U.S. 1, 37 (1949).
22. Fisher, supra note 9, at 43–44.
23. Ibid., at 2.
24. Ibid.
25. Ibid., at 40.
26. Ibid., at 53.
27. Ibid., at 64.
28. Ibid., at 64–65.
29. Ibid., at 53. See also ibid., at 46 ("Given a free people and a representative Government . . . the Legislature must be supreme. So it has happened in England, and so it will happen here. . . .").
30. Ibid., at 50.
31. It is a "universal law of nature, that the internal spirit is manifested by external form, that the invisible is represented by the visible, that mind rules matter, and makes of it an instrument to execute its will." Ibid., at 45.
32. Ibid., at 48.
33. Ibid., at 47. Compare Holmes, supra note 2, at 473 ("[Law] has the final title to respect that it exists, that it is not a Hegelian dream, but a part of the lives of men.").
34. Christopher G. Tiedeman, *A Treatise on the Limitations of Police Power in the United States Considered from Both a Civil and Criminal Standpoint* (St. Louis: F. H. Thomas Law Book Co., 1886).

35. Thomas M. Cooley, *A Treatise on the Constitutional Limitations Which Rest upon the Legislative Powers of the States of the American Union* (Boston: Little, Brown, 1868).

36. Notably, Cooley and Tiedeman were training a generation of elite lawyers whose professional roles would often include limiting the possibilities of new electoral majorities.

37. This lack of concern with jurisdiction in sources is reflected a little later in Langdell's use of British cases. See Chapter 5 above. This issue will reappear in contemporary constitutional law in the controversy over citations to foreign law. Again, those attracted to a constitutionalism of project will be disturbed by the practice; those who think of law as the immanent order of reason will see nothing problematic in the practice.

38. See Christopher Gustavus Tiedeman, *The Unwritten Constitution of the United States* (New York: G. P. Putnam's Sons, 1890), 5–6 ("The great majority of a people are a law unto themselves. And wherever this fundamental thought is lost sight of, legislation results in nothing but the production of dead letters, stillborn laws, that never did and never could have become a living rule of conduct.").

39. See David M. Rabban, *Law's History: American Legal Thought and the Transatlantic Turn to History* (New York: Cambridge University Press, 2013), 57–58.

40. See also Francis Wharton, *Commentaries on Law* (Philadelphia: Kay & Brother, 1884), 365, 424–25.

41. Tiedeman, supra note 38, at 80–81.

42. Ibid., at 76 ("There is, therefore, no such thing, even in ethics, as an absolute, inalienable, natural right.").

43. Ibid., at 80.

44. Appealing to public opinion—rightly understood—against popular legislation becomes a standard form of argument in the twentieth century. See, e.g., Alexander M. Bickel, *The Least Dangerous Branch: The Supreme Court at the Bar of Politics*, 2nd ed. (New Haven: Yale University Press, 1986).

45. Tiedeman was a professor of law—first at Missouri, then Columbia, and finally dean at Buffalo. See Rabban, supra note 39, at 57.

46. See Bruce A. Ackerman, *Private Property and the Constitution* (New Haven: Yale University Press, 1977) (on ordinary and expert frameworks); Jürgen Habermas, *The Theory of Communicative Action*, vol. 2: *Lifeworld and System: A Critique of Functionalist Reasoning*, trans. Thomas McCarthy

(Boston: Beacon Press, 1985) (on different forms of discourse for life-world and system).

47. Tiedeman, supra note 38, at 49–50. Wharton is writing in a similar vein at about the same time. See Wharton, supra note 40, at § 359, 410 ("Primary law-making is unconscious and instinctive . . . we must examine, in order to understand its processes, the forces by which it was produced, and the environments to which they were subjected. . . . [T]he Constitution was evolved in large measure unconsciously from the conditions in which the community was placed. . . .").

48. Tiedeman, supra note 38, at 1.

49. Ibid., at 9.

50. Ibid.

51. Ibid., at 12. In the dispute between those who saw evolutionary change as gradual and those who saw it as abrupt, Tiedeman sided with the latter. In this, he followed Rudolf von Jhering, with whom he had studied. Rabban, supra note 39, at 59.

52. Tiedeman, supra note 38, at 2.

53. Ibid., at 3.

54. Ibid., at 2.

55. Ibid., at 6. That "prevalent sense of right" will have a long history in political theory, where it will come to be understood as "public opinion."

56. Ibid., at 25 (footnote omitted).

57. Ibid., at 150.

58. Ibid., at 43–44 ("For, if by judicial interpretation, in obedience to the stress of public opinion or private interests, the express limitations of the written Constitution are made to mean one thing at one time, and at another time an altogether different thing, there is very little restraint imposed by these written limitations.").

59. Ibid., at 136.

60. Ibid., at 137–39.

61. Ibid., at 89.

62. Ibid., at 5.

63. Ibid., at 88.

64. Tiedeman's view of public opinion formation shares none of the modern demand for equal access and participation that characterizes, for example, the work of Habermas and Post. See Habermas, supra note 46; Robert Post, "Participatory Democracy and Free Speech," 97 *Virginia Law Review* 477 (2011).

65. Tiedeman, supra note 38, at 121.
66. Ibid., at 120–21.
67. Ibid., at 118.
68. Ibid., at 107.
69. Ibid., at 156.
70. Ibid., at 125.
71. Ibid., at 127.
72. Ibid.
73. Ibid., at 108.
74. Woodrow Wilson, *Congressional Government: A Study in American Politics* (New York: Meridian Books, 1956 [1885]), 24.
75. Wilson, as a self-imagined "scientist," places himself in relation to a disciplinary school. Here the dominant influence is that of Walter Bagehot, who finds the American Constitution a very poor competitor with the British. See Walter Bagehot, *The English Constitution* (London: Chapman and Hall, 1867).
76. Wilson, supra note 74, at 27.
77. Ibid., at 28.
78. Ibid.
79. Ibid.
80. Ibid.
81. Ibid., at 54.
82. On the centrality of public opinion to modern democratic theory, see Jürgen Habermas, *The Structural Transformation of the Public Sphere: An Inquiry into a Category of Bourgeois Society*, trans. Thomas Burger (Cambridge, Mass.: MIT Press, 1989).
83. Wilson, supra note 74, at 29.
84. Woodrow Wilson, *Constitutional Government in the United States* (New York: Columbia University Press, 1908), 54–55.
85. See Herbert J. Hovenkamp, "Evolutionary Models in Jurisprudence," 64 *Texas Law Review* 645 (1985).
86. See ibid., at 651.
87. See John Milton Cooper, Jr., *The Warrior and the Priest: Woodrow Wilson and Theodore Roosevelt* (Cambridge, Mass.: The Belknap Press of Harvard University Press, 1983). Of course, in 1912 they ran against each other for the presidency, with Roosevelt running as the third-party candidate of the Progressive Party.
88. Wilson, supra note 84, at 192.
89. Ibid.

90. Ibid., at 157.
91. Ibid., at 142.
92. Public opinion has become the site of popular sovereignty. Compare Paul W. Kahn, *Putting Liberalism in Its Place* (Princeton: Princeton University Press, 2005), 264–79 (describing completeness of sovereignty in terms of Aristotle's four causes).
93. Wilson, supra note 84, at 23–24.
94. Ibid.
95. Benedict Anderson, *Imagined Communities: Reflections on the Origin and Spread of Nationalism* (London: Verso, 1983).
96. Here, Wilson anticipates Thomas Kuhn, *The Structure of Scientific Revolutions* (Chicago: University of Chicago Press, 1962).
97. Wilson, supra note 84, at 23.
98. Ibid., at 17.
99. Ibid., at 68.
100. Ibid., at 79.
101. Ibid., at 56.
102. Ibid., at 57.
103. Ibid., at 65.
104. See Ernst H. Kantorowicz, *The King's Two Bodies: A Study in Mediaeval Political Theology* (Princeton: Princeton University Press, 1957).
105. Just as there is no real scarcity in public opinion, there is nothing like the generation of random change. New ideas appear and succeed for reasons rooted in other ideas, i.e., not because they facilitate the survival of those who hold them.
106. The phrase "free trade in ideas" at work "in the competition of the market" is introduced by Justice Holmes in his dissent in *Abrams v. United States*, 250 U.S. 616, 630 (1919).
107. No doubt the privileging of public opinion was also a way to privilege the place of the scholar who claimed to articulate the content of that opinion.
108. See, e.g., *Citizens United v. FEC*, 558 U.S. 310 (2010); *Sorrell v. IMS Health Inc.*, 564 U.S. 552 (2011).
109. Habermas, supra note 46; Bruce A. Ackerman, *Social Justice in the Liberal State* (New Haven: Yale University Press, 1980).
110. See, e.g., *Nebbia v. New York*, 291 U.S. 502 (1934).
111. *Lochner v. New York*, 198 U.S. 45 (1905).
112. Ibid., at 75.

113. See William M. Wiecek, *The Lost World of Classical Legal Thought: Law and Ideology in America, 1886–1937* (New York: Oxford University Press, 1998).
114. See discussion above, pp. 198–208.
115. See Robert W. Gordon, "Legal Thought and Legal Practice in the Age of American Enterprise, 1870–1920," in *Professions and Professional Ideologies in America*, ed. Gerald L. Geison (Chapel Hill: University of North Carolina Press, 1983), 98 ("The rules determining the *limits* of legislation were given by the law of the constitution, which in Liberal legal thought simply incorporated all the neutral principles of the common law.").
116. *Lochner v. New York*, 198 U.S. 45, 53 (1905).
117. In *Meyer v. Nebraska*, 262 U.S. 390, 399 (1923), the Court makes the link explicit, stating that the liberty protected by the 14th Amendment extends "generally to . . . those privileges long recognized at common law as essential to the orderly pursuit of happiness by free men."
118. *Lochner*, 198 U.S. at 53.
119. *Allgeyer v. Louisiana*, 165 U.S. 578, 589 (1897) (emphasis added).
120. A similar phenomenon can be seen earlier in a developing formalism of private law—particularly in contract. For example, while the early nineteenth-century law emphasized a view of contract that gives primacy to the wills of the parties, by mid-century those reciprocal wills are framed in terms of "objective" categories. See Morton J. Horwitz, *The Transformation of American Law, 1780–1860* (Cambridge, Mass.: Harvard University Press, 1977), 263 ("[C]ontract law was no longer conceived of as simply implementing the parties' 'wills,' but rather its categories were often treated as existing somehow prior to individual bargains.") (footnote omitted). These categories of common-law contract were understood as the systemic object of a legal science—the same science that will receive constitutional expression in *Lochner*.
121. *Lochner*, 198 U.S. at 53.
122. Ibid., at 57.
123. See *Buck v. Bell*, 274 U.S. 200, 207 (1927).
124. See ibid. (upholding state statute providing for sterilization of "mental defectives").
125. Compare *Muller v. Oregon*, 208 U.S. 412 (1908) (upholding state law restricting working hours of women) to *Adkins v. Children's Hospital*, 261 U.S. 525 (1923) (striking down a minimum wage law for women).

126. *Adkins*, 261 U.S. at 553.

127. *Lochner*, 198 U.S. at 62.

128. 198 U.S. at 64.

129. *Carter v. Carter Coal Co.*, 298 U.S. 238 (1936).

130. See *NLRB v. Jones & Laughlin Steel Corp.*, 301 U.S. 1 (1937).

131. *Carter Coal*, 298 U.S. at 308.

132. Ibid., at 307–08.

133. Ibid., at 308.

134. Felix S. Cohen, "Transcendental Nonsense and the Functional Approach," 35 *Columbia Law Review* 809 (1935).

135. Jonathan Sheehan and Dror Wahrman, *Invisible Hands: Self-Organization and the Eighteenth Century* (Chicago: University of Chicago Press, 2015), 279. See also Daniel J. Boorstin, *The Mysterious Science of Law: An Essay on Blackstone's Commentaries* (Boston: Beacon Press, 1958), discussed in Chapter 5 above.

136. For example, the New York bakery regulation may have been aimed at excluding recent Jewish and Italian immigrants from competing with established bakeries. See David Bernstein, *Rehabilitating Lochner: Defending Individual Rights Against Progressive Reform* (Chicago: University of Chicago Press, 2011), 24–27.

Conclusion

1. Just before this pledge, the Declaration states, "with a firm reliance on the protection of Divine Providence. . . ." The significant word is "protection," not "direction."

2. On the difference between a pledge and a contract see Paul W. Kahn, *Sacred Violence: Torture, Terror, and Sovereignty* (Ann Arbor: University of Michigan Press, 2008), 112–14.

3. See Carl Schmitt, *Political Theology: Four Chapters on the Concept of Sovereignty*, trans. George Schwab (Chicago: University of Chicago Press, 2006), 36 (discussed above); see also Hannah Arendt, *The Human Condition* (Chicago: University of Chicago Press, 1958), chap. 5 (linking natality and miracle).

4. Oliver Wendell Holmes, Jr., "The Soldier's Faith," Memorial Address at Harvard University, May 30, 1895, in *The Occasional Speeches of Oliver Wendell Holmes*, ed. Mark Antony De Wolfe Howe (Cambridge, Mass.: The Belknap Press of Harvard University Press, 1962), 76.

5. Carl Schmitt, *The Concept of the Political*, trans. George Schwab (Chicago: University of Chicago Press, 1996), 38–39.

6. See ibid., at 36. See also Émile Durkheim on sacred as representation of the community. Émile Durkheim, *The Elementary Forms of the Religious Life*, trans. Joseph Swain (New York: Macmillan, 1915).

7. Compare Halbertal, who recognizes the danger of separating sacrifice from moral values, arguing that sacrifice should be grounded on an independent value. Moshe Halbertal, *On Sacrifice* (Princeton: Princeton University Press, 2012).

8. Carl Schmitt, *The Crisis of Parliamentary Democracy*, trans. Ellen Kennedy (Cambridge, Mass.: MIT Press, 1985).

9. See Paul W. Kahn, *Putting Liberalism in Its Place* (Princeton: Princeton University Press, 2005), 298–301 (on the romantic family).

10. Political science departments are still divided between those who do classic political theory and those who pursue an empirical science.

11. The classic expression of this point was in *Lochner*: "There are . . . certain powers, existing in the sovereignty of each state . . . somewhat vaguely termed police powers, the exact description and limitation of which have not been attempted by the courts." 198 U.S. 45, 53 (1905). Discussed in Chapter 6 above.

12. See, e.g., Herbert Spencer, *Social Statics* (London: John Chapman, 1851), 322–23 (on leaving windows and orphans "to struggle for life or death"). Even crime—of the right sort—has an optimal level in a society. See Gary S. Becker, "Crime and Punishment: An Economic Approach," 76 *Journal of Political Economy* 169 (1968).

13. See Paul W. Kahn, *Legitimacy and History: Self-Government in American Constitutional Theory* (New Haven: Yale University Press, 1992), 135.

14. For a similar reflection of the place of what he calls legal "ideologies," see Robert W. Gordon, "Legal Thought and Legal Practice in the Age of American Enterprise, 1870–1920," in *Professions and Professional Ideologies in America*, ed. Gerald L. Geison (Chapel Hill: University of North Carolina Press, 1983), 109 ("Such understandings, discourses, or ideologies . . . can never of course determine particular outcomes, but they are the tools that must be used to construct the framework for decision. They encourage the perception of some alternatives as reasonable and realistic and of others as visionary or offensive, and still others they suppress before they can even be imagined.").

15. See, e.g., George L. Priest, "The Common Law Process and the Selection of Efficient Rules," 6 *Journal of Legal Studies* 65 (1977).

16. Dworkin is often criticized for blurring the line between moral norms and legal rules. But from the systemic perspective, that line is always

blurred, for the immanent order is a function of all of our beliefs and practices.

17. Ronald Dworkin, *Law's Empire* (Cambridge, Mass.: The Belknap Press of Harvard University Press, 1986).

18. Ibid., at 228–32.

19. Dworkin's jurisprudence actually combines elements of project and system. While the development of law is understood systemically, each citizen interpreting the law is to imagine the law as a project she has given herself. Ibid., at 189.

20. See Eugene V. Rostow, "The Democratic Character of Judicial Review," 66 *Harvard Law Review* 193, 208 (1952) (describing the Supreme Court as "teaching in a vital national seminar").

21. See, for example, Bruce A. Ackerman and James Fishkin, *Deliberation Day* (New Haven: Yale University Press, 2004).

22. Edmund Burke, *Reflections on the Revolution in France*, ed. Frank M. Turner (New Haven: Yale University Press, 2003 [1790]), 40.

23. Today, when we speak of the politicization of the rule of law, we refer to the disappearance of this phenomenon. There can be no reverence for a Court that is perceived as only an instrument of party politics. Law, in that case, never separates from ordinary politics. Compare *Planned Parenthood v. Casey*, 505 U.S. 833, 867–68 (1992) (speaking of the Court's responsibility to those who accept a judicial decision even when they disagree with it).

24. See Paul W. Kahn, *The Cultural Study of Law: Reconstructing Legal Scholarship* (Chicago: University of Chicago Press, 1999), 117–19.

25. *Plessy v. Ferguson*, 163 U.S. 537 (1896).

26. Ibid., at 551.

27. See Gerald N. Rosenberg, *The Hollow Hope: Can Courts Bring About Social Change?* (Chicago: University of Chicago Press, 1991).

28. The problem for the modern sociologist is to explain why society resists the legal project of integration. This problem replicates the demand for an explanation of society's resistance to the project of the French Revolution, out of which modern sociology emerged. See Chap. 1 above.

29. *Nebbia v. New York*, 291 U.S. 502, 537 (1934). Discussed above in Chapter 6.

30. *Obergefell v. Hodges*, 135 S. Ct. 2584 (2015).

31. This is a secular replay of Manichaeism which also insisted that evil must have a source separate from that of the good.

32. See Paul W. Kahn, *Making the Case: The Art of the Judicial Opinion* (New Haven: Yale University Press, 2016).

33. Compare Philip Bobbitt, *Constitutional Interpretation* (Oxford: Basil Blackwell, 1991) (on different modalities of constitutional arguments).

34. See, e.g., H. Jefferson Powell, "The Original Understanding of Original Intent," 98 *Harvard Law Review* 885 (1985). For a recent example of synthesis, see Jack M. Balkin, *Living Originalism* (Cambridge, Mass.: The Belknap Press of Harvard University Press, 2011).

35. Michael Kammen, *A Machine That Would Go of Itself: The Constitution in American Culture* (New York: Knopf, 1986).

36. Roscoe Pound, *Interpretations of Legal History* (Cambridge: Cambridge University Press, 1923), 152.

37. See Chapter 6 above.

38. See Chapter 5 above.

39. See, for example, Emer de Vattel, *The Law of Nations: Or Principles of the Law of Nature Applied to the Conduct and Affairs of Nations and Sovereigns* (London: G. G. and J. Robinson, 1797), §7: "[T]he necessary law of nations . . . contains the precepts prescribed by the law of nature to states, on whom that law is not less obligatory than on individuals, since states are composed of men. . . ."

40. See ibid., at §21; Henry Wheaton, *Elements of International Law* (Philadelphia: Carey, Lea, & Blanchard, 1836), 56.

41. See Paul W. Kahn, "Nuclear Weapons and the Rule of Law," 31 *New York University Journal of International Law and Politics* 349, 390–401 (1999).

42. See William Blackstone, "The law of nations is . . . here adopted in its full extent by the common law, and is held to be a part of the law of the land." 4 William Blackstone, *Commentaries* *67 (chap. 5).

43. The international-law problem of incorporation appears in the somewhat different context of the citizen's ability to use international law to ground a private right of action. See *Sosa v. Alvarez-Machain*, 542 U.S. 692 (2004).

44. U.S. Constitution, art. 1, §8, cl. 10. See also *The Paquete Habana*, 175 U.S. 677 (1900).

45. Prior to the Constitution, state law was held to incorporate the law of nations. Whether customary international law has the status of federal common law became an issue after *Erie*. It remains controversial for some theorists. See Curtis A. Bradley and Jack L. Goldsmith,

"Customary International Law as Federal Common Law: A Critique of the Modern Position," 110 *Harvard Law Review* 815 (1997).

46. *The Antelope*, 23 U.S. (10 Wheat.) 66 (1825).

47. *Johnson v. M'Intosh*, 21 U.S. (8 Wheat.) 543 (1823).

48. See Paul W. Kahn, "Law of Nations at the Origins," in *International Law and Religion: Historical and Contemporary Perspectives*, ed. Martti Koskenniemi, Mónica García-Salmones Rovira, and Paolo Amorosa (Oxford: Oxford University Press, 2017).

49. On this shift in understanding the law of nations as moving from system to project—or, in more doctrinal language, from natural law to positivism, or from monism to dualism—see William S. Dodge, "*The Charming Betsy* and *The Paquete Habana* (1804 and 1900)," in *Landmark Cases in Public International Law*, ed. Eirik Bjorge and Cameron Miles (Oxford: Hart Publishing, 2017).

50. Alexis de Tocqueville, *Democracy in America*, trans. and ed. Harvey C. Mansfield and Delba Winthrop (Chicago: University of Chicago Press, 2000), 230.

51. See, e.g., Charles A. Beard, *An Economic Interpretation of the Constitution of the United States* (New York: Macmillan, 1913).

52. On super-statutes, see William N. Eskridge, Jr., and John Ferejohn, *A Republic of Statutes: The New American Constitution* (New Haven: Yale University Press, 2010).

53. Dworkin puts this idea, which he calls "integrity," at the center of his jurisprudence. Dworkin, supra note 17. Amar calls it "intratextuality," by which he means that interpretation shows us the systemic unity of the entire Constitution. Akhil Reed Amar, "Intratextualism," 112 *Harvard Law Review* 747 (1999). Ackerman calls it "synthesis" and describes it as the ordinary work of the Court. Bruce Ackerman, *We the People*, vol. 1: *Foundations* (Cambridge, Mass.: The Belknap Press of Harvard University Press, 1991). For a critical response to this approach, see Adrian Vermeule and Ernest A. Young, "Hercules, Herbert, and Amar: The Trouble with Intratextualism," 113 *Harvard Law Review* 730 (2000).

54. *Bowers v. Hardwick*, 478 U.S. 186 (1986).

55. Ibid., at 190.

56. *Obergefell v. Hodges*, 135 S. Ct. 2584 (2015).

57. See *United States v. Darby Lumber Co.*, 312 U.S. 100, 124 (1941).

58. *Obergefell*, 135 S. Ct. at 2598.

59. See Chapter 5 above.
60. See, e.g., Roberto Mangabeira Unger, *The Critical Legal Studies Movement* (Cambridge, Mass.: Harvard University Press, 1986); Catharine A. MacKinnon, *Toward a Feminist Theory of the State* (Cambridge, Mass.: Harvard University Press, 1989).
61. John Hart Ely, *Democracy and Distrust: A Theory of Judicial Review* (Cambridge, Mass.: Harvard University Press, 1980).

polarization, 16, 253
police power, 198–200, 226, 227, 239
political parties, 133
political theory, 13, 46, 47; democracy inseparable from, 121, 238; Founders' views of, 62, 80–82, 87–88; legal project underpinned by, 114–17; limitations of, 124; Marshall's reliance on, 96–97, 117–19, 139; practical application of, 125, 142; roles of, 58; separation of powers as tenet of, 88; social contract and, 37–38, 85–86; Wilson's turn to, 208
Pollock, Frederick, 260n3
Pope, Alexander, 31, 32–34, 40
positivism, 171
Posner, Richard, 272–73n4
Pound, Roscoe, 248, 291n16
pragmatism, 176, 272n4
precedent, 79, 124, 239, 253–54
predestination, 264n31
presidency, 135; powers of, 143; Wilson's view of, 210, 212, 215, 219–21, 222
prisoner's dilemma, 38
prisons, 186
private realm, 90
probability, 9, 67
procedure, 256
Progressive era, 231
project discourse, 14–16
project failure, 45
property rights, 39, 200; common-law protections of, 224; pleasure decoupled from, 50; as project vs. system, 45–46;

Utopian rejection of, 49, 51, 59; winners vs. losers and, 240
protectionism, 65
Protestant Reformation, 4
provincial assemblies, 103
psychology, 46, 190
public goods, 108
public health, 227–28
public opinion, 55, 133, 231, 232; capriciousness of, 182, 203; constructing vs. following, 205–6; law as reflection of, 179–80, 182; revolution and, 207; social evolution linked to, 222–23; Wilson's view of, 213, 215, 217–19, 221
Puritans, 34, 110

Radical Republicans, 209, 245
Rawle, William, 87, 128, 277n29
Rawls, John, 88, 179
reason, 109, 283n25; in adjudication, 79, 255; consent linked to, 166; in constitution-making and legislating, xiii, 62–63, 79, 83, 84, 87, 124, 255; custom linked to, 168, 169, 170–71; for the elite, 107–8, 110; as force of order, 31; God's will and, xi–xii, 159, 165; intergenerational ethics and, 89; Kant's view of, 162; Langdell's view of, 176, 185, 197; laws of nature provided by, 127; multiple meanings of, 163–64; the people linked to, 123–24; philosopher's rule and, 51–53; Pope's view of, 34, 40; religion linked to, 50–51, 55, 73, 74;

Milton Keynes UK
Ingram Content Group UK Ltd.
UKHW040849091024
449443UK00004B/81